Copyright © 2019 Eric L. Green, TG Publishing

All rights reserved. No part of this publication may be reproduced, distributed, or transmitted in any form or by any means, including photocopying, recording, or other electronic or mechanical methods, without the prior written permission of the publisher, except in the case of brief quotations embodied in critical reviews and certain other non-commercial uses permitted by copyright law. for permission request, right to the publisher, addressed "Attention: Permissions Coordinator," at the address below.

TG Publishing
One Audubon Street, Third Floor
New Haven, CT 06511
(203) 285-8545

Table of Contents

About the Author 6

The Lure of Offers-in-Compromise 8

The Collection Process 10

    The IRS Collection Division 12

    Collection Appeals 13

    The Statute of Limitations 15

    Federal Tax Liens 16

    Federal Tax Levies 17

    Tax Compliance 17

    Estimated Taxes 18

    Withholding Taxes 20

Financial Analysis: It's All in the Numbers 21

    RCP: Reasonable Collection Potential 22

    Net Equity in Assets 23

    Future Income Calculation 25

    One-Spouse is Liable 34

    Community Property States 35

Installment Agreements & Uncollectible Status 37

    Automatic Installment Agreement 39

    Streamlined Installment Agreement 40

    Regular Installment Agreement 40

    Partial-Pay Installment Agreement 41

    One-Year Rule 42

Six-Year Rule... 42

Defaulting on an Installment Agreement 43

Uncollectible Status 43

Offers-in-Compromise 47

The Offer-in-Compromise Program.. 49

Lump-Sum Offers... 49

Short-Term Deferred Offer (Periodic Payment)... 50

Reasonable Collection Potential ("RCP")... 51

Common Issues with Offers 53

Non-Compliance 53

Ability to Full-Pay 55

Dissipated Assets 55

Non-Cash Expenses 57

Averaging the Taxpayer's Income.. 57

Orders of Restitution 58

The Firearms Excise Tax Improvement Act of 2010 (FETI) 59

The IRC § 6204 Assessment 60

Dealing with the Civil Assessment 60

No Compromise 61

Compromise with Restitution Paid in Full.. 61

Effective Tax Administration Offers ("ETA") and Doubt-as-to-Collectability with Special Circumstances ("DCSC") 62

Doubt-as-to-Liability Offers ("DATL") 64

The Offer-in-Compromise Outcome 64

Bankruptcy 66

The Automatic Stay.. 68

    Discharging Taxes 68

    Payment Plans 73

    74

    Tax Liens 74

Collection Appeals 75

    Collection Due Process 76

    The Appeals Hearing 78

    Equivalent Hearings 79

    Offer-in-Compromise Appeals 80

Payroll Taxes & Personal Liability 81

    Introduction to Payroll Taxes 82

    Internal Revenue Code § 6672 84

    The Willfulness Requirement 85

    The Trust Fund Investigation 85

    The Payroll Liability Assessment Process 86

    Recent Payroll Tax Initiatives by the IRS 86

    Federal Tax Deposit ("FTD") Alerts 87

    So, what is an FTD Alert? 88

Case Studies 89

    1. Streamlined Installment Agreement 90

    2. "Pay-Down" to a Streamlined Installment Agreement 91

    3. Currently-Not-Collectable 92

    4. Regular Installment Agreement 95

    5. Offer-in-Compromise: Joint-Liability 97

    6. Offer-in-Compromise: One Spouse Responsible 99

Checklist: Offer-in-Compromise 102

Exhibits 105

About the Author

Eric is a partner in Green & Sklarz LLC, a boutique tax firm with offices in Connecticut and New York. The focus of Attorney Eric L. Green's practice is civil and criminal taxpayer representation before the Department of Justice Tax Division, Internal Revenue Service and state Departments of Revenue Services, as well as handling probate matters and estate planning for individuals and business owners and tax planning for closely held businesses. He is a frequent lecturer on tax topics for CCH, the NAEA, the NATP, the ABA Tax Section and the Connecticut Society of CPAs. Attorney Green has served as adjunct faculty at the *University of Connecticut School of Law*. He was the author and lecturer of the *CCH IRS Representation Certificate Program*, and he is a columnist for *CCH's Journal of Practice & Procedure*. He is the founder of *Tax Rep LLC* which coaches accountants and attorneys on building their own IRS Representation practices, and has the weekly Tax Rep Network podcast.

Mr. Green is the author of *The Accountant's Guide to IRS Collection* and *The Accountant's Guide to Resolving Tax Debts*. He is a contributing author for *Advocating for Low Income Taxpayers: A Clinical Studies Casebook, 3rd Edition*, and has also been quoted in *USA Today, Consumer Reports, The Wall Street Journal's Market Watch, TheStreet.com, The Wall Street Journal* and *CreditCard.com*.

Prior to practicing law Attorney Green served as a senior tax consultant for KPMG and Deloitte & Touche.

Attorney Green was the 2010 Nolan Fellow of the American Bar Association and has served as Chair of the American Bar Association's Closely Held Businesses Tax Committee. Attorney Green is the current Chair of the Executive Committee of the Connecticut Bar Association's Tax Section. Eric is a Fellow of the *American College of Tax Counsel* ("ACTC").

Attorney Green is also a member of the Connecticut, Massachusetts and New York Bar Associations, as well as the American Bar Association. Attorney Green is admitted to practice in Massachusetts, New York and Connecticut Superior Courts, the United States Tax Court, The Federal Court of Claims and the Federal District Court for

Connecticut. Attorney Green received his Bachelor of Business Administration degree in Accounting with a minor in International Business from Hofstra University and is an honors graduate from New England School of Law. He earned a Masters of Laws in Taxation (LL.M.) from Boston University School of Law.

The Lure of Offers-in-Compromise

Everyone is in love with the idea of making tens of thousands of dollars of tax debt vanish for pennies. Taxpayers who owe back taxes sit up at night stressed out, and listen to those late-night commercials and think, "What I really need is a knife that can cut up my shoes, an expensive piece of workout equipment I'll never use, and to settle my tax debt with these people who promise they can get rid of a gazillion bazillion dollars for 50 cents! Why not send them $10,000 right now?"

The reality is that taxpayers who owe back taxes can take advantage of the Offer-in-Compromise program, *IF THEY QUALIFY!* So, how do we know if they qualify?

The IRS utilizes a formula (yes, it's just a formula) to determine a taxpayer's ability to pay. This formula is called "Reasonable Collection Potential," or "RCP." Knowing how to calculate a taxpayer's RCP is why we get 90% of our Offers-in-Compromise accepted, and why so few other practitioners find success. Practitioners need to understand how the IRS will evaluate the taxpayer's situation so that the practitioner can determine if the client is an Offer-in-Compromise candidate, and if so what the correct amount is to offer the IRS.

The same situation exists for Installment Agreements. Taxpayers have options when it comes to resolving their back taxes, including several variations of installment agreements. There are automatic agreements, streamlined agreements, regular agreements and even partial-pay installment agreements. There is a one-year rule and a six-year rule, either of which might apply and help your taxpayer. If the practitioner does not understand these special rules, then the opportunities presented by the special rules are meaningless to the taxpayer.

Confused? Not certain what to do for your taxpayers?

Fear not! This guide will walk you the practitioner through the variations of installment agreements and offers so that you too can start the process of becoming a tax resolution master. The area of taxpayer representation continues to grow despite IRS cutbacks. Currently there are almost 14 million taxpayer accounts in the Collection Division's inventory and nearly 7 million non-filers that the IRS has ifdentified. The need for practitioners who can help taxpayers through the process and resolve their tax issue has never been greater.

This guide will explain in detail how to resolve the taxpayer's outstanding tax debt. I hope you find it illuminating and profitable.

Eric L. Green, Esq.

The Collection Process

1

"I owe back taxes."

This is usually the phrase we hear at our firm when a new client calls us. In fact, owing back taxes is generally why anybody calls our firm, especially for me. Resolving tax issues is sort of what we do, or at least, it's what we are best known for.

Accountants are well placed to help clients – they are the first professional who taxpayers usually turn to when seeking help with anything to do with the IRS. Usually, however, the Certified Public Accountant ("CPA"), Enrolled Agent ("EA") or unenrolled preparer either has no idea how to help the client, or worse, thinks they do when they really do not and end up doing more harm than good. Why is this? The truth is that the accountant simply does not understand either the IRS collection process or how to resolve an outstanding tax debt. It's not what they do, and most accounting programs do not teach tax resolution.

To help clients resolve their outstanding tax debt, the practitioner needs to understand:

1. The IRS "Collection Process"
2. The role of the IRS financial guidelines
3. The collection alternatives

None of the three items listed above is complicated nor are they beyond your understanding; you just need to get familiar with them. Once you understand how they work, you are close to mastering a process that is in high demand and only growing year-by-year.

So how does the IRS collection process work?

The IRS Collection Division

The Mission Statement of the IRS Collection Division is as follows:

The mission of Field Collection is to provide SB/SE [Small Business/Self-Employed] taxpayers with top quality post-filing services by helping them understand and comply with all applicable tax laws and by applying the tax laws with integrity and fairness.

Despite the Collection Division's "warm & fuzzy" mission statement, our experience is that most clients don't find the IRS "post-filing services" to be either top quality or educational. They find them to be abusive, scary, and financially devastating. Clients often don't understand what is expected of them and how to work with collection division personnel, and the government employees of the Collection Division don't bother to explain the process to the taxpayer.

Once a tax liability is assessed, a billing notice CP-14 is mailed to the taxpayer requesting payment (see Exhibit 1). If the tax is paid in full, including interest and penalties, then the issue for that year is closed.

If the tax continues to go unpaid, then additional notices are sent to the taxpayer. These include:

Types of Additional Notices	
CP-501	You have a balance due (money you owe the IRS) on one of your tax accounts. (see Exhibit 2)
CP-503	We have not heard from you, and you still have an unpaid balance on one of your tax accounts. (see Exhibit 3)
CP-504	Intent to Levy. You have an unpaid amount due on your account. If you do not pay the amount due immediately, the IRS will seize your assets in an attempt to pay the balance due. (see Exhibit 4)

After the notices listed above have been sent to the taxpayer, another notice will arrive: "Notice of Intent to Levy," ("Final Notice")[1] (see Exhibit 5). With the Final Notice also comes a blank Form 12153, "Request for a Collection Due Process or Equivalent Hearing," also referred to as "CDP." (see Exhibit 6). The Final Notice is a critical notice, because 30 days after the date of this notice, levy action may commence against the taxpayer. The way you stop the levy action is by requesting the hearing with the Form 12153.

It is critical for the taxpayers to understand where they are in the collection process, because at any point the taxpayer can call collection, and start working out a deal. There is no reason why the taxpayer should be so remiss as to reach the point of receiving a Letter 11. Some critical points to consider:

- Get any missing returns filed as soon as possible;
- Open the mail! It is stunning to me, even after doing this for 20 years, how often taxpayers don't even open the mail and, therefore, have no idea what's going on. Opening the mail is critical to understanding the tax situation and knowing when to call the IRS, or more critical, when to seek professional tax help.
- Respond to IRS requests in a timely fashion.
- Every response should be sent in a way that the taxpayers can prove when they sent it: fax with a fax receipt, certified or registered mail, or overnight service that can be tracked. It may become critical for the taxpayers later to have proof they sent in something by a particular date, so this is no time to get cheap! They should spend the extra money and send the filing by certified mail.

Collection Appeals

It is critical that the Form 12153 be filed within 30 days of the date on the Final Notice. In fact, with the exception of some very limited circumstances, it is (in the author's

---

[1] There are three versions of the "Final Notice" that may arrive depending upon which division sends it: Letter 1058 is sent from IRS Headquarter Collections; Letter 11 is sent from the Automated Collection Service area of Collections ("ACS"); CP-90 is used by the Field Collection Force (i.e. Revenue Officers).

opinion) malpractice *not* to file the CDP request. By filing the CDP request, a number of things will happen in the taxpayer's case:

- The IRS ceases all collection action against the taxpayer for the tax periods listed on the Final Notice;
- The taxpayer's case is forwarded to Appeals;
- The taxpayer has the right to go to the Tax Court if the taxpayer can't work out an arrangement with Appeals; and
- The taxpayer has additional time to prepare any missing returns and sort out the proposal for resolving the outstanding tax debt.[2]

Unfortunately, many taxpayers (and their equally clueless practitioners) don't realize the seriousness of the need to file the appeal. The National Taxpayer Advocate reports that less than 3% of taxpayers ever take advantage of their appeal rights!

What if the taxpayer misses the 30-day deadline to request the CDP hearing? On page 2 of Form 12153 there is a box, line item 7, that if the request is late, the taxpayer would like a hearing equivalent to a CDP hearing (see Exhibit 6). The taxpayer has up to one year to request an equivalent hearing in this manner, that is, by filing the Form 12153 and checking line item 7. This still gets the case to Appeals. However, by requesting an equivalent hearing (having missed their 30-day CDP request deadline) the taxpayer has lost some significant rights:

1. Collection action does *not* stop for an equivalent hearing, so the taxpayers or their representative still have to continue dealing with the collection division while they await their appeal;
2. There is no right to go to the United States Tax Court, as anything the appeals officer decides at the equivalent hearing is final.

---

[2] The taxpayer must quickly get into compliance in order for their appeal request to be honored. Taxpayers must be in compliance to qualify for a hearing with the Appeals Division.

The IRS cannot extend more time to the taxpayer. The CDP right is statutory, created by Congress, and IRS personnel have no authority to grant the taxpayer more time. Many times, taxpayers call the IRS, and the IRS tells the taxpayers they will give them more time to get information. This additional time is the IRS agreeing to voluntarily hold off on levy action. If later the IRS Collection Division and the taxpayer don't come to terms, the taxpayer has lost the right to a CDP hearing and an appeal to the Tax Court.

The Statute of Limitations

The IRS has 10 years from the date of assessment to collect a tax debt. That is all, 10 years. In most cases, after 10 years the debt becomes unenforceable. For example, if the 2004 tax return were filed on October 1, 2005, and the tax was assessed on October 5, 2005, the IRS would have until October 4, 2015, to collect that tax.

How does a practitioner know the date of assessment? Practitioners should obtain what are called "Account Transcripts" from the IRS that list everything that has occurred with that particular tax year for the taxpayer, including when the return was received, when the tax was assessed, the penalty and interest charged, and payments received. (see Exhibit 7). Even better, the practitioner should ask the IRS for the "Mod A," which will have an estimated CSED (Collection Statute Expiration Date).

The reason the statute of limitations is so important is that the amount of time remaining on the collection statute determines which solution the practitioner should select to resolve the client's tax liability.

The other key point about the statute of limitations is that certain actions on a client's part will toll, or freeze, the statute, preventing it from running. Such actions include the filing of an Offer-in-Compromise, filing a CDP request, requesting an installment agreement, and filing for bankruptcy.[3] These actions prevent the IRS from taking collection action, and therefore stop the 10-year collection statute from running. The rationale is that it would be unfair to allow the statute to run against the government

---

[3] The filing of a bankruptcy by statute not only tolls the statute from running but adds an additional six months. A bankruptcy filed on January 1 that was discharged on May 31 would add 11 months to the collection statute: the five for the bankruptcy plus the extra six-months by statute.

while it is prevented from taking collection action. The time remaining on the collection statute is therefore critical for the practitioner to advise the client about which of the collection alternatives make the most sense to resolve the client's tax issue.

For instance, if the liability is recent and most of the 10-year limitations period remains, an Offer-in-Compromise may make the most sense, as clients don't want the liability and tax hanging over their head for years to come. If, however, the tax liability is already older and not much more time remains on the limitations period, perhaps having the liability deemed currently-not-collectable makes sense, as this would allow you to hold the IRS Collection Division at bay while the 10-year statute continues running on the old tax debt.

The tolling of the collection statute is why filing Offers-in-Compromise that have no chance of success accomplishes nothing but wasting the practitioner's valuable time and the client's limited resources.

Federal Tax Liens

The federal tax lien arises automatically by law and will be in place automatically once the taxpayer owes money and fails to pay it upon demand (the billing notice). However, nobody knows about it but the IRS and the taxpayer (assuming the taxpayer even opened their mail). If the taxpayer owes more than $10,000 the IRS believes it must protect its interest in the taxpayer's assets and income, and will therefore the IRS will file a Notice of Federal Tax Lien ("NFTL") on both the land records where the taxpayer resides and with the Secretary of the State (Exhibit 8).

Taxpayers are often put off by the IRS's inflexible nature when it comes to the NFTL. "Why can't they just withdraw it if I do not own anything anyway?" The reason is that the IRS has done a number of studies that all conclude the same thing: The Notice of Federal Tax Lien gets the IRS paid. Hence the IRS is not interested in removing the Notice of Federal Tax Lien simply because a taxpayer requests it, as it believes that long term the NFTL will help it recover the money that it is owed.

Federal Tax Levies

A tax levy is the seizing of a taxpayer's assets to pay the back-tax debt. This can include a garnishment of wages, a seizure of everything in the taxpayer's bank account at a given moment in time, and a seizure of money owed to the taxpayer by third parties. Levies, unlike liens, can cause not only embarrassment but immediate economic devastation. (Exhibit 9)

Thankfully, the IRS has a process that it must follow before it gets to the point of issuing levies (see the notices listed previously). However, it is all too often that clients ignore the IRS notices and then seem shocked when the levies are served. Worse, now they have to borrow the money to hire the professional to help them!

Tax Compliance

What is "tax compliance?"

Tax Compliance may be the most difficult part of tax resolution work. This is because of the client themselves. For a taxpayer to work out any kind of a deal with the IRS, the taxpayer must be in tax compliance, meaning that all tax returns have been filed and they are making their current tax payments properly. They need to understand that, if they do work out a deal with the IRS, a critical term of that deal is that they will maintain their tax compliance. Any failure to do so results in a default of the installment agreement or a voiding of the Offer-in-Compromise they worked so hard to get.

So often we fight to get a client's Offer-in-Compromise accepted only to have the client incur a new debt later and void the offer. Therefore, it is critical from the beginning that clients understand the need to get into tax compliance and maintain compliance going forward.

This means that:

- All tax returns due are filed when you begin trying to work out a deal with the IRS;
- If your client is an employee, that sufficient taxes are withheld to cover the tax bill at the end of the year;

- If the clients are self-employed that they are making estimated tax payments each quarter as required;
- If the client is a business, it is depositing its payroll taxes on time each period; and
- All future tax returns due are filed on time. [4]

Clients need to understand that without their tax compliance there can be no deal reached with the IRS because lack of compliance automatically voids the deal the client just reached with the government. Why should the IRS agree to anything for the future when the client can't even stay compliant now?

Tax compliance is something the client must take care of immediately. Get the old returns completed and filed, and have the clients adjust their ways so they can make the proper tax payments to avoid running up yet another debt.

Estimated Taxes

Green: *Mr. Smith, I will call the Revenue Officer and try to get the wage garnishment lifted so you can pay your rent. The Revenue Officer is going to ask about your current year taxes. Have you made your estimated tax payments for this year?*

Client: *What's an estimated tax payment?*

It is unbelievable to me still that there are self-employed people wandering around unsupervised who do not understand that they are expected to pay their taxes on a quarterly basis. Many Americans believe they can simply file their tax return at the end of the year and just pay the tax bill then. Unfortunately, that is not how our tax system works.

---

[4] For purposes of collection, the IRS generally considers a taxpayer in compliance when they have filed the last 6 years.

Our tax system requires taxes to be paid into the government quarterly: Employers file and pay the taxes withheld from their employees quarterly, with a Form 941, and self-employed individuals are expected to file quarterly estimated tax payments with a Form 1040-ES (see Exhibit 10).

The quarterly deadlines for self-employed individuals are:

- April 15
- June 15
- September 15
- January 15

In most cases, your client must pay estimated taxes if both of the following apply.

1. They expect to owe at least $1,000 in tax, after subtracting their withholding and refundable credits.
2. They expect their withholding and refundable credits to be less than the smaller of:
    - 90% of the tax to be shown on their current year's tax return, or
    - 100% of the tax shown on their prior year's tax return. If they earn more than $150,000 per year, it is increased to 110% of the tax shown on the prior year's tax return.

Now, I know what the client is thinking. "I've never done that before. I just file my return and send them a check and the IRS has never gone after me before."

And they would be correct: so long as they can pay the tax liability in full, plus penalty and interest at the end of the year, they won't be bothered by the IRS. Once a taxpayer ends up in collection, however, the rules change.

Taxpayers need to prove that they are in tax compliance and will not create a new liability to make a deal with the IRS. Making current payments is part of that process.

Withholding Taxes

For wage earners, "tax compliance" means having the proper amount of tax withheld. Though this sounds obvious, it is amazing how frequently this issue arises when handling IRS cases.

The conversation usually goes something like this:

Client: *Every year I end up owing money to the government!*

Green: *How about increasing your withholding to make sure you cover the taxes due?*

Client: *Wow, that's a great idea!*

Green: *Thanks.*

Compliance is something the taxpayer needs to understand and maintain, because even after we solve the client's problem, no matter how we solve the problem, blowing their compliance will undo all the good we have done and the money they spent. For instance:

- If an Offer-in-Compromise is accepted, the taxpayers must maintain compliance for five years or the offer is deemed to be void and the original liability (less whatever they paid in with the offer) is put back, and they get the fun of having the IRS chase them all over again. Sort of like a bizarre game of tag, except that this one costs the client tens of thousands of dollars.
- If the taxpayers have an installment agreement and they fail to file a return, pay a tax, or receive a penalty, they have defaulted on the terms of their agreement. By defaulting on their agreement, the terms of the old agreement cease, and the taxpayer gets the pleasure of starting the process all over again.

The most difficult part of tax resolution work is dealing with the client's tax compliance. Hence this is where you need to focus your initial efforts, because without tax compliance there is no deal, and no chance of resolving the back-tax debt.

Financial Analysis: It's All in the Numbers

2

"Can the client file an Offer-in-Compromise?"

We hear this daily from accountants who are desperate to want to settle the debt for their client. This is the equivalent of our calling you and asking "Our client needs you to do their tax return. How much money can you get them back in a refund?" Your answer should be "How the hell do I know you idiot, I haven't seen their information yet!"

Our answer is similar, though slightly nicer: "It depends. What is your client's RCP?"

RCP: Reasonable Collection Potential

The IRS utilizes a formula to determine what the taxpayer's "RCP" is when considering an Offer-in-Compromise. There are other factors involved, which we will discuss, but the whole process begins with RCP.

The taxpayer's RCP consists of two elements: net equity in assets and future income. These two elements added together will calculate the RCP. Success in the area of IRS collection will depend upon our ability to calculate the taxpayer's RCP. This is why so many taxpayer's Offers are rejected, and why so many of our firm's Offers are ultimately successful. We get a very high percentage of our Offers accepted, probably north of 90%. I tell you this for four reasons:

1. To brag
2. To point out the necessity of calculating the RCP correctly so we file Offers that have a very good chance of success
3. Notice I did not say we get 100% of our Offers accepted. Our client's fail to follow through and maintain compliance just like your clients. Our client's lie to us and forget to mention things to us, just like your clients. It's the nature of this type of work that some people either do not want to be saved or cannot be saved
4. The client's situation can change. The reality is that it can take the IRS almost a year to complete its review, and often the client's income and asset picture can change enough to alter their ability to complete the Offer.

Now there are some differences between how installment agreements and Offers-in-Compromise are approached by the IRS, and we will go through those differences in the separate chapters, but for now we want to cover the basics of how the IRS will go through its process of calculating a taxpayer's ability to pay.

Net Equity in Assets

The first step in the process is to determine the fair-market-value of the taxpayer's assets. When we submit our financial packages to the IRS, we will include copies of the documents that support our numbers. When it comes to assets, we would generally include the following:

Asset	Documentation
Cash	3 months of bank statements all accounts
Investments & Retirement Accounts	Latest statement of value
Cash value Life Insurance	The latest statement showing the cash value in the policy[5]
Real Estate	A printout of value from Zillow[6]
Vehicles	A printout of value from Kelly Blue Book
Personal Assets	A listing and valuation of any collectables[7]

---

[5] For permanent life insurance policies with cash value, often the company will not allow the policy holder to take 100% of the cash value out as a loan because there is a need to maintain some cash in the policy to absorb investment ups and downs. We have our client's obtain a letter or email from their agent explaining how much of the policy can be borrowed without collapsing the policy and include that with our collection package to the IRS to explain why we can only borrow what we said we could borrow of the cash value.

[6] I suggest Zillow because that is the site I know the IRS checks, so before I submit the package I want to know what the IRS will see so I can prepare for it. If the value of Zillow is much higher than what the client thinks I can have the client obtain two statements of value: one from a realtor and one from an actual appraiser (which they need to pay for). It is not uncommon for taxpayers to have homes that are in need of much repair that Zillow cannot take into account, so it sometimes is worth obtaining the other two statements of value and including them.

[7] For personal assets the IRS is interested in collectables – artwork, jewelry, collections, etc – that can be sold to raise money. They do not mean the daily items used like clothing and furniture. Be sure to check

There are two other "assets" that are exempt for collection purposes: Tools of the Trade and Household Assets.

- Tools of the Trade: There is a statutory exemption from levy that applies to an individual taxpayer's tools used in a trade or business, which will be allowed in addition to any encumbrance that has priority over the NFTL. The levy exemption amount is updated on an annual basis and is currently $4,770.[8]
- Household Assets: This covers the personal effects in the household that are NOT of extraordinary value, such as furniture and personal effects. There is a statutory exemption amount that is updated on an annual basis and is currently $9540.[9]

Once the fair-market-value of the various assets is established the IRS will proceed with its analysis to determine how much of the equity in each asset, if any, is available for collection purposes. To determine the available equity the IRS assumes that it would obtain the "Quick-Sale" value of the asset.

The "Quick-Sale" value of the asset is generally 80% of its fair-market-value. The reason is the IRS assumes that this would be the value that would be obtained if the IRS seized the assets and sold it at a government auction. The reality is that the IRS would get much less value if it sold the asset at a government auction, but this is what it assumes when pursuing collection, so it is what we need to deal with then trying to help our taxpayers.

As an example, a taxpayer owns a home worth $300,000 with a mortgage of $250,000. He also owns some stock worth $20,000 and a car worth $5,000 without any loan against it. Here is how the IRS would look at a taxpayer's assets as far as availability:

---

the taxpayer's homeowner's policy for riders: those items specifically listed to be additionally insured, because the IRS will to see if there are valuable collections listed.
[8] See IRS Revenue Procedure 2018-57
[9] Id.

Asset	Fair Market Value	Quick Sale Value	Loan Balance Outstanding	Available Equity
House	$300,000	$240,000	$250,000	$0
Stocks	$20,000	$16,000	$0	$16,000
Car	$5,000	$4,000	$3,450 (exemption)	$550

The IRS would assume there is no equity in the home (the mortgage is larger than the quick-sale-value that could be obtained). The IRS would expect the stocks to be sold and used to pay the tax debt. The IRS, at the author's urging,[10] created an exemption for automobiles that matches that found in bankruptcy court (currently $3,450). The IRS would assume the remaining amount beyond the exemption would be available for an Offer-in-Compromise. For an installment agreement, the IRS may want the taxpayer to attempt to get a loan against the asset (the car is necessary for the production of income so the IRS would not require it be sold). Assuming the used car could not be used to obtain a loan, IRS would expect at least $16,000 to come from the sale of the stock.

The next step will be to see if the taxpayer can make payments from their future income.

Future Income Calculation

The Future Income calculation is where most practitioners go wrong when trying to help their wayward taxpayers. When calculating a taxpayer's ability to pay the IRS will utilize

---

[10] This is one accomplishment the author is very proud of. During a presentation with the Director of Collection Policy the author raised the issue of the exemption in federal bankruptcy court and that the IRS should adopt a similar policy given that both are supposed to allow taxpayers a fresh start. The IRS ultimately agreed and adopted this position, now a formal exemption for automobiles in the Offer-in-Compromise program. Your welcome!

the Taxpayer's gross monthly income and then allow certain expenses ("allowable expenses").

The ability to pay for IRS purposes is not a taxable income analysis but rather a cash-flow analysis. The IRS is attempting to determine the taxpayer's free monthly cash to pay down their tax debt, so all sources of money are considered. These include:

- Wages
- Net business income (the bottom line profit and loss from a business)
- Net Rental Income (the bottom line profit after all expenses)
- Social Security
- Dividends & Interest
- Pension Distributions
- Alimony
- Child Support Payments
- Other sources of cash

> **HOT TIP**
>
> The ability to pay for IRS purposes is not based upon taxable income but rather cash-flow from all sources! Therefore, when determining a taxpayer's ability to pay all income sources into the household will be considered.

The IRS will want the gross monthly amount of cash flow into the household and then deduct the monthly allowable expenses (see below).

For wages the IRS will want to utilize the taxpayer's gross monthly income and not the taxpayer's net income from their job. The reason for using gross monthly income is that the IRS knows the taxpayer may be having all sorts of things deducted from their pay that the IRS will not allow for determining collectability. These items include 401(k) contributions, charitable contributions, etc. The IRS has no issue with people saving for retirement or donating money to charity, but they should only do those things after they have paid their taxes.

On the expense side there are basically three types of expenses: actual, national standard and local standard. We have created a chart for you to see how the IRS treats each expense.

The key to mastering IRS collection is, aside from understanding the collection process, to be able to properly apply these rules to calculate the amount of income remaining for the IRS.

Expense	Actual or Allowable
Food, Clothing, and Miscellaneous	National Standard
Housing and Utilities	Lesser of Actual or Local Standard
Automobile - Ownership	Lesser of Actual or National Standard
Automobile - Operating	Local Standard
Public Transportation	National Standard
Health Insurance	Actual
Out of Pocket Health Care Costs	Higher of Actual or National Standard
Court Ordered Payments	Actual
Child/Dependent care expenses	Actual (must be necessary)
Life Insurance	Actual (must be reasonable)
Current Year Taxes	FIT, FICA or SE, SIT, Local
Secured Debts	Actual
Delinquent State Taxes	Percentage of State v. Federal Debt

We will review each of these in detail so that you can understand how the IRS will calculate the allowable expense for each category and determine the taxpayer's ability to pay their back taxes.

As background information, the IRS does not merely make up its standard expenses but rather obtains them from the Bureau of Labor Statistics. It generally updates them in March of each year, although it has been known to make periodic changes to the tables, so it is important for practitioners to check back and confirm the expenses before submitting information for a taxpayer.

Food, Clothing & Miscellaneous: This expense is a national standard expense, which means the taxpayer automatically gets what is on the IRS table[11], and that is it. We have attached the current national standard table (Exhibit 21). Practitioners should note that the Food, Clothing & Miscellaneous table includes the following expenses: food, house-keeping supplies, apparel, personal care products and a "miscellaneous" category. The Miscellaneous portion of the expense is designed to cover those expenses that people often incur but that do not fall into any other category, such as credit card payments, bank fees and charges, reading material and school supplies.

The taxpayer does not need to provide any supporting documentation to obtain this expense. The IRS will give them the amount on the table regardless of what the taxpayer claims or submits for documentation. As a practice point I usually just take the amount from the table and do not review records or attach documentation to support it, as the IRS will not budge from its standard amount.

Housing & Utilities: The Housing & Utilities Expense category is a local standard expense, which means that the taxpayer will be allowed the LESSER of the amount they actually spend or the amount listed on the table[12]. The table is done by state and by county. We have attached the Connecticut table as an exhibit so that you can see

---

[11] https://www.irs.gov/businesses/small-businesses-self-employed/national-standards-food-clothing-and-other-items
[12] https://www.irs.gov/businesses/small-businesses-self-employed/local-standards-housing-and-utilities

what the table looks like (Exhibit 21). The housing and utilities expense category includes all of the following expenses incurred by the taxpayer: mortgage or rent, property taxes, interest, insurance, maintenance, repairs, gas (for heating), electric, water, heating oil, garbage collection, residential telephone service, cell phone service, cable television, and Internet service. The taxpayer must provide supporting documentation to claim the expense, so copies of lease agreements, mortgage statements, utility bills, bank statements showing the payments, etc, must all be provided with the collection package when it goes into the IRS to support the claim for the expense.

There are often a few issues that come up with the housing expense. Among these are what to do with the expense for a home equity line of credit and what about a second home?

The expense of paying a home equity line of credit should be deducted on the Secured Debts line, not the housing expense line. The main reason for deducting the home equity line as a secured debt is that the line of credit is truly a secured debt not a housing expense. The other reason is so that the taxpayer can take the full expense of the credit line payments. Most taxpayer's housing expense exceeds the local IRS standard. Hence, if the practitioner includes the home equity line expense with the housing there is a very good chance that the expense will be limited/not considered. By claiming the home equity expense on the secured debts line the taxpayer can use the expense to their advantage.[13]

Regarding second homes, the IRS will not allow payments for second homes as it is unnecessary for the taxpayer to have two homes. In the unlikely event a taxpayer requires the second property for some legitimate business reason than it would be allowed, but the taxpayer must sustain the argument that it is necessary. For instance, if the taxpayer has a division of their business in another state and the mortgage on the second property is cheaper than paying for hotel rooms. In that instance, the second home may be allowable as a business expense but expect to have to fight for it.

---

[13] Note on the IRS Local Housing Standards table that the home-equity line of credit expense is NOT listed as one belonging on the housing line.

Automobile Ownership Expense: A single taxpayer is normally allowed one automobile (two if married, one for each spouse). For each automobile, taxpayers will be allowed the lesser of:

- the monthly payment on the lease or car loan, or
- the ownership costs shown in the table below.

If a taxpayer has no lease or car loan payment, the amount allowed for Ownership Costs will be $0. In the instance a taxpayer has multiple vehicles, the IRS will allow the payment that is the least per month. So, if a taxpayer has one car with a loan and monthly payment and owns another car outright with no payment, the IRS will assume the taxpayer can use the car with no loan on it and disallow the car payment in its analysis.

Automobile Operating Expense: Taxpayers are allowed a monthly amount for operating a vehicle.[14] These amounts vary based upon the regional and metropolitan area where the taxpayer lives. The taxpayer is allowed the lesser of the actual amount spent or the amount on the table. If a taxpayer spends more than the standard and can substantiate the expense and why it is necessary for either the health & welfare of the family or the production of income, they may be able to get the higher amount. There are a couple of things to watch for in automobile operating expense when practitioners are completing the financial analysis. These include:

- Self-Employed people often already deduct this expense against their business income if they use one vehicle for both business and personal, so practitioners should make sure that they do not factor automobile operating expense personally if it has already been deducted against the business income.
- For Offers-in-Compromise (and only for Offers) there is an additional $200 of operating expense allowed for older vehicles, which are vehicles that are either more than 8 years old or have more than 100,000 miles.[15]

---

[14] https://www.irs.gov/businesses/small-businesses-self-employed/local-standards-transportation
[15] IRM 5.8.5.22.3.6

Public Transportation: There is a single nationwide allowance for public transportation based on Bureau of Labor Statistics expenditure data for mass transit fares for a train, bus, taxi, ferry, etc. Taxpayers with no vehicle are allowed the standard amount monthly, per household, without questioning the amount actually spent.

If a taxpayer owns a vehicle and uses public transportation, expenses may be allowed for both, provided they are needed for the health and welfare of the taxpayer or family, or for the production of income. However, the expenses allowed would be actual expenses incurred for ownership costs, operating costs and public transportation, or the standard amounts, whichever is less.

Health Insurance: Health insurance premiums are allowed so long as they are actually being paid and the coverage is reasonable.

Out of Pocket Health Care Costs: Out-of-pocket health care expenses include medical services, prescription drugs, and medical supplies (e.g. eyeglasses, contact lenses, etc.). Elective procedures such as plastic surgery or elective dental work are generally not allowed. Taxpayers and their dependents are allowed the standard amount monthly on a per person basis, without questioning the amounts they actually spend. If the amount claimed is more than the total allowed by the health care standards, the taxpayer must provide documentation to substantiate those expenses are necessary expenses.

Court Ordered Payments: Court-Ordered Payments include alimony, child support, including orders made by the state, and other court ordered payments. If the payments are court ordered, reasonable in amount, and actually being paid by the taxpayer than they are allowable. If payments are ordered, but the taxpayer is not actually making the payments, then the IRS will not allow the expense unless the non-payment was due to temporary job loss or illness.

Child & Dependent Care Expenses: Child Care & Dependent Care expenses include things such as baby-sitting, day care, summer day-camp (not overnight camp), nursery and preschool. The expense must be reasonable and necessary for the taxpayer to produce income. For example, if the taxpayer works but his wife is a stay-at-home parent then day care expenses would not be allowed as it would be unnecessary because the child's mother does not work and is capable of watching the child.

Life Insurance: Life insurance is allowed so long as the coverage is reasonable and the premiums are actually being paid. Term policies are generally allowed without question. Permanent insurance that builds cash value such as universal life, whole life and variable life policies will generally not be allowed but the cash value will be viewed as an asset and the IRS will expect the cash value to be taken and used to pay the taxes.

Taxpayers should also include disability insurance here if they are paying for a disability policy to protect their family's income in the event of a long-term disability.

Current Year Taxes: Current taxes include federal income taxes, FICA, Medicare, state and local taxes. Current taxes are allowed regardless of whether the taxpayer made them in the past or not, the theory being that the taxpayer is required to remain current with taxes going forward, so the IRS must allow the money to be available to pay the taxes. The taxpayer's past aside, they must be in current tax compliance during and after the collection alternative is put in place.

Secured Debts: A debt that is secured will be allowed if the taxpayer can show they are making the payments. An example of a secured debt would be a home equity line of credit.

Delinquent State & Local Taxes: The ability to factor in the delinquent state & local taxes will depend upon whether there is a payment plan in place and when it was put in place. The rules are as follows:

IF	AND	THEN
the taxpayer **does not** have an existing agreement for payment of the delinquent state or local tax debts,	provides a complete Collection Information Statement (CIS) and verification of state or local tax debts,	Use the procedure to calculate the allowable percentage of the available future income (below)
the taxpayer has an existing agreement for delinquent state or local tax debts, and that agreement was established **after** the earliest IRS date of assessment,	the payment amount on the state or local agreement is **less** than the calculated percentage amount,	The monthly amount due on the existing state or local agreement will be allowed
the taxpayer has an existing agreement for delinquent state or local tax debts, which was established **after** the earliest IRS date of assessment,	the payment amount on the agreement, is **more** than the calculated percentage amount,	Use the procedure to calculate the allowable percentage of the available future income (below)
the taxpayer has an existing agreement for delinquent state or local tax debts, which was established **prior to** the earliest IRS date of assessment,	allowing the amount on the existing state or local agreement will not result in the case being reported uncollectible,	Allow the existing state or local tax payment

Page 33

The "allowable percentage of future income" calculation is designed to take the remaining allowable income and allocate it between the IRS and state & local tax debt based on the percentage each is owed of the total tax debts of the taxpayer.

For instance, assume the taxpayer has $300 remaining of their income after all allowable IRS expenses are deducted except for delinquent state & local taxes. If the taxpayer is paying $180 to the State, which is owed $10,000, and they owe the IRS $20,000, then they would be allowed to use 1/3 of the $180 state payment as an allowable expense. The reason is that the State is 1/3 of the tax debts ($10,000 State Debt / $30,000 IRS & State Debt). So, the IRS would allow 1/3 of the $180 payment, or $60, to be deducted. In addition, once the state debt was paid then the IRS would increase the taxpayer's monthly payment by the $60.

One-Spouse is Liable

What happens if only one of the spouses is responsible for the tax debt?

This situation arises either when one spouse came to the marriage with the tax debt, the spouses file married-filing-separate, or during the marriage one spouse was deemed responsible for a business's unpaid payroll taxes (also called the "Trust Fund Recovery penalty"). How will the IRS perform the analysis, and will the non-debtor spouse be forced to pay the other's tax debt?

In state's that are not community-property states, the non-debtor spouse will not be required to disclose his or her assets. They will be required to disclose their income.

> **PRACTICE TIP**
>
> For taxpayers who have not filed their tax returns, it may make sense to file the STATE returns first, and set-up an installment agreement with the state before filing the federal tax returns. This way the state liability is ahead of the federal and the state payment plan is in place, allowing the taxpayer to use 100% of the payment as an allowable expense for their federal Offer-in-Compromise!

This disclosure is neither because they are responsible nor because they are expected to pay any of the other spouse's tax debts. The non-debtor spouse's income is required in order for the IRS to do an allocation of joint expenses between the two spouses.

Example: Joe and Mary have two children, so their standard Food, Clothing & Miscellaneous expense on the IRS table would be $1,650 (the amount for a family of four). Assume only Joe owes the tax debt from a failed business with payroll tax problems. Joe is currently earning $6,000 a month and Mary earns $4,000 a month. Joe would be allocated 60% of the joint expenses because he earns 60% of the household income, or in this case $990 of the Food, Clothing & Miscellaneous expense ($1,650 x 60% = $990).

The IRS will insist on having proof of Mary's income so they can do this allocation.

Community Property States

Community property is not an issue when a joint OIC is submitted by spouses who reside in a community property state, and both spouses are liable for the tax. In this circumstance, the assets and income of both are considered available for IRS collection. There is an issue, however, when only one spouse is liable for the tax and they reside in a community property state.

Where only one spouse is liable for a tax and that spouse files an OIC, community property rules apply as follows:

1. Anything that could be classified as the liable spouse's separate property or income should be considered in the offer. In addition, the liable spouse's share of community property and community property income should be considered. If, under the community property laws of the state involved, part or all of the non-liable spouse's share of community property or income would be available to satisfy the tax liability, the portion available should also be considered in the offer in compromise.[16]

---

[16] Treas. Reg. 301.7122-1(c)(2)(ii)(B).

2. However, where spouses demonstrate that collection from assets or income of the non-liable spouse would have a "material and adverse impact" on the standard of living of the taxpayer, the non-liable spouse, and their dependents, these assets will not be considered in determining the acceptability of the offer.[17]
3. Community property assets or income will not be disregarded under this regulation to allow the taxpayers to maintain what the IRS perceives to be a luxurious or affluent lifestyle. In most cases, it is anticipated that any "material and adverse impact" of considering community property income in an offer will be eliminated by the allowance of necessary living expenses in accordance with the IRS's allowable expense guidelines.
4. In addition, community property assets will not be disregarded under this regulation unless inclusion in an offer would have an adverse impact on the taxpayer's ability to meet reasonable living expenses.[18]

The key to handling a collection case is to understand the rules for how the IRS will calculate the amounts available in assets and the taxpayer's future income. We will go through actual case studies with these numbers in the final chapter as we review Installments Agreements, Uncollectible Status and Offers-in-Compromise.

---

[17] Id.
[18] See IRM 25.18.4.14 (06-05-2017), Effect of Community Property on Offers-in-Compromise

Installment Agreements & Uncollectible Status

"Some debts are fun when you are acquiring them,

but none are fun when you set about retiring them."

- Ogden Nash

An "installment agreement" is an agreement between the IRS and a taxpayer to allow the taxpayer to pay their back-tax debt in monthly payments. There are various forms of installment agreement, each of which has special rules.

There is something practitioners and taxpayers need to understand when setting out to negotiate an agreement with the IRS, and that is that the IRS knows that installment agreements historically will default within 48 months, and therefore the IRS is told to collect as much as it can as fast as it can. This is an issue when taxpayers try and negotiate smaller payments for longer periods of time.

The IRS will utilize (usually) the financial guidelines covered in the previous chapter and seek to maximize the monthly payment. This often comes as a shock to taxpayers who get upset when the IRS will not give them "just a little more time" to pay the money back.

Example: a taxpayer who owes $95,000 to the IRS shows the ability to pay $1,000 a month based on his actual expenses but can pay $2,000 a month based upon his income less IRS allowable expenses. The taxpayer also has an IRA with $50,000. The IRS will want the IRA liquidated and paid ($35,000 after taxes and early withdrawal penalty) and the balance paid at $2,000 a month. "But can't the IRS just allow me to keep the IRA and allow me to pay it over another 3 years?"

The IRS could, but it will not. The IRS knows the agreement will default in less than 4 years (or at least believes it will), and therefore is told to collect it all as quickly as possible. The IRS marching orders to its Collection Division personnel is to collect as much as possible as quickly as possible.

With that information as background as to how the IRS will approach the payment issue, there are four types of installment agreements:

- Automatic (if the taxpayer owes less than $10,000)
- Streamlined (if the taxpayer owes less than $50,000)
- Regular
- Partial-Pay

Automatic Installment Agreement

An automatic installment agreement is an agreement where the taxpayer owes less than $10,000 in tax and:

- During the past 5 tax years the taxpayer has not owed any tax or had an installment agreement and
- The taxpayer agrees to pay the full amount owed within 3 years.

The practitioner simply either goes online to the IRS or completes IRS Form 9465 and submits it to the IRS (see Exhibit 11). There is no need for the taxpayer to provide any financial information. The IRS will set up the payment plan, as well as charging a fee for the creation of the agreement.

HOT TIP

The IRS charges for setting up installment agreements. The current fees for doing so are $225 for an installment agreement requested by phone or through filing the paper request, though this fee will be reduced to $107 if the taxpayer agrees to set-up the agreement as a direct-debit (where the IRS drafts the amount each month automatically from the taxpayer's bank account. Taxpayer's who meet the low-income threshold will pay a reduced fee of $43. There are two reasons why it is preferable for taxpayers to agree to a direct-debit agreement: the reduced fee and a smaller risk of defaulting on the agreement once it is set-up by sending in their payment late. To incentivize taxpayers to use their online portal (and reduce the need for staff time), the IRS has reduced the fee for online installment agreement requests to just $10.

Streamlined Installment Agreement

A streamlined installment agreement is very similar to the automatic installment agreement. If a taxpayer meets the following criteria, they can simply make a phone call to the IRS and arrange an installment agreement:

- The taxpayer owes less than $50,000[19]
- The taxpayer has not had a back-tax debt or an installment agreement in the last 5 years
- The taxpayer agrees to full pay the liability within 72 months or before the Collection Statute Expiration Date ("CSED"), whichever occurs first.

Just like an automatic agreement, with a streamlined agreement the taxpayer does not have to provide any financial information. The taxpayer can create an agreement with just a phone call (or going to the IRS website).

Regular Installment Agreement

Where a taxpayer cannot meet the requirements of a streamlined installment agreement either because they owe more than $50,000 or because they are unable to repay the amount back at the rate required by a streamlined installment agreement (i.e. within 72 months), then the taxpayer will be required to complete a Collection Information Statement (IRS Form 433, see Exhibit 12). The IRS will review the taxpayer's gross monthly household income and reduce it by the allowable expenses (see the prior chapter on Financial Guidelines). The IRS will set-up an installment agreement for the monthly available cash remaining after the allowable expenses are deducted. If this monthly amount will result in the IRS debt being repaid within the time remaining on the 10-year collection statute, then the agreement will be a "regular installment agreement."

---

[19] The IRS ran a pilot program in 2017 and 2018 that increased the streamlined agreement thresholds from $50,000 to $100,000, and the payment time from 72 months to 84 months. This was made permanent for ACS streamlined agreements (but not the Field Collection Force, or Revenue Officers) in September 2018. The Field Force, as of the date of this book, is still utilizing the old $50,000/72 month rule.

If a Taxpayer owns an entity, like an LLC or Corporation, they are required to include a financial for each business called Form 433-B (see Exhibit 14). If the taxpayer is submitting a form to Automated Collections ("ACS) to be deemed uncollectible they should use IRS Form 433-F (see Exhibit 13). If submitting a financial and a request for an installment agreement to ACS they should use Form 433-H (see Exhibit 15). When a taxpayer reaches an agreement with the IRS for a payment arrangement, they will be required to complete the authorization form, IRS Form 433-D (see Exhibit 16).

The benefit of a regular installment agreement is that, so long as the taxpayer remains in tax compliance, they will not have to revisit their payment plan again. If there is a change in circumstances so that the taxpayer can no longer afford their current payment plan, then the taxpayer can contact the IRS and provide updated information to modify their agreement. Failure to make the current payments or contact the IRS to modify the agreement will result in a default of the agreement, which will make it more difficult to set another agreement up.

Partial-Pay Installment Agreement

Similar to a Regular Installment Agreement, a Partial-Pay Installment Agreement ("PPIA") is reached when a taxpayer provides financial information to the IRS and the information shows that the taxpayer can make payments but they will not result in full-payment of the tax liability within the time remaining on the collection statute. When a taxpayer's RCP analysis indicates that they can make payments, but those payments will not be enough to full-pay the liability within the time remaining on the Collection Statute, the IRS will still agree to the payment plan. These agreements, called "partial-pay" installment agreements, will be just like a regular agreement except that the IRS will revisit the taxpayer every 18 months or so to see if the taxpayer's ability to pay has improved.

One-Year Rule

The IRS allows taxpayers negotiating for an installment agreement to base the payment arrangement on their actual expenses (instead of the allowable IRS standards) for up to one-year.[20] The rationale for this "one-year rule" is to allow the taxpayer a one year period to adjust their living expenses and bring them into line with the IRS allowable expenses.

When you propose this to the IRS the installment agreement proposal must include an amount for 12 months (cannot be zero), increasing to the amount calculated based on the IRS allowable expenses thereafter.

For example, assume Taxpayer Joe's financials show that he is currently unable to make his monthly installment payments because his housing expense is too high (not an uncommon situation). He is negative $100 a month, but his IRS analysis shows he can pay $500 a month once the IRS standards are applied, limiting his housing to the local housing expense standard. So long as Joe shows that he can pay the balance in full over the time remaining on the collection statute, he can request one-year to use his actual expenses for a payment plan. Now, the IRS cannot make someone uncollectible for a year and then start an installment agreement, so Joe should propose one-year of minimal payments (i.e. $25 a month), then increasing to $500 a month thereafter. Joe would have one-year to either change his housing situation to come into line with the IRS allowable standard or to find another means of paying the IRS.

Six-Year Rule

When a taxpayer is unable to full pay immediately and does not qualify for a streamlined installment agreement, the taxpayer may still qualify for the six-year rule. Taxpayers are required to provide financial information in these cases but are not required to provide substantiation of reasonable expenses. So long as the taxpayer can full-pay the amount owed within six-years and can show they will be able to maintain their tax

---

[20] IRM 5.14.1.4.1.2

compliance, the IRS generally will allow the actual expenses being paid by the taxpayer, even if they exceed the allowable standards, so long as they are not unreasonable.[21]

Defaulting on an Installment Agreement

A taxpayer will default on his or her installment agreement by doing any of the following:

- Incurring a new tax debt by filing a tax return with a balance due
- Failing to file a tax return timely and incurring a late filing penalty
- Failing to make their installment payments as agreed

Once a taxpayer defaults on his or her installment agreement the IRS will send them a letter (CP 523) Intent to Terminate your Installment Agreement (see Exhibit 17). The taxpayer must either pay the balance due in full, request an Appeal under the Collection Appeal Process (see IRS Form 9423, see Exhibit 18), or contact collections to begin renegotiating for a new installment agreement.

This is why tax compliance is such a critical aspect to tax resolution work. The failure of the taxpayer to maintain his or her tax compliance will void any deal we reach with the IRS for the taxpayer.

Uncollectible Status

What happens when a taxpayer has no available equity in assets and his or her income is not sufficient to cover their IRS allowable expenses? The taxpayer would be deemed "uncollectible", or "CNC" in tax-speak, and would receive Letter 4223 (see Exhibit 19).

When a taxpayer is deemed uncollectible it simply means the taxpayer's accounts will be coded so that the IRS does not take any levy action against him or her. Being

---

[21] 5.14.1.4.1.1

uncollectible does not actually resolve the outstanding tax issue, but it does a number of things for the taxpayer:

- The 10-year collection statute continues to run
- The IRS will not take enforcement action against either the taxpayer's assets or income

The taxpayer technically still owes the money, so interest continues to run on the outstanding debt, and the IRS may still file a Notice of Federal Tax Lien to secure its interest in assets the taxpayer either owns or after-acquires.

So, if having a taxpayer deemed uncollectible does not really resolve the issue, why consider this as a collection alternative?

There are times when it will behoove a taxpayer to simply buy time. These may include the following situations:

- The 10-year collection statute will expire soon. If the collection statute expiration date ("CSED") is approaching, then the last thing we want to do is stop the collection statute from running. By filing the documentation to have the taxpayer placed in CNC status, we hold-off enforcement action by the IRS, and allow the time remaining on the statute to continue to run;
- The taxpayer is not eligible for an Offer-in-Compromise due to a dissipated asset issue. Dissipated assets will be covered in greater depth in the Offer-in-Compromise chapter, but when a taxpayer has either transferred away assets or used assets to pay for unsecured debts instead of the IRS, that money will be required to be added to any Offer-in-Compromise filed for the next three years. The rationale is that the IRS should have received that money, so the taxpayer needs to include it in their Offer. This is usually the end to any Offer by the taxpayer for three years. In these situations, making a taxpayer Uncollectible may be desirable to ride out the three year wait before they can file an Offer.
- The taxpayer has past compliance problems that they have been unable to fix. One of the situations that comes up often with low income taxpayers (as well as other taxpayers) is a lack of records to get back returns filed. The general rule for IRS collection is the taxpayer must be in compliance in order to obtain a collection

alternative (Installment Agreement, Offer-in-Compromise or Uncollectible Status). However, there is a statutory exception for those taxpayers who are in economic hardship (ie. uncollectible). For taxpayers who are uncollectible the IRS is not to issue levies against them, even if they are not in compliance. Therefore, a taxpayer who has missing returns can still file a Collection Information Statement (IRS Form 433) with the IRS Collection Division and, if they are CNC, it should stave off any levies against bank accounts or wages. This will give the taxpayer time to prepare and file the back returns and get into tax compliance.

- If the taxpayer cannot get into current tax compliance with their payments and we need to buy-time with the IRS Collection Division. This is frequent once we get past the first quarter of the year. Many taxpayers in tax trouble are unable to make up multiple estimated tax payments and therefore are unable to get into tax compliance to pursue an Offer-in-Compromise. By submitting documents to have the taxpayer's account placed in CNC status we can buy time to get past the current year so they can start the new year being compliant.

So, uncollectible status can be used effectively to prevent the IRS from taking enforced collection action against the taxpayer for a period of time, which may be just what the taxpayer needs.

The concern with real property is that if the taxpayer owes significant money, and has a piece of property with any equity in it, then the IRS

HOT TIP

It is critical that you know how much time is remaining on your taxpayer's collection statute. If the debt is new and most of the ten-year collection statute remains then an Offer-in-Compromise may be the way to go, rather than making your client uncollectible. If, however, the ten-year statute does not have much time remaining, then uncollectible status may be the best option, particularly if they do not own any real property. Simply make the client CNC and allow the ten-years to run on the debt, allowing the whole problem to just expire.

may refer the case over to the Department of Justice to sue and bring the federal tax lien to judgment so it can seize and sell the home. (see Exhibit 36)

Offers-in-Compromise

4

One of the most popular yet misunderstood programs the IRS has for settling an outstanding tax debt is the Offer-in-Compromise, or "OIC" in practitioner speak.

An Offer-in-Compromise is where the IRS accepts less than the total owed by a taxpayer to settle the taxpayer's outstanding tax debt. What many taxpayers do not understand is the OIC program, at its core, is a formula. Hence many Offers filed by taxpayers and practitioners are not accepted because they fail to consider the formula, thereby filing Offers with the IRS that stand no chance of success from the moment they are filed.

Many of the myths circulating around the Offer program we hear include:

1. You have to Offer at least 30% (or pick whatever your favorite number is) or the IRS will not consider it;
2. You have to file the Offer during tax season as the IRS is less likely to look closely at it, increasing its chance of getting through and being accepted;
3. Do not bother filing an Offer – the IRS never accepts Offers anyway.

The IRS does accept many Offers, but they are Offers that meet the IRS's Reasonable Collection Potential ("RCP") calculation (see Chapter 2). What we will do in this chapter is review the Offer-in-Compromise program, discuss the various forms of Offers that can be pursued, review the financial analysis the IRS uses to calculate the amount of the Offer and common issues that arise when you are preparing Offers. We will review the documents that should be submitted with the Offer and will cover appealing a denied Offer.

In this book are samples of the forms you would file and of the various letters you can expect to receive while involved with an OIC. We have also included sample Allowable Expense tables and case studies to illustrate how these cases are actually done.

So, how does the IRS determine what a taxpayer should Offer? It is all about the client's RCP calculation. So long as the taxpayer's Offer meets or exceeds the IRS calculated RCP, then the Offer should be accepted.

The Offer-in-Compromise Program

The Offer-in-Compromise program allows a taxpayer to settle their back-tax debt for less than the amount owed under certain circumstances. In order for a taxpayer to obtain an Offer-in-Compromise the taxpayer must be in tax compliance, meaning at least the last 6 years of tax returns must be on file and they must be making their current tax payments.

There are two types of Offers-in-Compromise:

- **Doubt-as-to-Collectability Offer:** This is an Offer where the taxpayer does not dispute the amount owed in back taxes but cannot afford to pay the tax debt back in full. The taxpayer makes an Offer to the IRS based upon their particular financial circumstances and provides back-up to support their proposal.
- **Doubt-as-to-Liability Offer:** This is an Offer where the taxpayer offers to settle the debt based upon being able to show they do not actually owe all of the underlying tax. In many ways a Doubt-as-to-Liability Offer is similar to audit reconsideration. Here the taxpayer provides documentation as to why they do not owe the money the IRS claims.

When dealing with the IRS Collection Division it is much more common that you will be arguing about collectability rather than the underlying liability, however issues of liability do come up, and the practitioner should be aware of the methods of challenging an underlying liability. We will review this process later in this chapter.

For Offers as to collectability there are two forms the Offer can take: lump sum and short-term deferred.

Lump-Sum Offers

A "Lump Sum" Offer is one in which the taxpayer agrees to pay the Offered amount within five months of the date of acceptance. Once the taxpayer and/or practitioner calculate the taxpayer's Reasonable Collection Potential, or "RCP", then the following steps occur:

1. Taxpayer files the Offer based upon two components to calculate RCP:
   a. Net Equity in Assets
   b. 12 months of Future Income
2. Taxpayer sends in two checks that accompany the Offer (Form 656, see Exhibit 20):
   a. $186 for the Offer application fee[22]
   b. One for 20% of the amount offered (for instance, if a taxpayer Offered $10,000, he would send in a check for 20% of the amount offered, or $2,000)
3. Upon acceptance of the Offer, the taxpayer would have 5 months to pay the balance of the amount offered.

Short-Term Deferred Offer (Periodic Payment)

A short-term deferred offer, also known as a "Periodic Payment Offer", is one in which the taxpayer will begin making monthly payments while the Offer is pending and will pay the balance of the Offer in more than 6 months but not more than 24 months. It operates exactly the same as a lump sum Offer, except that the taxpayer must begin making monthly payments and continue making his or her monthly payments while the Offer is being considered, just like an installment agreement. The other difference between Short-Term Deferred Offers and Lump Sum Offers is the IRS will calculate the RCP using 24 months of future income instead of 12 months.

---

[22] This fee does change from time to time. As of this writing there is suggestion that the IRS may increase it to $300. Please make sure to pull the most updated forms and information when you submit your Offers. Failure to submit the correct fee will result in your Offer being returned and the money being kept – the fee and the deposit. Client's will not be impressed if that happens!

For a comparison of the two types of Offers, please review the chart below:

	Lump-Sum	Short-Term Deferred
Application Fee	$186	$186
Deposit	20% of Offer	1st Monthly Payment
Monthly Payments	No	Yes
Length of Time to Pay	Up to 5 months	6 – 24 months
Future Income Included	12 months	24 months
Balloon Payment Allowed	Yes	Yes
Refundable	No	No

So how does the IRS calculate how much a taxpayer needs to Offer? Let's discuss Reasonable Collection Potential as it pertains to Offers-in-Compromise.

Reasonable Collection Potential ("RCP")

The IRS will calculate Reasonable Collection Potential based upon the financial guidelines we discussed earlier in this book: net equity in assets and future income. There are slight differences, however, that practitioners need to be familiar with to master the art of filing Offers that get accepted.

For net equity in assets, the IRS will seek the equity in all assets. We say this because for an installment agreement the IRS generally does not seek the equity in a taxpayer's vehicle (unless it is a collectable or extremely expensive). With an Offer the IRS will add in all the equity. The way the author generally approaches Offers (and explains it to clients) is to think about what would the IRS get if it foreclosed its lien, sold everything at quicksale value (80%), paid off any loan ahead of its lien and took the net equity? That is the RCP from the assets the IRS would expect, and it's what has to be added into the taxpayer's OIC.

There are some exceptions to this rule. Those include the following:

Asset	Exception
Cash	Exemption of $1,000 for personal bank accounts[23]
Automobiles	There is currently a $3,450 exemption for the equity in each vehicle[24]
Retirement Accounts	Use 70% of value instead of 80% quicksale value due to the income taxes due and 10% early withdrawal penalty (if the taxpayer is under the age of 59.5. If older than 59.5 years of age then use 80%). The IRS is said to "step into the shoes of the taxpayer", meaning if the taxpayer can liquidate the account then the IRS can reach it as well and it will be considered available for collection purposes.
Professional Books & Tools of the Trade	There is a $4,770 exemption for books and tools used in the taxpayer's trade or business
Household Effects	There is a $9,540 exemption for personal household effects

Once the IRS calculates the taxpayer's RCP that will probably be the number the service will look for when considering compromising the tax debt. I say "probably" because there are a number of other issues the IRS will look at, which we will cover next.

---

[23] The IRS allows cash equal to one month of allowable expenses – see IRM 5.8.5.7.1. Try exempting one month of the taxpayer's allowable expenses and see if the IRS allows it. You can always fall back on the $1,000 exemption if this fails.
[24] You're welcome.

Common Issues with Offers

When considering whether to file an Offer-in-Compromise or not, a practitioner should consider several issues beyond just that of the RCP calculation. These include:

- Is the client in compliance and if not, can they get into compliance and then remain in compliance?
- Does the taxpayer have the ability to full-pay the liability?
- Are there any dissipated asset issues?
- Are there non-cash expenses (i.e. depreciation)?
- Are there any orders of restitution involved?

These issues will not only impact the RCP calculation, but may very well disqualify the taxpayer from filing an OIC. It is therefore critical that the practitioner consider each of these prior to filing the OIC.

Non-Compliance

One of the biggest issues practitioners will need to deal with when it comes to Offers-in-Compromise (though truthfully it's an issue with any collection alternative) is the issue of tax compliance. In Chapter 1 we discussed tax compliance and what it means for taxpayers to work out an arrangement with the IRS. Compliance becomes a huge issue for taxpayers seeking to file an Offer-in-Compromise, as they not only must be in compliance when they file the case but then remain in compliance while the Offer is pending and for 5 years *AFTER* the Offer is accepted.

Practitioners will probably find that the biggest challenge to doing a successful Offer is not the process, the forms or the numbers but rather the client themselves! So what do you do when the taxpayer is non-compliant and wants to file an Offer? Easy – they can't!

If the taxpayer must be in tax compliance for the current tax period with estimated tax payments to file an Offer that is acceptable, what do we do with taxpayers who cannot fix their current compliance?

Example: Joe comes to us in October 2016. He watched some late-night commercials and knows he can do an Offer for "pennies on the dollar" because he saw this good-looking couple on a golf course in the commercial who said he could. The conversation will go like this:

Me: "Okay Joe, I went through your numbers and yes I believe you can do an Offer and get rid of the $50 billion you owe the IRS for $1,700, which is just the equity in your car. Now it's October of 2016. Have you made your estimated tax payments for 2016?"

Joe: "No! Besides…who cares about 2016, that is not due until next October."

Me: "Actually that is not correct. You must be in tax compliance in order to file and Offer, then you must maintain compliance while it is pending and, when accepted, you have to maintain compliance for 5-years following the acceptance. Failure to do any one of those things and your Offer is dead."

Joe: "So now what?"

Me: "Can you make the 3 estimated payments for 2016 that you should have done as of today?"

Joe: "I don't have that kind of cash. So, no. The IRS is threatening to levy me again. What do we do now?"

Me: "Okay. What is means is that we cannot file the Offer yet. We will file the 433 and argue you should be made uncollectible because you show no ability to pay, and the only asset is the used car. That should hold off levy action while the IRS reviews your financial disclosures. You need to hurry up and get that tax return for 2016 filed as-soon-as possible when the forms are released, that way we can roll it into the Offer. On April 15th of 2017 you MUST make your first estimated tax payment and continue to do so for the future."

Joe: "Okay, that makes sense."

What I hope this shows you is that, in situations where the taxpayer cannot get into compliance in the current period, we need to look at other options to give them time to get into compliance. Here, I would suggest filing the 433-A with the IRS and negotiate for uncollectible or an installment agreement because we need to deal with collection to avoid the enforcement action by the IRS (ie. the proposed levy). Meanwhile, the taxpayer has some breathing room to make those moves necessary to put themselves in position to do an Offer-in-Compromise. So, it's not that they cannot do an Offer, they just cannot do the Offer right now.

Ability to Full-Pay

The IRS will not consider an OIC if the taxpayer shows the ability to full-pay the liability within the time remaining on the statute. It is therefore critical that the practitioner look at how much time remains on the collection statute and calculate if the taxpayer could full pay the liability. To do this the practitioner needs to look at the net equity calculated from assets and assume the taxpayer made their future income payments until the end of the statute. If the taxpayer's equity in assets and future income will cover the liability within the time remaining, then the taxpayer is not considered eligible to file an OIC. The taxpayer would be required to get into an installment agreement.

Dissipated Assets

A dissipated asset is an asset that was sold or transferred by the taxpayer which should have/could have been used to pay the IRS.

Example: Joe owes the IRS $75,000 for tax years 2011, 2012, 2013 and 2014. In 2015 he sells stock that he owns for $20,000 and uses the money to pay off a personal loan from a friend. The IRS would insist on the $20,000 paid to the friend for an unsecured debt being added into Joe's OIC, as it was an asset it should have received but instead Joe decided to pay off a non-priority, unsecured creditor (the friend) instead.

The rationale behind this is that it is unfair to the IRS to have to compromise a debt when a taxpayer decides they would prefer to pay-off other creditors whose debts are behind the IRS in priority. In the example above, Joe would be out from under his personal loan and would then be able to get the IRS to settle his tax debt without any assets. To avoid the government being taken advantage of the IRS will review the last three years of tax returns and look for any sales or transfers of assets. The IRS will review Schedule D, Form 4797 and any Gift Tax returns filed. If the IRS notes there have been any sales it will insist on finding out what happened to the funds. If the funds were used for paying off non-priority debts, then the amount so used will be added into the OIC calculation.

It is worth noting that the money has to have been used for a non-priority debt. The money could be used for allowable expenses and therefore not be considered "dissipated." These situations could include the following:

- The asset was sold and used to pay the taxpayer's taxes. It is a perfectly viable strategy where a taxpayer is unable to get into tax compliance with current year tax payments, so they either sell assets or draws money from a retirement account to pay their current taxes. These funds would not be dissipated because the assets were used to pay an allowable expense.
- The asset or funds were used to pay an allowable expense, such as mortgage, real estate taxes, alimony, child support or medical expenses. These expenses are allowable IRS expenses, and the money used to pay these expenses should not be considered dissipated (unless the expense was considered unnecessary – like payments on a second home, cosmetic surgery, etc).

Knowing the IRS will review the last three-year's tax returns for dissipated assets means that we, as practitioners, should review the same-three-years. Look for Schedule D (capital gains and losses), Form 4797 (sale of business assets) and see if the taxpayer has filed any gift tax returns (transferring away of assets). If so the taxpayer may have to wait until three-years has passed before he or she can consider filing an OIC.

Non-Cash Expenses

Practitioners should review the profit and loss for self-employed taxpayers very closely and look at the expenses that are being paid. One expense the IRS will disallow is depreciation/amortization, as it is an expense that is not an actual cash payment the taxpayer is making. Business use of the home will also be denied, as the living expenses are included on he personal side of the collection analysis.

The key concept to understand is that the ability to pay focuses on cash flow, not taxable income. Depreciation expenses is not an actual cash payment and is therefore not an allowable expense. The IRS will add it back to the profit and loss for purposes of calculating the taxpayer's gross monthly income.

Practitioners need to look beyond the depreciation expenses and see what is creating the deduction. If the taxpayer is making payments on the vehicle or equipment that is the source of the depreciation expense on the profit & loss statement, then those payments should be considered when calculating the net income from the taxpayer's business.

Example: Taxpayer's profit and loss shows $10,000 of depreciation expense. The taxpayer is paying off equipment that they financed at $500 a month, which for tax purposes must be capitalized when purchased and then depreciated over time. The IRS will add back the depreciation expense of $10,000, but should allow the $6,000 for the payments the taxpayer is actually making on the equipment, as it is reducing cash flow.

Averaging the Taxpayer's Income

The IRS does not want to accept the taxpayer's Offer just because the taxpayer is having a bad year. The IRS will look back over the last three years, and if the income seems down it will average the income to come up with a number for the taxpayer. For instance, a taxpayer whose income was $80, $150 and now $60 would be given a gross monthly income of the average, or $90.

Practitioners should review the last three years of returns as well and see if the taxpayer's income should indeed be averaged, and do so when calculating the gross monthly income for the RCP calculation. A potential issue practitioners should watch for is the IRS averaging the income to increase the gross monthly income for RCP purposes but leaving the current tax number alone. (Example: Average the income so instead of $60 its now $90, but leave the current tax number based upon the original $60!) If the IRS is going to increase the gross monthly income than it has to allow the taxpayer to pay the current taxes on such income, and the current tax number should be increased accordingly. Assume the IRS will not do this, and be prepared to point it out to the Offer Specialist reviewing the OIC.

In short, though calculating the RCP for a taxpayer's Offer is the critical first-step in the analysis, practitioners need to look at these other potential issues in making his or her determination to recommend the OIC filing. By reviewing returns for average income, dissipated assets, non-cash expenses and making sure the taxpayer does not show the ability to full-pay the liability, we can help our clients avoid wasting a lot of time and limited resources on an OIC that does not have potential for being accepted by the IRS.

Orders of Restitution

For those practitioners who have handled IRS Collection matters since before 2010, there has been a change recently in IRS Collection when it comes to taxpayers who emerge from the criminal tax process. The impact of the Firearms Excise Tax Improvement Act of 2010 ("FETI") now empowers the IRS to assess and collect on a restitution order from the criminal tax prosecution. This impact has changed the way taxpayers and their practitioners have to deal with the IRS, making it almost impossible for taxpayers to do anything with these assessments other than full-pay them. Practitioners need to be aware of what these restitution-based assessments are before they go filing Offers-in-Compromise to try and resolve these debts.

The Firearms Excise Tax Improvement Act of 2010 (FETI)

Federal district courts may sentence a defendant to pay restitution upon conviction of certain criminal offenses. Criminal restitution serves to compensate a victim for the loss caused by that defendant. In tax cases, the victim is often the Internal Revenue Service, and therefore a court may order a defendant to pay restitution to the Internal Revenue Service for a tax-related loss. Restitution is ordered pursuant to 18 U.S.C. § 3556, and the enforcement of that order is retained by the government under Title 18. In criminal tax cases, taxpayers may agree to an order of restitution through the plea agreement process. In contested cases that go to trial, the court may order restitution as a condition of probation or supervised release. Prior to 2010 the Service could accept payments of restitution as the victim, but neither Title 18 nor Title 26 provided the Service with the power to administratively collect on a restitution order because restitution is not a tax. That all changed with the enactment of The Firearms Excise Tax Improvement Act of 2010 ("the FETI Act").

With the enactment of the FETI Act, Congress has empowered the Service to use its administrative collection tools to enforce a restitution-based assessment. The IRS accomplishes this not by collecting on the restitution order itself, but by assessing the amount of Title 18 criminal restitution as a tax under Title 26.

In addition, the FETI Act amends IRC § 6213(b) by adding IRC § 6213(b)(5), which provides that a restitution-based assessment is not subject to deficiency procedures. Finally, the FETI Act amends IRC § 6501(c) by adding IRC § 6501(c)(11), which provides that the restitution-based assessment may be made at any time. So to summarize the impact of the FETI Act, the IRS must create a civil assessment to match the amount ordered for restitution resulting from the taxpayer's criminal tax case, said assessment can be done anytime once the restitution order becomes final, and the assessment is not subject to challenge by the taxpayer.

The IRC § 6204 Assessment

The amendment to IRC § 6204 requires the civil assessment to match the order of restitution made after August 16, 2010. The assessment cannot be more than or less than the amount ordered for restitution, so tax crimes not involving an order of restitution will not be subject to civil assessment under IRC § 6204(a)(4)(A). Crimes under Title 18 that are traceable to a tax crime under Title 26 may be assessed. However, crimes in which the order of restitution is not traceable to a tax may not result in assessable restitution. The decision will be case and fact specific and will be made by IRS Criminal Investigation in consultation with IRS Office of Chief Counsel/Associate Chief Counsel for Criminal Tax.

So, when a taxpayer has served his or her sentence and emerges from prison to rejoin society, their tax problem will continue with both the Department of Justice and IRS pursuing collection of the restitution order.

Dealing with the Civil Assessment

When the civil assessment is made based upon the order of restitution, it will trigger the standard ten-year collection statute for all civil tax debts. However, once the ten-year collection statute expiration date begins to draw near, the IRS may request that the Department of Justice to file a suit to reduce the restitution-based assessment to judgment in order to avail itself of the twenty-year judgment lien under 28 USC § 3201(c). Interest shall accrue on the restitution-based assessment, and the IRS Collection Division will pursue the amount owed like any other debt. If the taxpayer is already paying the Department of Justice a monthly amount, the IRS will allow that payment as an allowable expense and, utilizing its financial standard guidelines, will determine if there is any remaining money available to make payments to it.

The Taxpayer will be provided with a Collection Due Process hearing prior to levy action, just like any other tax assessment. A Notice of Federal Tax Lien will be filed against the taxpayer, which will also grant the taxpayer the right to a Collection Due Process hearing.

No Compromise

One of the critical differences with a restitution-based assessment is that neither the IRS nor Department of Justice has any authority to compromise the debt. The order of restitution that underpins the assessment is a court order, and therefore may not be compromised by either agency. The court itself could theoretically modify the order if it can be shown that the amount ordered is incorrect. However, an inability to pay or a change of economic circumstances are not reasons to modify the court order. Hence, once the restitution is ordered, and the IRS does its assessment based on such order, the taxpayer will own that debt until they either pay it in full or die. Given this situation, a taxpayer's options for dealing with the restitution-based assessment are extremely limited.

Compromise with Restitution Paid in Full

The author has had the chance to work out an Offer-in-Compromise with the IRS involving both a restitution-based assessment and non-restitution assessments. In that situation, the taxpayer had gone to prison for willfully violating IRC § 7202 by not accounting for and paying over payroll taxes for their business. The court entered an order of restitution for $175,000, which the IRS had also assessed under IRC § 6201. They also owed unpaid income taxes for another $250,000. With total taxes assessed (including voluntary assessments and the restitution-based assessment) of $425,000, the taxpayer's family agreed to lend $200,000 to resolve the debt.

We calculated the taxpayer's Reasonable Collection Potential ("RCP") to be $78,000. We offered $180,000 to resolve the tax debt (the "Offer"), explaining that, although the RCP was only $78,000, the taxpayer would need to pay the restitution-based assessment in full, and could borrow the funds needed from family, hence the Offer of $180,000. Though Centralized Offer-in-Compromise denied our Offer, at the Appeals hearing the Settlement Officer accepted the Offer we had filed. Admittedly, this is a situation that will not come up frequently, but it is worth noting that offers can work so long as any restitution-based assessment is paid in full. Otherwise, Offers-in-

Compromise filed for an restitution-based assessment will not be considered by either the IRS or Department of Justice.

Effective Tax Administration Offers ("ETA") and Doubt-as-to-Collectability with Special Circumstances ("DCSC")

An ETA Offer-in-Compromise is an Offer in which the taxpayer can full-pay the tax but where, for public policy reasons, the IRS should not require them to do so and should accept less than the full amount due.

A DCSC is an Offer-in-Compromise where the taxpayer does not have the ability to full-pay the tax liability and has proven special circumstances that warrant acceptance for less than the amount of the calculated RCP. The factors considered by the IRS for both an ETA and DCSC include the following: economic hardship, public policy or equity grounds and the compromise would not undermine compliance with the tax laws.

1. **Economic Hardship:** Economic hardship occurs when a taxpayer is unable to pay reasonable basic living expenses and is generally considered under the same 433-A analysis. Because economic hardship is defined as the inability to meet reasonable basic living expenses, it applies only to individuals (including sole proprietorship entities). Compromise on economic hardship grounds is not available to corporations, partnerships, or other non-individual entities.

An example would be where a 72-year-old retired taxpayer owed the IRS $450,000, and had $500,000 in a savings account. Every month he is required to use $1,000 a month of his savings to pay his necessary living expenses. On paper the taxpayer can full-pay his liability, but the author filed an ETA OIC and argued that the IRS would need to allow the taxpayer to keep $180,000 of the account: $1,000 a month for the 15 years of his life expectancy on the IRS tables. The IRS agreed and accepted $320,000 to settle the $450,000, allowing the taxpayer to keep $180,000.

2. **Public Policy or Equity Grounds:** Here the taxpayer's actions will be viewed to see if the taxpayer is someone sympathetic and therefore worthy of

a compromise. The author has had these situations where the taxpayer owed payroll taxes due to being the victim of embezzlement by a bookkeeper. All non-hardship ETA offers should meet the following requirements:

- The taxpayer has remained in compliance since incurring the liability and overall their compliance history does not weigh against compromise;
- The taxpayer must have acted reasonably and responsibly in the situation giving rise to the liabilities; and
- The circumstances of the case must be such that the result of the compromise does not place the taxpayer in a better position than they would occupy had they timely and fully met their obligations, unless special circumstances justifying the compromise are present.

3. **Compromise Would Not Undermine Compliance with Tax Laws:** Compromise under the ETA economic hardship or non-economic hardship provisions are permissible if acceptance does not undermine compliance. The public should not perceive that the taxpayer whose offer is accepted benefited by not complying with the tax laws. Factors supporting (but not conclusive of), a determination that compromise would undermine compliance include, but is not limited to:

- The taxpayer has an overall history of noncompliance with the filing and payment requirements of the Internal Revenue Code
- The taxpayer has taken deliberate actions to avoid the payment of taxes.
- The taxpayer has encouraged others to refuse to comply with the tax laws.

Practitioners need to be aware that these Offers exist, but also that they are generally reviewed in Washington, DC by IRS Counsel and are very rarely given. The taxpayers seeking these generally have to have very strong facts and circumstances for the IRS to agree to accept less than the total owed.

Doubt-as-to-Liability Offers ("DATL")

A DATL is an Offer where the taxpayer requests the IRS to compromise the assessed liability not because they cannot make payments, but rather because the taxpayer does not truly owe the tax. The taxpayer who believes they do not owe the IRS the money claimed may file a DATL with the IRS, which is done by completing Form 656-L. The Form (Exhibit 35)

The taxpayer who submits a DATL should submit with the Offer any and all supporting documentation that supports the claim that he or she does not owe the money claimed by the government. There is no need to provide a 433 Collection Information Statement, as the issue here is not one of ability to pay but rather that the Taxpayer does not really owe the money. The taxpayer must Offer something to the IRS: a Taxpayer cannot Offer zero, even if they believe they do not owe the tax. Also, the Taxpayer who has overpaid the tax or who has had money levied by the IRS for the tax year or years in question cannot seek a refund through this process. The DATL is meant to Offer the IRS something for resolving the debt. Taxpayers who want to pursue refunds would have to either pay and then file a refund request or seek audit reconsideration.

Finally, the DATL is an Offer, just like the Doubt-as-to-Collectability Offers, and therefore have the same compliance requirements. Therefore, Taxpayers must be in Tax Compliance when they file their DATL and must maintain said compliance throughout the process and for five-years afterward.

The Offer-in-Compromise Outcome

Once the Offer is filed the IRS will send a letter confirming it has received the Offer (see Exhibit 22). Later the Taxpayer will receive either a letter accepting the Offer (see Exhibit 23), or a letter explaining that the Offer is insufficient based upon the IRS's calculation of RCP (see Exhibit 24). The IRS will include its tables showing the calculation for how it arrived at its RCP number (see Exhibit 25). The taxpayer can either send additional information as to why he or she disagrees with the IRS's calculation, or simply agree to the increased Offer. If the taxpayer agrees to the increased Offer then IRS will send an addendum (see Exhibit 26) for the taxpayer to sign, agreeing to the higher RCP. At that time the taxpayer will need to make an additional payment so that the twenty percent of a lump-sum offer is properly paid in.[25]

Example: Taxpayer made an Offer-in-Compromise of $10,000, paying in the $186 application fee and a $2,000 deposit (20% of the amount offered for their lump sum Offer). If the IRS calculates the RCP should be $18,000, and if the taxpayer agreed to the increased Offer, the IRS would send an addendum for the taxpayer to sign and send back with an additional $1,600. The additional $1,600 is for the amount that should have been submitted ($18,000 Offer 20% = $3,600 deposit, less the $2,000 that was submitted previously, or $1,600). Had the Offer been a deferred Offer where the taxpayer was making monthly payments the taxpayer would need to increase the monthly payments so that they paid in accordance with the new Offer and payment schedule.

If the Offer is ultimately accepted then the IRS will send an acceptance letter indicating it has been accepted and reviewing the terms of the Offer, including the due date for final payment and the need for the taxpayer to maintain his or her compliance (see Exhibit 23). When the taxpayer does make their final payment, another letter indicating that the taxpayer has met the terms of their agreement will be sent (see Exhibit 27). If later the taxpayer defaults on his or her Offer a letter threatening the default will be sent (see Exhibit 28).

If the Offer is rejected, then a letter indicating it has been rejected will be sent (see Exhibit 29) and providing the taxpayer with time to submit an appeal of the denial.

---

[25] 5.8.4.24.1.12

Bankruptcy

5

There are many myths and rumors surrounding the issue of bankruptcy when it comes to tax debts. Most practitioners tell clients that taxes are not dischargeable in bankruptcy. Fortunately, they are only partially correct. The general rule is that taxes are not dischargeable unless they meet several exceptions. Thankfully, we often can use bankruptcy to great effect, and bankruptcy is one of the best ways to deal with tax and other debts. It's critical that practitioners understand when to use bankruptcy and what taxes may be dischargeable. Obviously, these decisions need to be made by a knowledgeable bankruptcy attorney, but it is useful to understand when bankruptcy should be considered as an option.

There are many benefits to using bankruptcy to resolve back tax issues. These include the automatic stay on collection activities, possibly the discharge of taxes, interest and penalties, challenging the underlying tax liability, and forcing the government to accept payment agreements it otherwise may not be interested in accepting.

The first thing to understand is the basics of the various forms of bankruptcy. In a Chapter 7 bankruptcy, the taxpayers seek to have their debts simply discharged. If a Chapter 7 bankruptcy is filed for a business, then it is done with the intent of a complete liquidation of the business.

Chapter 13 is a plan of reorganization for individuals who need to restructure their debts in order to pay back their creditors. There may be some discharged debts through Chapter 13, but otherwise it is a forced plan of repayment to creditors, usually lasting no longer than 60 months, that is overseen by a bankruptcy trustee.

Chapter 11 is for reorganizing business debts, although some individuals do use Chapter 11 to reorganize their personal debts as well. Similar to Chapter 13, it allows the filer to discharge those debts that can be discharged, and then reorganizes the remaining debts into a plan of repayment that is overseen by a bankruptcy trustee. The payment plans generally must be completed within 60 months of filing, though creditors may agree to allow a longer repayment period.

With that as a quick overview of the various forms of bankruptcy, let's review the potential benefits of using the bankruptcy code to resolve our client's outstanding tax debts.

The Automatic Stay

Section 362 of the Bankruptcy Code provides that, with few exceptions, all collection activity by creditors must cease once the client files for bankruptcy.[26] This includes the IRS and its efforts to pursue collection of back taxes. So one of the immediate benefits of filing a bankruptcy is that it can put a stop to all IRS and state revenue departments' collection efforts against the taxpayers and their property. The bankruptcy effectively removes the case from the IRS Collection Division and moves it to the IRS's Insolvency Unit, which deals with bankruptcy cases. This can give a taxpayer immediate relief to work out a plan through a bankruptcy when the IRS may have otherwise been unwilling to work with the taxpayer.

Discharging Taxes

The issue of discharging taxes can be complicated. It depends upon a number of factors, including the type of tax, how old the tax year is, when it was filed, and what the taxpayer has done since filing the return. What we focus on here are the basics of discharge-ability, and when we should consider having the taxpayer talk to a bankruptcy attorney.

There are 10 rules for discharge-ability of tax obligations in a Chapter 7 bankruptcy filing. The first six relate to income taxes. All 10 of the following rules must be satisfied in order to discharge a tax obligation.

1. *The three-year rule.*[27] The tax in question must be more than three years old, dated from the most recent date the tax return was due to be filed. The three-year period is computed from the most recent date the tax return is due for the tax year (typically April 15 of the year following the tax year) including any more recent due date resulting from a taxpayer's filed extension, or if April 15 falls on a weekend or holiday. The critical date for the three-year look back period to

---

[26] 11 U.S.C. § 362.
[27] 11 U.S.C. § 507(a)(8)(A)(i).

commence is when the return was last due, including extensions, not when the return was filed, which is immaterial.[28]

2. *The 240-day rule.*[29] The tax in question must have been assessed more than 240 days prior to the bankruptcy (plus any period of time during which an offer in compromise was pending, plus 30 days). An amended return, an examination of a return, or an audit may trigger a new or second assessment showing an increase in the tax claim. If any of these events occur, the subsequent audit assessment triggers a new 240-day period applicable to the increase in the tax assessment. The original portion of the tax, if dischargeable prior to the audit, would still be dischargeable.

3. *The two-year rule.*[30] A late-filed tax return must have actually been filed more than two years before the bankruptcy petition date. "[I]n order for a document to be considered a 'return,' under either the bankruptcy or the tax laws, it must (1) purport to be a return; (2) be executed under penalty of perjury; (3) contain sufficient data to allow calculation of tax; and (4) represent an honest and reasonable attempt to satisfy the requirements of the tax laws."[31] Therefore, although a substitute for return (SFR) generally doesn't count as a return,[32] if the debtor signs the SFR it may constitute a return.[33]

4. *The non-fraudulent return rule.*[34] The return for the tax year in question must have been non-fraudulent. Generally, the IRS must establish (1) a debtor's knowledge of the falsehood of the return, (2) an intent to evade taxes, and (3) an underpayment of taxes. The test is a fact-sensitive inquiry requiring culpability on the part of a debtor.[35]

---

[28] *U.S. v. McDermott (In re McDermott)*, 286 B.R. 913 (M.D. Fla. 2002).
[29] 11 U.S.C. § 523(a)(1)(B).
[30] 11 U.S.C. § 523(a)(1)(B).
[31] *Moroney v. US (In re Moroney)*, 352 F.3d 202 (4th Cir. 2003), *but see, Colsen v. United States*, 446 F.3d 836 (8th Cir. 2006) (SFRs are returns – minority rule).
[32] *In re Payne*, 431 F.3d 1055 (7th Cir. 2005) (SFR's are not "returns" – majority rule).
[33] *See Bergstrom v. United States (In re Bergstrom)*, 949 F.2d 341 (10th Cir. 1991).
[34] 11 U.S.C. § 523(a)(1)(C).
[35] *Riley v. United States (In re Riley)*, 202 B.R. 169 (Bankr. M.D. Fla. 1996).

5. *The non-tax evasion rule.*[36] A taxpayer must not have willfully attempted to evade or defeat taxes. There is both a conduct and mental state requirement under Section 523(a)(1)(C). Many courts have held that the government need only establish that the debtor (1) had a duty to pay the tax; (2) knew of that duty; and (3) voluntarily and intentionally violated that duty in order to prove that the debtor willfully attempted to evade or defeat a tax. Mere nonpayment of taxes has been held to be insufficient, but a debtor can't engage in affirmative acts to evade or defeat collection of taxes.[37]

6. *Unassessed income tax.*[38] Income tax must be assessed as of the petition date and must not be assessable post-petition.[39] For example, if the underlying tax is dischargeable, but the IRS can still audit the tax year in question (three years from when a return is filed or longer by agreement), any additional taxes assessed by an audit would then be non-dischargeable.

7. *Payroll, Withholding, and Other Trust Fund Taxes.*[40] A tax required to be collected or withheld and for which the debtor is liable in any capacity (that is, payroll taxes and sales taxes), regardless of when the tax claim was incurred, is a trust-fund tax and ordinarily not dischargeable.[41] This includes federal and state payroll withholding taxes and sales taxes.

8. *Property taxes.*[42] Property taxes assessed and payable without penalty more than one year before the petition date are dischargeable. Property taxes that are assessed and payable without penalty within one year of the petition date are non-dischargeable.

9. *Employment, excise taxes and custom duties.*[43] Certain employment and excise taxes imposed on transactions within three years of the petition date

---

[36] 11 U.S.C. § 523(a)(1)(C).
[37] See In re Griffith, 206 F.3d 1389; In re Haesloop, 2000 Bankr. LEXIS 1104.
[38] 11 U.S.C. 507(a)(8)(A)(iii).
[39] Pilya v. Commissioner (In re Pilya), 282 B.R. 640 (Bankr. S.D. Ohio 2002); In re Williams, 183 B.R. 43 (Bankr. E.D.N.Y. 1995).
[40] 11 U.S.C. § 507(a)(8)(C).
[41] DeChiaro v. New York State Tax Comm'n (In re DeChiaro), 760 F.2d 432 (2nd Cir. 1985).
[42] 11 U.S.C. § 507(c)(8)(B).
[43] 11 U.S.C. § 507(a)(8)(D), (E) and (F).

(including any extensions) and customs duties arising out of the importation of merchandise are non-dischargeable. Examples of excise taxes include gift, estate and highway use taxes.

10. *Gap Claims.*[44] A "Gap Claim" is a tax claim that arises after a taxpayer is forced by creditors into an involuntary bankruptcy but before a bankruptcy trustee is appointed or before the order for relief is granted (the "gap period"). Such tax claims would be non-dischargeable in bankruptcy.

To summarize the basic rules that impact most clients, a tax may be dischargeable if:

- The tax return was due (including extensions) more than three-years ago,
- If the return was filed late, and it's been on file with the IRS for at least two years,
- Any additional assessments (from an exam or an amended return) are at least 240 days old,
- The taxpayer did not commit fraud or attempt to evade a tax, and
- It's an income tax and not a "trust" tax that was collected on behalf of the government.

Example: Joe filed his 2008 to 2012 tax returns in October 2013 with the IRS. Joe would go on extension each year but then never got around to filing the actual return until the IRS pursued him. Joe came to see us in August 2016 about a bankruptcy due to vendors pursuing him for unpaid bills. Which of the tax years can he discharge in the bankruptcy?

The taxes are all income taxes. Assuming there has been no fraud or tax evasion, and that a bankruptcy attorney determines whether Joe meets the qualifications for a Chapter 7 bankruptcy (called the means test, which is beyond the scope of this Guide), Joe should be able to discharge the tax years 2008 – 2011 if he filed bankruptcy that day (August 2016). The 2012 tax year was due October 2013 on extension, so it won't meet the three-year rule until October of 2016. The other years are all more than three

---

[44] 11 U.S.C. § 507(a)(2).

years old, and though being late filed, have been on file with the IRS for more than two years.

Note of Caution: It is critical that a qualified bankruptcy attorney review the IRS transcripts and make a determination on the "means test" and other issues. The critical issue here is that we as tax practitioners must be able to identify when a bankruptcy filing may be a useful tool for the taxpayers to resolve their tax (and non-tax) creditor issues. The client's case may be quite complicated, as the taxpayer may have extended the three-year rule by filing Offers-in-Compromises, CDP requests, and other actions with the IRS. In addition, depending on the federal circuit in which the taxpayer resides, some of the circuits have taken the position that late filed returns are never dischargeable. If you think you have a taxpayer who can benefit from a bankruptcy filing, please send them to a qualified bankruptcy attorney who understands the tax rules!

Non-Discharge-ability of Payments of a Non-Dischargeable Tax. If you pay a non-dischargeable tax with what would otherwise be a dischargeable method of payment (that is, a credit card), the credit card balance for the tax paid would also be non-dischargeable in bankruptcy. Taxpayers are not going to be permitted to turn otherwise non-dischargeable debts into a dischargeable one because they used a credit card to pay the debt. So, not paying the Trust Fund taxes with a credit card and then trying to discharge the credit card debt!

Discharge-ability of Penalties. The rule is that penalties that are designed to repay the government are non-dischargeable in bankruptcy; however, penalties designed to punish the taxpayer may be dischargeable in bankruptcy. For income tax penalties (accuracy, failure-to-file, and failure-to-pay) the government is already collecting the tax and interest, so the penalty is purely to punish the taxpayer's behavior, and therefore may be discharged. The penalty is treated as a non-priority, unsecured debt (like a credit card) and may be discharged through the bankruptcy.[45] The Trust Fund Recovery Penalty assessed against responsible individuals who failed to pay over the company's

---

[45] 11 U.S.C. § 523(a)(7). *See Roberts v. United States* (*In re Roberts*), 906 F.2d 1440 (10th Cir. 1990); *Polston v. United States* (*In re Polston*), 239 B.R. 277 (Bankr. M.D. Pa. 1999).

payroll taxes are non-dischargeable, as they relate to a non-dischargeable debt (a Trust Tax).

Discharge-ability of Interest. Interest on tax debts follows the underlying tax: If the tax is dischargeable then the interest is also dischargeable.[46] If the tax is not dischargeable, then the interest will not be either. The government is entitled to interest on its money and is allowed to collect the money owed and the interest that accumulates during the bankruptcy.

Payment Plans

One of the other major benefits of using a Chapter 11 or Chapter 13 bankruptcy filing is that the taxpayers can create an installment agreement with the government to repay their taxes over time (generally up to 60 months) whether the IRS likes it or not. We have used this in cases in which a taxpayer had a valuable business but just could not get out from under some old tax debt and the IRS would not work with the taxpayer any longer.

Example: Taxpayers had a childcare business with nearly 400 children that was fully committed and making very nice money. They owed $275,000 in payroll taxes, plus $30,000 in interest, and $85,000 in penalties from several years back when the company owner became sick and the business faltered. The company had already defaulted on two installment agreements. The taxpayer came to us, and we offered the IRS $7,500 a month through a new installment agreement to repay the debt based upon the company's current Collection Information Statements; however, the Revenue Officer felt the taxpayers had already had their opportunities and refused any agreement. The clients filed a Chapter 11 bankruptcy. All collection action by the IRS against the company stopped. We were able to discharge the penalties ($85,000) and credit card debt ($50,000) and create a monthly payment plan for the tax and interest of $5,500, much better than

---

[46] *Jones v. United States* (*In re Garcia*), 955 F.2d 16 (5th Cir. 1992).

the amount the 433 CIS statements showed when we gave them to the IRS! Guaranteed payment arrangement, $135,000 in savings (credit cards and tax penalties), and a lower monthly payment plan.

Tax Liens

It is often said that bankruptcy can't disturb liens and that security interests pass through bankruptcy. This is particularly important in the context of a federal tax lien because the federal tax lien passes through bankruptcy and attaches to the debtor's future interests. Thus, while the underlying tax debt may be sufficiently old to be discharged in bankruptcy, if the federal tax lien remains and the debtor owns or later acquires lienable property (that is, real estate) the IRS is still able to execute on its tax lien.[47]

The impact is that, when clients have a federal tax lien, they can use bankruptcy to discharge tax debts; however, those assets they have that the lien attached to are still subject to collection, and other resolution options may be considered for dealing with those, such as an Offer-in-Compromise.

HOT TIP

Bankruptcy can be a wonderful tool for helping taxpayers clean up both tax and non-tax debts, make payment arrangements, and bring their financial nightmare to an end. However, it's critical that we as tax practitioners not make these decisions without the input of an experienced bankruptcy practitioner who understands the impact of the tax debts and what can and cannot be accomplished through the bankruptcy filing.

---

[47] *IRS v. Orr* (*In re Orr*), 180 F.3d 656 (5th Cir 1999).

Collection Appeals

6

Prior to 1998 taxpayers who owed the IRS money were at the mercy of the IRS Collections Division. There was no appeal, no audit reconsideration, and no United States Tax Court rights. The Collection Division could simply seize assets whenever it deemed it administratively efficient to expedite payment.

In 1998 Congress held hearings and deemed the IRS collection methods abusive. From the hearings came the 1998 IRS Restructuring & Reform Act. Embodied in the act are Collection Due Process ("CDP") rights for every taxpayer, which each taxpayer must be advised of before enforced collection action can take place.

When a taxpayer invokes their CDP rights a number of good things happen:

- Collection activity ceases
- The case is forwarded to an Appeals Officer to review
- The taxpayer ensures they have the right to take their case to the United States Tax Court

Yes, despite the benefits of invoking a taxpayer's CDP rights, very few taxpayers and practitioners ever invoke them. According to the National Taxpayer Advocate less than 3% of taxpayers request a CDP hearing. The failure to request a taxpayer's collection due process right is in most cases a serious mistake made by practitioners and taxpayers who do not understand the process.

Collection Due Process

A taxpayer is provided the opportunity to invoke their CDP appeal rights whenever either a Notice of Federal Tax Lien ("NFTL") is filed or when the IRS issues a final notice of threat to levy assets of the taxpayer.[48] Upon receipt of either if NFTL or threat to levy the taxpayer has 30 days to request the CDP hearing with an Appeals Officer, also referred to as a Settlement Officer. The request is made by filing IRS Form 12153, Request for Collection Due Process Hearing or Equivalent Hearing.

---

[48] This "Final Notice" could come in the form of either a Letter 11, Letter 1058 or CP-90

Once the IRS receives the formal request for a CDP hearing all collection activity will stop as to the tax periods on the threat to levy. Collection may continue on older tax periods where the CDP rights have expired.

Example: Joe owes money to the IRS for tax years 2007 and 2008. He was in an installment agreement but defaulted when he filed his 2013 return with a new balance owed that he could not pay. He has received a Ltr 11, Final Notice of Intent to Levy for the new 2013 year and has filed his Form 12153 to request a CDP hearing. Collection will cease for 2013, but the IRS Collection Division may continue taking action on the 2007 and 2008 years, which are not covered by the CDP request.

In cases like the example above where taxpayers owe for back years as well as newer tax periods that are covered by a CDP request, practitioners need to continue to deal with the Collection Division if he or she wants to avoid levy action against his or her taxpayer's assets.

Example (continued): Joe's CPA, while waiting for the CDP hearing with an IRS Settlement Officer, will put together a Collection Information Statement (Form 433-A) and mail it into the IRS Collection Division with a new installment agreement proposal. Later, when he hears from the Appeals office he can submit the same package to it. By providing the package to Collection with a request for an agreement there should be no enforcement activity by the IRS against Joe for the older tax years. Joe's CPA can now see which division will give him the installment agreement: Collection or Appeals.

HOT TIP

When you complete a Form 12153 for a taxpayer on Page 2 in Box 8 there are a list of collection alternatives. Practitioners MUST pick one: a request for a hearing without proposing a collection alternative in Box 8 means you have no proposal, and the hearing will be over before you ever meet with someone. You must pick one! Our recommendation is to select all three alternatives. By selecting all three options the message to Appeals when the request is received is that the taxpayer is keeping his or her options open.

The Appeals Hearing

Once Appeals has the case it will be assigned to a Settlement Officer, who will mail a letter to the practitioner and the taxpayer informing them that the case has been received. The letter will also tell the taxpayer and practitioner what he or she should expect from Appeals, when the hearing is scheduled for, and what the Settlement Officer will want from the taxpayer in order for it to consider the taxpayer's case. Generally, Appeals will send a letter confirming it has received the taxpayer's case (see Exhibit 33), and then request the following be submitted from the taxpayer in advance of the scheduled hearing:

- Any unfiled tax returns must be filed prior to the hearing
- Proof of the taxpayer's tax compliance regarding current tax payments
- A Collection Information Statement (Form 433)
- A proposal from the taxpayer – what is it that the taxpayer wants?

The hearing with Appeals is generally done by phone, though if requested, the practitioner can go into the IRS Appeals Office for a face-to-face hearing. If you are new to this area of practice, then we recommend requesting face-to-face hearings and going in and meeting your local Settlement Officers. It is good to get to know your local folks and to start building professional relationships with them.[49]

The hearing will be informal, usually held by phone or in a conference room where the Settlement Officer will tell you what they see from their review and you can have a discussion of the taxpayer's situation and your proposal. After the conference the Settlement Officer will issue a Notice of Determination (see Exhibit 34). If the taxpayer agrees with the determination by Appeals then he or she will be asked to sign a waiver form, waiving their right to pursue the case to United States Tax Court. This is routine, and it allows the IRS to go through the work to set up the proposal agreed to without the

---

[49] Due to budget issues the IRS has been closing many appeals offices, and no longer will guarantee a taxpayer a face-to-face hearing. It is still worth requesting but is no longer guaranteed.

risk of doing all the work to put the agreement in place to just have the taxpayer later file their case in the United States Tax Court anyway.

If the taxpayer disagrees with the determination by the Settlement Officer, they will have 30-days to file a case in the United States Tax Court. Collection cases that proceed to the United States Tax Court have to do so on what is called an "abuse of discretion standard" of review, meaning that the taxpayer will have to carry the burden of showing why the IRS abused its discretion in not giving the taxpayer whatever collection alternative he or she wanted.

Equivalent Hearings

If the taxpayers miss the 30-day window to request the CDP hearing they still have up to one year to request an Equivalent Hearing, which is an appeals hearing equivalent to a CDP hearing, with three significant differences.

1. The Equivalent Hearing request gets the case to a Settlement Officer in Appeals to consider, but it doesn't grant the taxpayers the right to proceed to the Tax Court if they disagree. Whatever the Settlement Officer decides is final.
2. With an Equivalent Hearing the IRS Collection Division does not need to cease its collection efforts. Practitioners need to be aware that when they request the equivalent hearing, they must continue working with Collection to avoid a levy action against the taxpayer's income and assets.
3. The collection statute does not toll for an equivalent hearing.

The request for the Equivalent Hearing is done exactly the same as the request for a CDP hearing. Either the taxpayer or the practitioner files the Form 12153 to request the case be sent to Appeals. In order to obtain the Equivalent Hearing though, it must be filed within one year of the date on the letter, and Box 7 must be checked on page 2, specifically requesting the Equivalent Hearing. If Box 7 is not checked then the taxpayer is given nothing: They failed to file a timely CDP request (within 30 days) and failed to ask for the equivalent hearing (by not checking the box).

Offer-in-Compromise Appeals

Unless an Offer-in-Compromise is filed pursuant to a Collection Due Process hearing, the Offer appeal will be ultimate decision. This means that if a taxpayer simply files an OIC, that OIC is denied at the centralized unit and then the taxpayer takes his or her appeal, the Settlement Officer hearing the appeal will make the final decision and there will be no review by the United States Tax Court. Hence, usually it is beneficial to file an OIC pursuant to a CDP hearing, but if that is not available to the taxpayer, then the practitioner needs to know that the Appeal is the final word on that OIC.

HOT TIP

Many practitioners check Box 7 on page 2 of the Form 12153 every time they file the form just in case they have miscalculated the 30 days. Failure to do so means the taxpayers did not request an Equivalent Hearing and lost their opportunity to get to Appeals.

Payroll Taxes & Personal Liability

7

Payroll taxes are the number one reason why businesses and their owners end up in our office. The issue is why?

Given that most businesses fail due to cash-flow issues, it should not be surprising that taxes collected and withheld by the business also get spent when the business starts to struggle. Add to that most businesses start their life cycle under-capitalized, and it is easy to see why payroll taxes become an issue for struggling businesses.

A former senior partner of mine once explained that payroll taxes were the easiest loan to take and the hardest to pay back: easy because there are no loan documents to fill out or permission to ask. Just keep and spend the money. It is the hardest loan to pay back because, with all of the various penalties and interest, the struggling business soon finds itself in a financial hole that it has no hope of getting out from.

The worst part about payroll tax debts is the personal liability to the owners and key employees. A business is an asset of the owner, no different than any other asset, like a stock or a bond. However, because of the potential personal liability, the business has the potential to be destroyed by the unpaid payroll taxes, as do the other assets of the owner. That makes payroll tax debts one of the most common issues business owners deal with, and one of the largest opportunities for the knowledgeable tax practitioner to save financial lives and make money.

Introduction to Payroll Taxes

Payroll taxes are a significant stream of revenue for the United States Government. In 2018 more than $1.05 trillion was collected in federal employment taxes and more than $1.35 trillion collected in income taxes withheld by employers. The total taxes paid over by employers on behalf of employees represents more than 72% of all the taxes collected by the United States Government.

Income tax and Federal Insurance Contributions Act ("FICA") taxes are withheld from each employee's paycheck by the employer and paid over to the United States Government on either a weekly, monthly, quarterly or annual basis depending upon the size of the employer's payroll.

These taxes are reported using the following forms:

Form	Description
Form CT-1	Employer's Annual Railroad Retirement Tax Plan
Form 720	Quarterly Federal Excise Tax Return
Form 941	Employer's Quarterly Federal Tax Return
Form 943	Employer's Annual Federal Tax Return for Agricultural Employees
Form 944	Employer's Annual Federal Tax Return
Form 945	Annual Return of Withheld Federal Income Tax
Form 1042	Annual Withholding Tax Return for U.S. Source Income of Foreign Persons

FICA consists of a 6.2% tax for Social Security and a 1.45% tax for Medicare withheld from an employee's gross pay, with a corresponding match from the employer. The amounts withheld by an employer from the employees for the employee's share of the FICA taxes and federal income tax are referred to as "Trust Funds" because the employer is holding these funds in trust for the United States Government.

In an effort to protect this revenue source, Congress created Internal Revenue Code ("IRC") § 6672 to allow the Commissioner of the Internal Revenue Service, when payroll taxes are not paid over to the government, to assess a penalty against individuals and/or businesses whom it deems to be responsible for accounting for and paying over the payroll taxes and who willfully failed to do so. The penalty is equal to 100% of those trust funds taxes not properly accounted for and paid over to the United States Government by the employer.

In addition to IRC § 6672, the IRS also has available IRC § 3505, which allows it to collect unpaid Trust Fund taxes from third party lenders who knowingly loaned funds to cover a company's net payroll knowing that the company either could not or would not deposit the payroll taxes.

In addition to the civil penalties there are criminal aspects of failing to withhold and/or pay over payroll taxes. IRC § 7202 makes it a crime punishable by both fine and/or incarceration for those parties that willfully try to evade or defeat the accounting and payment of the trust funds to the United States Government. Congress also created IRC § 7215 which is a misdemeanor for the failure to pay over the payroll taxes. IRC § 7215 reduced the fines and potential time for incarceration from those imposed by the felony section IRC § 7202 but, because it is a misdemeanor, there is no requirement on the part of the Government to prove criminal intent to obtain a conviction.

Historically, despite having IRC § 7202 and IRC § 7215 in their arsenal of weapons, there were very few criminal payroll taxes cases brought by the government. However, since 2010 there has been a significant increase in criminal payroll tax prosecutions and convictions. The identification of the role of unpaid payroll taxes in the "Tax Gap" and the number of failed businesses during to the economic downturn has increased the focus of the IRS on payroll tax enforcement.

Internal Revenue Code § 6672

IRC § 6672 allows the Internal Revenue Service to recover "trust funds" withheld from employee's pay from "any person required to collect, truthfully account for, and pay over any tax imposed" and "who willfully fails to collect such tax, or truthfully account for and pay over such tax, or willfully attempts in any manner to evade or defeat any such tax or the payment thereof"

There are two key elements required for an individual or business to be held responsible for the Trust Fund Recovery Penalty under IRC § 6672:

1. The person had to be required to collect, account and pay-over the payroll taxes, and
2. The person's failure to do so must have been willful.

The Willfulness Requirement

For purposes of IRC § 6672 the failure to account and pay over the payroll taxes must have been willful. The IRS' stated position is that willfulness exists where "money withheld from employees as taxes, in lieu of being paid over to the Government, was knowingly and intentionally used to pay the operating expenses of the business, or for other purposes." The fact that there are insufficient funds to pay both employees and taxes is not a defense. In such a case, employers are expected to prorate the payments so that the employees get a portion of their pay and the IRS obtains the proper amount of withholding for the pay distributed. Individuals with sufficient control over the payroll process will be deemed responsible when the company fails to pay-over the payroll taxes, even if they are not the ultimate decision maker.

The Trust Fund Investigation

The IRS Revenue Officer assigned to the taxpayer's case will conduct an investigation to determine who was responsible for the company's failure to pay over the employment taxes. The IRS will utilize Form 4180 for the interview (see Exhibit 30). The goal of the Form 4180, if you look at it, is to identify who may have been responsible for the employer's failure to pay over the payroll taxes.

> **HOT TIP**
>
> We never allow our client to participate in the Form 4180 interview. The Forms have, over the years, become shorter and the questions loaded. We complete the Form with our clients and submit them, but with attachments, so we can explain the answers. For instance, In Section II, Letter C, the Yes/No question is: "Did You prepare, review, sign, or authorize transmit payroll tax returns?" What if you prepared them but had no authority to sign them or send the payment? A "Yes" answer could mean personal liability and a hard fight at appeals. Better to check "No", write in "See attached" and submit an attached statement explaining the taxpayer's role and what really happened. It avoids a lot of headaches later on!

The Payroll Liability Assessment Process

When a company owes payroll taxes, the process the IRS will pursue is the following:

1. The payroll returns are filed
2. The Taxes are assessed
3. Demand for payment is made on the Company
4. If the company cannot make payment within a short time, the IRS Revenue Officer will attempt to determine who the responsible parties are
5. The Form 4180 Trust Fund interviews will be conducted
6. The IRS will then make proposed assessments against all the parties it believes are responsible with Letter 1153 (see Exhibit 31)
7. The Letter 1153 also includes a waiver form, Form 2751 (see Exhibit 32)
8. Taxpayers can either sign the 2751 and be deemed responsible, or file a written protest denying responsibility within 60 days of receiving the Letter 1153
9. Those taxpayers held responsible will either pay or have to pursue a collection alternative

Recent Payroll Tax Initiatives by the IRS

In 2015, the IRS began a new payroll tax initiative. The initiative is designed for the IRS to try and get out ahead of a business's payroll tax problem before it mushrooms into something much larger. The "FTD Alert X Coded Pilot" tests whether accelerating the timing of alerts to taxpayers and the IRS will impact and identify which taxpayers would benefit most from alerts. These began to be implemented by the IRS in April of 2015.

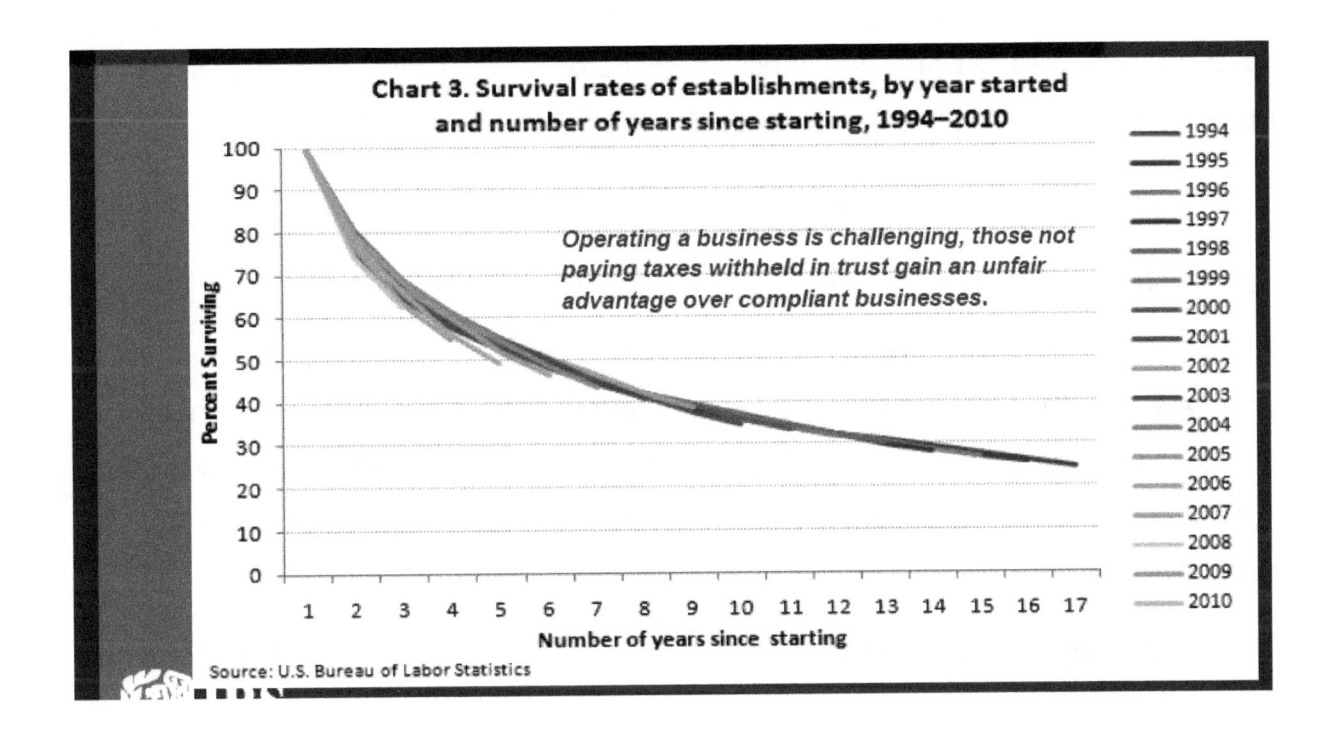

Chart 3. Survival rates of establishments, by year started and number of years since starting, 1994–2010

Operating a business is challenging, those not paying taxes withheld in trust gain an unfair advantage over compliant businesses.

Source: U.S. Bureau of Labor Statistics

In 2016, the IRS Collection Division began implementing its EFTPS Early Alerts. This modified the payment platform to create a real-time system to identify variances in FTDs that will enable/expand treatment streams.

The goals of these initiatives is to expand early intervention program, educate taxpayers and modify taxpayer behavior to enhance compliance. The hope is that they will improve collection case selection and assignment and enable data-driven decisions regarding taxpayers.

Federal Tax Deposit ("FTD") Alerts

The FTD Alert Program is the only Collection tool available that identifies anomalies in an employer's pattern of payroll tax deposits. Using this tool to anticipate deposits that are missed allows Field Collection the opportunity to interact with the taxpayer and proactively address potential problems as they develop, but before the amount owed exceeds the taxpayer's ability to pay.

In IRC § 6302 Congress mandated that the IRS establish a system of making deposits by electronic fund transfer in order to expedite the collection of depository taxes. In doing so, Congress has provided special procedures for the collection of depository taxes held in a special fund in trust for the United States in IRC § 7501(a).

So, what is an FTD Alert?

FTD Alerts are issued on taxpayers who are classified as semiweekly depositors and who have not made FTDs during the current quarter or who have made them in substantially reduced amounts. The IRS actually analyzes past compliance history and current deposit patterns to identify taxpayers who are least likely to self-correct their tax deposit issues.

There are three types of Alert issuances that are assigned for field contact y a Revenue Officer:

- Potential Pyramider - The taxpayer had notices issued in each of the prior two quarters.
- Potential Noncompliant – Here the taxpayer is considered to be likely to owe without intervention based on the ITRS's knowledge of their history.
- Potentially At Risk – Here the taxpayer is considered at risk of falling behind on their FTDs in the current quarter.

When an FTD Alert is received in the field the Revenue Officer will review the taxpayer's history and do some pre-contact analysis to determine if there is an explanation before making a field visit.

If the RO determines that contact the taxpayer makes sense, the IRM indicates that the RO make contact within 15 days of assignment of the alert. If the Taxpayer has a Power of Attorney, then the contact will be with the POA.

Case Studies

8

We will review a variety of taxpayer situations as "case studies" so that you can understand each situation and how we approach these. The goal is to help you determine how to approach each issue when your client is faced with a similar situation. Where appropriate, we have completed the forms and attached the source materials for the IRS allowable standards. The various client situations we will be reviewing include:

1	Streamlined Installment Agreement
2	"Pay-Down" to a Streamlined Installment Agreement
3	Currently-Not-Collectable taxpayer
4	Regular Installment Agreement (with a discussion about partial-pay arrangements)
5	Offer-in-Compromise: Joint Liability
6	Offer-in-Compromise: One Spouse Liable only

CAVEAT: We have completed these using the forms available and allowable expense tables in place during the third quarter of 2019. It is highly likely that these may change by the time you are reading this. Please do not rely on what we have provided but instead go the IRS website and pull the current form and use the current expense tables!

1. Streamlined Installment Agreement

Facts: Mary arrives in your office in August 2019 holding threats to levy for the tax years 2014 and 2015. They show a total balance of $42,368. She used to be self-employed but now has a W-2 job, so since 2016 all her income taxes have been withheld by her employer.

Analysis: Mary qualifies for a streamlined installment agreement: she owes less than $50,000 and is in current tax compliance. Her month payment over 72 months would be approximately $588 plus interest, so maybe $600-$625 a month. If she can pay this then you can easily arrange her payment plan by calling the IRS Collections number (800-829-3903), or going online to www.irs.gov and setting up a payment plan online. There are no financial forms to complete and no additional documents to provide.

If Mary told you she could not afford the $600 or so a month, then you would need to complete the Collection Information Statement (Form 433-A) and submit it with supporting documentation to arrange either a regular or partial-pay installment agreement.

2. "Pay-Down" to a Streamlined Installment Agreement

Facts: Assume the same facts as the "Streamlined Installment agreement" above but now Mary owes $112,368. She has $100,000 in an IRA that she would like to keep if possible.

Analysis: On the surface Mary does not qualify for a streamlined installment agreement because she owes more than $100,000.[50] She will complete a Form 433-A, which will show the IRS the $100,000 IRA. The IRS, with its marching orders to collect as much as possible as quickly as possible, will insist she cashed in the IRA, her early-withdrawal penalty and taxes paid (about 30%) and the balance used to pay the tax bill in full. Not what Mary wants!

The other option is to take enough of the IRA to pay the balance she owes down below the $100,000 threshold for a streamlined installment agreement. So, if Mary takes $18,000 from her IRA, pays 30% in taxes and penalty ($5,400), she can then use the remaining $12,600 to pay her tax debt down. Mary will then owe $99,768 and can request a streamlined installment agreement. Now she does not have to complete the 433-A and disclose the IRA and any other assets she has to the IRS!

Perhaps she could borrow the money from family to pay the balance down below $100,000 and not take IRA money, or maybe the client wants to cash the IRA and pay it and just be done with the IRS. We would always give the client the choice and let them

---

[50] We are assuming that because Mary is dealing with automated collections that a Revenue Officer is not involved and she can make use of the expanded streamlined procedures of $100,000 over 84 months.

decide how they want to handle the situation. It's our job to provide the client with the information so they can make a choice.

3. Currently-Not-Collectable

Facts: Mike comes to see us with a pile of IRS notices. He owes money for 2016, 2017, and 2018, when he was still an independent contractor. Now he is an employee for a large manufacturing business and his wages all have taxes withheld. He rents an apartment, has a checking account with $1,800 in it and owns a pick-up truck. He is borrowing money from his parents to pay our fee of $2,500. He lives in New Haven, Connecticut, and his income and expenses are as follows:

Salary	$48,000/year
Rent	$1,850/month
Utilities	$350/month (electric, heat)
Car Payment	$0
Health Insurance	$500/month
Current Taxes	$800/month
Out of Pocket Healthcare Costs	$15/month
United Way Donation	$10/month (taken directly on his paystub)

Analysis: Mike is uncollectible. His current monthly income of $4,000 a month is completely absorbed by the $4,184 of IRS monthly allowable expenses. See the analysis and Form 433-A on the following page.

To have Mike placed in uncollectible status we would submit the 433-A, our analysis sheet, and the following supporting documentation:

- His most recent 3 paystubs
- His last 3 month of bank statements

- Proof of his rent and utilities (either lease and bills, or highlight the payments for the IRS in the bank statements)
- Proof of his health insurance (probably on his paystub)
- Proof of his current tax payments (probably on his paystub)

The analysis is basically using the following numbers:

- The $727 a month for Food, Clothing & Miscellaneous is a national IRS standard, so just use that (you do not need receipts)
- The housing of $1,925 is the local standard for housing for New Haven County in Connecticut for one person. His actual expense is higher ($1,850 rent + $350 utilities = $2,200), but the IRS will limit the expense to the standard
- The $237 a month claimed for his automobile operating expense is the local standard on the IRS table
- The $500 for health insurance is allowed based upon his proof of payment (his paystubs)
- His $800 a month for current taxes includes federal Income Tax, State Income Tax and FICA taxes, all shown on his paystub
- The United Way donation is not allowed
- Out of Pocket Healthcare Costs is the national standard of $55. Mike could get more if he could prove he was spending more, but given that he only spends $15 a month, we will take the standard $55.

To have Mike placed in uncollectible status, submit the 433-A and the documentation discussed earlier with a cover letter explaining that the taxpayer currently does not have the ability to make payments nor has any assets that can be used to pay the debt, and ask that the account be placed in uncollectible status until sometime in the future when his situation turns-around.

Income	Actual	Expenses	Actual	Allowable
Wages (yourself)	$ 4,000	Food, Clothing and Misc.	$ 727	$ 727
Wages (spouse)	$ -	Housing & utilities	$ 2,200	$ 1,925
Interest - Dividends	$ -	Vehicle Ownership	$ -	$ -
Net Business Income	$ -	Vehicle Operating Costs	$ 237	$ 237
Net Rental Income	$ -	Public Transportation	$ -	$ -
Distributions	$ -	Health Insurance	$ 500	$ 500
Pension/Soc Sec (taxpayer)	$ -	Out of Pocket HealthCare	$ 55	$ 55
Pension/Soc Sec (spouse)	$ -	Court ordered payments	$ -	$ -
Social Security (taxpayer)	$ -	Child/Dep Care	$ -	$ -
Social Security (spouse)	$ -	Life Insurance	$ -	$ -
Child Support	$ -	Current Year Taxes	$ 800	$ 800
Alimony	$ -	Secured Debts	$ -	$ -
Other Income	$ -	Delinquent State Taxes	$ -	$ -
	$ -	Student Loans	$ -	$ -
	$ -	Total Living Expenses	$ 4,519	$ 4,244
Total	$ 4,000	**Net Difference**	$ (519)	$ (244)
Analysis - Future Income				
Income	$ 4,000			
Expense	$ 4,244			
Monthly Available	$ (244)			

4. Regular Installment Agreement

John comes to see us in August 2019. He lives in New Haven, Connecticut, is unmarried and has no children. John owes the IRS $137,000 for the tax years 2014 – 2017 when he was self-employed. He landed his current job in 2018 and then filed his outstanding 2014-2017 returns on June 30, 2018. John also owes Connecticut $30,000, which he is paying back through an installment agreement at $300 a month. He now has a job and would like to try and do an Offer in Compromise.[51] His income and expenses are as follows:

Income (per month)	$7,500
Expenses (per month)	
Rent	$1,800
Utilities	$375
Health Insurance	$575
Medical Co-Pays	$175
Current Taxes	$1,875
Connecticut Installment Agreement	$300

John cannot compromise his tax debt because he shows the ability to full-pay the liability: there are 102 months remaining on the collection statute (18 months have run since he filed the returns, so 102 remain on the 10 years), and he shows $1,932 available. That would allow him to pay $197,064 over the statute, which is more than the $137,000 owed, so he is not eligible for an Offer-in-Compromise. John should request an installment agreement and invoke the one-year rule at $1,436/month for the first 12 months based on his actual rent and his actual state payment, after which it will increase to $1,932. So long as John remains current with his taxes and makes his payments the IRS will not require him to revisit the payment arrangement. If, however,

---

[51] Yes, we know we are discussing "regular" installment agreements, but this is often how they start: the client wants an Offer and finds out they cannot do an Offer.

John has a change in circumstances (a loss of pay, etc.), he should contact the IRS and submit new information to modify the existing agreement.

John – Regular Installment Agreement

Income	Actual	Expenses	Actual	Allowable
Wages (yourself)	$ 7,500	Food, Clothing and Misc.	$ 727	$ 727
Wages (spouse)	$ -	Housing & Utilities	$ 2,175	$ 1,925
Interest - Dividends	$ -	Vehicle Ownership	$ -	$ -
Net Business Income	$ -	Vehicle Operating Costs	$ 237	$ 237
Net Rental Income	$ -	Public Transportation	$ -	$ -
Distributions	$ -	Health Insurance	$ 575	$ 575
Pension/Soc Sec (taxpayer)	$ -	Out of Pocket HealthCare	$ 175	$ 175
Pension/Soc Sec (spouse)	$ -	Court ordered payments	$ -	$ -
Social Security (taxpayer)	$ -	Child/Dep Care	$ -	$ -
Social Security (spouse)	$ -	Life Insurance	$ -	$ -
Child Support	$ -	Current Year Taxes	$ 1,875	$ 1,875
Alimony	$ -	Secured Debts	$ -	$ -
Other Income	$ -	Delinquent State Taxes	$ 300	$ 54
	$ -	Student Loans	$ -	$ -
	$ -	Total Living Expenses	$ 6,064	$ 5,568
Total	$ 7,500	Net Difference	$ 1,436	$ 1,932

5. Offer-in-Compromise: Joint-Liability

John and Mary smith come to see us in August 2019. They live in New Haven Connecticut and have two children, ages 17 and 14. John now works for a large contractor in New Haven and Mary works for a local hospital as an administrative assistant. Previously John was a self-employed contractor and ran up $185,000 of federal income tax debt. He does not owe the State of Connecticut anything, as he managed to pay those taxes each year. John makes $60,000 per year, and Mary makes $36,000.

The have the following assets:

- Checking account with $1,000
- Savings Account with $750
- Mary has a defined benefit plan with no cash value through the hospital where she works
- They own their home worth $300,000. It has a mortgage to the bank of $260,000
- John owns a 2014 Cadillac Escalade with 68,000 miles on it worth $12,000 with no loan
- Mary owns a 2014 Honda Accord with 65,000 miles on it worth $4,500 with no loan

Their monthly expenses are as follows:

- They pay $3,500 a month for mortgage, real estate taxes, homeowners insurance and utilities
- They pay $875 a month for health insurance through Mary's employer
- They pay $50 for term life insurance covering John and $35 covering Mary
- They pay $1,760 in current taxes for federal state and FICA taxes

John & Mary
Joint Offer & Compromise

Income	Actual		Expenses	Actual	Allowable
Wages (yourself)	$ 5,000		Food, Clothing and Misc	$ 1,786	$ 1,786
Wages (spouse)	$ 3,000		Housing & utilities	$ 3,500	$ 2,656
Interest - Dividends	$ -		Vehicle Ownership	$ -	$ -
Net Business Income	$ -		Vehicle Operating Costs	$ 474	$ 474
Net Rental Income	$ -		Public Transportation	$ -	$ -
Distributions	$ -		Health Insurance	$ 875	$ 875
Pension/Soc Sec (taxpayer)	$ -		Out of Pocket HealthCar	$ 220	$ 220
Pension/Soc Sec (spouse)	$ -		Court ordered pmts	$ -	$ -
Social Security (taxpayer)	$ -		Child/Dep Care	$ -	$ -
Social Security (spouse)	$ -		Life Insurance	$ 85	$ 85
Child Support	$ -		Current Year Taxes	$ 1,760	$ 1,760
Alimony	$ -		Secured Debts	$ -	$ -
Other Income	$ -		Delinquent State Taxes	$ -	$ -
	$ -		Student Loans	$ -	$ -
	$ -		Total Living Expenses	$ 8,700	$ 7,856
Total	$ 8,000		Net Difference	$ (700)	$ 144

Analysis - Future Income		
Income	$ 8,000	
Expense	$ 7,856	
Monthly Available	$ 144	
Offer Analysis - Future Inc.	$ 1,728	$144 x 12 months
Offer Analysis - Assets		
House	$ -	$300,000 x 80% - $260,000
Auto - Accord	$ 150	$4,500 x 80% - $3,450 exemption
Auto - Caddillac Escalade	$ 6,150	$12,000 x 80% - $3,450 exemption
Cash	$ 750	$1,750 - $1,000 exemption
Available equity in assets	$ 7,050	
RCP (assets and future Inc)	$ 8,778	

The issue here in John and Mary's offer is the housing, which exceeds the allowable local housing standard by $844, so instead of the future income being a negative $700 it is now a positive $144.

John and Mary would submit their Offer. Assuming it is a Lump-Sum Offer we calculated, would use the 12 months of future income. John and Mary would send in the Offer package with two checks: $186 for the application fee and one for $1,755.60, representing 20% of the amount offered. Upon acceptance of the Offer the balance would need to be paid within 5 months ($7,022.40).

If John and Mary chose to do a deferred Offer instead, they could pay it over 24 months but would need to increase their Offer for the 24 months of future income. Now the Offer would increase to $10,506 ($7,050 for assets and $3,456 for the 24 months of $144 future income), and they would have to begin making monthly payments and continue to make monthly payments while the Offer is pending. If accepted, they would continue the payments until the end of the Offer period, and it was paid in full.

6. Offer-in-Compromise: One Spouse Responsible

Let's assume all the facts are the same as in the last case study, except that now the tax liability comes from John only. John's business failed and he was deemed responsible for the unpaid payroll taxes.

Now the IRS will allocate the joint expenses so that John will be given his share of the expense based upon the fact that he brings in 63% of the household expense ($5,000 of the $8,000 monthly income). Joint expenses are all those that cover multiple house members, so Food & Clothing, Housing, health insurance and out of pocket medical (includes the kids). John will get his own $237 a month for the operating of his car, his own current taxes, and the term insurance on his life.

Mary would not have to disclose her own assets[52], so the Honda Accord is not included in the Offer calculation. Mary would have to disclose her income, not because she is responsible, but because the IRS needs it to do the allocation.

---

[52] In Community Property states this might not hold true. In most community property states property of each spouse become community property of the couple and it would therefore be disclosed and potentially included in the Offer. Practitioners need to look at the state's particular version of the community property rules to know what property may be exempt.

The analysis now looks like this: 152

John & Mary
John Responsibility Offer & Compromise

Income	Actual	Expenses	Allowable	63% Allocated
Wages (yourself)	$ 5,000	Food, Clothing and Misc	$ 1,786	$ 1,116
Wages (spouse)	$ 3,000	Housing & utilities	$ 2,656	$ 1,660
Interest - Dividends	$ -	Vehicle Ownership	$ -	$ -
Net Business Income	$ -	Vehicle Operating Costs	$ 598	$ 237
Net Rental Income	$ -	Public Transportation	$ -	$ -
Distributions	$ -	Health Insurance	$ 875	$ 547
Pension/Soc Sec (taxpayer)	$ -	Out of Pocket HealthCare	$ 220	$ 138
Pension/Soc Sec (spouse)	$ -	Court ordered pmts	$ -	$ -
Social Security (taxpayer)	$ -	Child/Dep Care	$ -	$ -
Social Security (spouse)	$ -	Life Insurance	$ 85	$ 50
Child Support	$ -	Current Year Taxes	$ 1,760	$ 1,100
Alimony	$ -	Secured Debts	$ -	$ -
Other Income	$ -	Delinquent State Taxes	$ -	$ -
	$ -	Student Loans	$ -	$ -
	$ -	Total Living Expenses	$ 7,980	$ 4,848
Total	$ 8,000	Net Difference	$ 20	$ 152

Analysis - Future Income		
Income	$ 5,000	
Expense	$ 4,848	
Monthly Available	$ 152	
Offer Analysis - Future Inc.	$ 1,824	$152 x 12 months
Offer Analysis - Assets		
House	$ -	$300,000 x 80% - $260,000
Auto - Caddillac Escalade	$ 6,150	$12,000 x 80% - $3,450 exemption
Cash	$ 375	$1,750 - $1,000 exemption x 50%
Available equity in assets	$ 6,525	
RCP (assets and future Inc)	$ 8,349	

John would submit his Offer. Assuming it is a Lump-Sum Offer we calculated, would use the 12 months of future income. John would send in the Offer package with two checks: $186 for the application fee and one for $1,670, representing 20% of the amount offered. Upon acceptance of the Offer the balance would need to be paid within 5 months ($6,679).

If John chose to do a deferred Offer instead, he could pay it over 24 months but would need to increase his Offer for the 24 months of future income. Now the Offer would increase to $10,173 ($6,525 for assets and $3,648 for the 24 months of $152 future income), and he would have to begin making monthly payments and continue to make monthly payments while the Offer is pending. If accepted, he would continue the payments until the end of the Offer period, and it was paid in full.

Checklist: Offer-in-Compromise

1. **New Client**
    a. Retainer agreement
    b. Retainer check
    c. Power of Attorney

2. **Compliance**
    a. Have the tax returns due been filed?
    b. Have current tax payments been made?

3. **Obtain Taxpayer's Financial Information**
    a. Bank Statements – last three months
    b. Retirement Accounts
        i. Recent statement of value
        ii. Copy of the plan document (to see if the taxpayer can access the funds)
    c. Investment Accounts – recent statement of value
    d. Life Insurance – statement of current cash value
    e. Real Estate
        i. Statement of Value (Zillow, etc)
        ii. Recent Mortgage Statement showing loan balance and monthly payment
    f. Automobiles
        i. Statement of Value (Kelly Blue Book)
        ii. Current lease or loan statement showing outstanding balance and monthly payment amount
    g. Collectibles, Artwork, etc. – statements of values on collectables that can be used to pay the tax debt
    h. Proof of income
        i. Profit & Loss
        ii. Paystubs

i. Utility Bills – last 3 months (get proof of payments or highlight in the bank statements)

   j. Proof of health insurance premium (get proof of payments or highlight in the bank statements)

   k. Proof of term life insurance and premium amount (get proof of payments or highlight in the bank statements)

   l. Proof of disability insurance (get proof of payments or highlight in the bank statements)

   m. Proof of out-of-pocket medical expenses (get proof of payments or highlight in the bank statements)

   n. Proof of alimony (Divorce Agreement or Decree)

   o. Proof of child support (Divorce Agreement or Decree)

   p. Proof of dependent care expenses (get proof of payments or highlight in the bank statements)

   q. Proof of judgments and payments to creditors

   r. Proof of current taxes being paid/withheld

   s. Written agreement with state department of revenue and proof of payments

4. **Prepare Collection Information Statement (IRS Form 433)**

   a. Individual – 433-A (OIC)

   b. Each Business Interest – 433-B (OIC)

5. **Analyze taxpayer's assets for collection**

   a. Analyze taxpayer's income vs. IRS allowable expenses

   b. Calculate Net Equity in Assets

   c. Calculate RCP

6. **Prepare package for IRS**

7. **File with the IRS with a proposed Collection Alternative**

   a. Form 433-A (OIC)

   b. Form 4330-B (OIC) if necessary

   c. Form 656

   d. Application fee (currently $186)

e. Payment

　　i. 20% of offer for Lump-Sun

　　ii. 1st monthly payment if a Deferred Offer

Exhibits

Exhibit Number	Exhibit
1	CP-14: Request for Payment
2	CP-501: Billing Notice
3	CP-503: Reminder Notice
4	CP-504: Threat To levy
5	Letter 11: Final Notice of Intent to Levy & Taxpayer's Right to a Hearing
6	Form 12153: Request for a Collection Due Process or Equivalent Hearing
7	IRS Account Transcript
8	IRS Letter 3172 – Notice of Federal Tax Lien
9	IRS Form 668-A – Notice of Levy
10	IRS Form 1040-ES – Estimated Tax Payment Vouchers
11	IRS Form 9465 – Installment Agreement Request
12	IRS Form 433-A – Collection Information Statement for Wage Earners and Self-Employed Individuals (Field Collections)
13	IRS Form 433-F – Collection Information Statement (ACS Form)
14	IRS Form 433-B – Collection Information Statement for Business
15	IRS Form 433-H – Installment Agreement Request and Collection Information Statement
16	IRS Form 433-D – Installment Agreement

17	IRS Letter CP-523 – Notice of Intent to Terminate Your Installment Agreement
18	IRS Form 9423 – Collection Appeal Request
19	IRS Letter 4223 – Case Closed as Currently Not Collectable
20	IRS Offer-in-Compromise Form 656
21	Sample IRS Allowable Standard Expenses for Collection
22	IRS Letter Confirming Receipt of the Offer
23	IRS Letter of Acceptance of the Taxpayer's Offer
24	IRS Letter indicating that the offered amount is insufficient
25	IRS tables supporting its RCP calculation
26	IRS Offer-in-Compromise Addendum
27	IRS Letter that the offer terms have been met
28	IRS Letter threatening to default offer
29	IRS Letter rejecting the taxpayer's Offer and providing an opportunity to file an Appeal
30	IRS Form 4180 – Report of Interview with Individual Relative to Trust Fund Recovery Penalty or Personal Liability for Excise Taxes
31	IRS Letter 1153 – Notice of Proposed Trust Fund Assessment
32	IRS Form 2751 – Proposed Assessment of Trust Fund Recovery Penalty Waiver
33	IRS Letter 4837 – Letter Confirming Appeals has Received the Taxpayer's Case

34	IRS Form 12257 – Summary Notice of Determination, Waiver of Right to Judicial Review of a Collection Due Process Determination, Waiver of Suspension of Levy Action, and Waiver of Periods of Limitation in Section 6330€(1)
35	IRS Form 656-L – Offer in Compromise (Doubt as to Liability) booklet
36	Notice of Lis Pendens

Department of the Treasury Internal Revenue Service P.O. Box 9019 Holtsville, NY 11742-9019	

Notice	CP14
Tax year	2017
Notice date	January 30, 2018
Social security number	nnn-nn-nnnn
To contact us	Phone 1-800-xxx-xxxx
Your caller ID	nnnn
Page 1 of 6	

JOHN AND MARY SMITH
123 N HARRIS ST
HARVARD, TX 12345

You have a balance due for 2017
Amount due: $1,075.21

Our records show you have unpaid taxes and/or penalties and interest on your 2017 Form 1040.

If you already paid your balance in full within the last 21 days or made payment arrangements, please disregard this notice.

If you already have an installment or payment agreement in place for this tax year, then continue with that agreement.

Billing Summary

Tax you owed	$3,183.00
Payments and credits	−3,328.00
Failure-to-file penalty	318.30
Failure-to-pay penalty	633.30
Interest charges	145.00
Failure-to-pay estimated tax penalty	123.61
Amount due by February 20, 2018	**$1,075.21**

If you are a debtor in a bankruptcy case, this notice is for your information only and is not intended to seek payment outside of the bankruptcy process of taxes due before you filed your petition. You will not receive another notice of the balance due while the automatic stay remains in effect.

What you need to do immediately

If you agree with the amount due and you're not working with an IRS representative

- Pay the amount due of $1,075.21 by February 20, 2018, to avoid penalty and interest charges.
- Pay online or mail a check or money order with the attached payment stub. **You can pay online now at www.irs.gov/payments.**

Continued on back...

Payment

John and Mary Smith
123 N Harris Street
Harvard, TX 12345

Notice	CP14
Notice date	January 30, 2018
Social security number	nnn-nn-nnnn

- Make your check or money order payable to the United States Treasury.
- Write your social security number (nnn-nn-nnnn), the tax year (2017), and the form number (1040) on your payment.

INTERNAL REVENUE SERVICE
CINCINNATI, OH 45999-0149

Amount due by February 20, 2018	$1,075.21

0000 0000000 0000000000 0000000 0000

Exhibit 1

Notice	CP14
Tax year	2017
Notice date	January 30, 2018
Social security number	nnn-nn-nnnn
Page 2 of 6	

What you need to do immediately – continued

If you agree with the amount due and you're not working with an IRS representative – **continued**

If you disagree with the amount due
Call us at 1-800-xxx-xxxx to review your account with a representative. Be sure to have your account information available when you call.

We'll assume you agree with the information in this notice if we don't hear from you.

Payment options

Pay now electronically
We offer free payment options to securely pay your tax bill directly from your checking or savings account. When you pay online or with your mobile device, you can:
- Receive instant confirmation of your payment
- Schedule payments in advance
- Reschedule or cancel a payment before the due date

You can also pay by debit or credit card for a small fee. To see all of our payment options, visit www.irs.gov/payments.

Payment plans
If you can't pay the full amount you owe, pay as much as you can now and make arrangements to pay your remaining balance. Visit www.irs.gov/paymentplan for more information on installment agreements and online payment agreements. You can also call us at 1-800-xxx-xxxx to discuss your options.

Offer in Compromise
An offer in compromise allows you to settle your tax debt for less than the full amount you owe. If we accept your offer, you can pay with either a lump sum cash payment plan or periodic payment plan. To see if you qualify, use the Offer in Compromise Pre-Qualifier tool on our website. For more information, visit www.irs.gov/offers.

[Back of payment stub]

Notice	CP14
Tax year	2017
Notice date	January 30, 2018
Social security number	nnn-nn-nnnn
Page 3 of 6	

Payment options—continued

Account balance and payment history

For information on how to obtain your current account balance or payment history, go to www.irs.gov/balancedue.

If you already paid your balance in full within the past 21 days or made payment arrangements, please disregard this notice.

If you think we made a mistake, call 1-800-xxx-xxxx to review your account.

If we don't hear from you

Pay $1,075.21 by February 20, 2017, to avoid penalty and interest charges.

Penalties

We are required by law to charge any applicable penalties

Failure-to-file

Description	Amount
Total failure-to-file	**$318.30**

We assess a 5% monthly penalty for filing your return late for each month or part of a month the return is late, for up to 5 months. When a penalty for paying late applies for the same month, the amount of the penalty for filing late for that month is reduced by the amount of the penalty for paying late for that month. The penalty for paying late is ½% for each month or part of a month. We base the monthly penalty for filing late on the tax required to be shown on the return that you didn't pay by the original return due date, without regard to extensions. We base the monthly penalty for paying late on the net unpaid tax at the beginning of each penalty month folowing the payment due date for that tax. When an income tax return is more than 60 days late, the minimum penalty is $210 or 100% of the tax required to be shown on the return that you didn't pay on time, whichever is less.

(Internal Revenue Code Section 6651)

Notice	CP14
Tax year	2017
Notice date	January 30, 2018
Social security number	nnn-nn-nnnn
Page 4 of 6	

Penalties – continued

Failure-to-pay

Description	Amount
Total failure-to-pay	**$633.30**

We assess a 1/2% monthly penalty for not paying the tax you owe by the due date. We base the monthly penalty for paying late on the net unpaid tax at the beginning of each penalty month following the payment due date for that tax. This penalty applies even if you filed the return on time.

We charge the penalty for each month or part of a month the payment is late; however, the penalty can't be more than 25% in total.

- The due date for payment of the tax shown on a return generally is the return due date, without regard to extensions.
- The due date for paying increases in tax is within 21 days of the date of our notice demanding payment (10 business days if the amount in the notice is $100,000 or more).

If we issue a Notice of Intent to Levy and you don't pay the balance due within 10 days of the date of the notice, the penalty for paying late increases to 1% per month.

Failure-to-pay proper estimated tax

Description	Amount
Total failure-to-pay proper estimated tax	**$145.00**

When you don't pay enough taxes due for the year with your quarterly estimated tax payments, we charge a penalty for not properly estimating your tax. For information about estimated tax requirements, download Instructions for Form 2210 or Tax Withholding and Estimated Tax (Publication 505) from www.irs.gov or call us for a copy. (Internal Revenue Code section 6654)

Removal or reduction of penalties

We understand that circumstances—such as economic hardship, a family member's death, or loss of financial records due to natural disaster—may make it difficult for you to meet your taxpayer responsibility in a timely manner.

We can generally process your request for penalty removal or reduction quicker if you contact us at the number listed above with the following information:
- Identify which penalty charges you would like us to reconsider (e.g., 2016 late filing penalty).
- For each penalty charge, explain why you believe it should be reconsidered.

If you write us, include a signed statement and supporting documentation for penalty abatement request.

We'll review your statement and let you know whether we accept your explanation as reasonable cause to reduce or remove the penalty charge(s).

Notice	CP14
Tax year	2017
Notice date	January 30, 2018
Social security number	nnn-nn-nnnn

Removal of penalties due to erroneous written advice from the IRS

If you were penalized based on written advice from the IRS, we will remove the penalty if you meet the following criteria:
- You wrote us asking for written advice on a specific issue
- You gave us adequate and accurate information
- You received written advice from us
- You relied on our written advice and were penalized based on that advice

To request removal of penalties based on erroneous written advice from us, submit a completed Claim for Refund and Request for Abatement (Form 843) to the address shown above. For a copy of the form, go to www.irs.gov or call 1-800-TAX-FORM (1-800-829-3676).

Interest

We are required by law to charge interest when you do not pay your liability on time. Generally, we calculate interest from the due date of your return (regardless of extensions) until you pay the amount you owe in full, including accrued interest and any penalty charges. Interest on some penalties accrues from the date we notify you of the penalty until it is paid in full. Interest on other penalties, such as failure to file a tax return, starts from the due date or extended due date of the return. Interest rates are variable and may change quarterly. (Internal Revenue Code Section 6601)

Description	Amount
Total interest	**$145.00**

The table below shows the rates used to calculate the interest on your unpaid amount due. For a detailed calculation of your interest, call 1-800-xxx-xxxx.

Period	Interest rate
October 1, 2016 – December 31, 2016	3%
Beginning January 1, 2017	3%

Notice	CP14
Tax year	2017
Notice date	January 30, 2018
Social security number	nnn-nn-nnnn

Additional interest charges	If the amount you owe is $100,000 or more, please make sure that we receive your payment within 10 work days from the date of your notice. If the amount you owe is less than $100,000, please make sure that we receive your payment within 21 calendar days from the date of your notice. If we don't receive full payment within these time frames, the law requires us to charge interest until you pay the full amount you owe.
Additional Information	- Visit www.irs.gov/cp14. - For tax forms, instructions, and publications, visit www.irs.gov/formspubs or call 1-800-TAX-FORM (1-800-829-3676). - Paying online is convenient, secure, and ensures timely receipt of your payment. To pay your taxes online or for more information, go to www.irs.gov/payments. - You can contact us by mail at the address at the top of the first page of this notice. Be sure to include your social security number and the tax year and form number you are writing about. - Keep this notice for your records. If you need assistance, please don't hesitate to contact us.

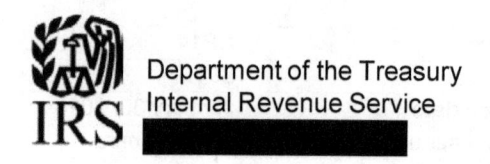

![IRS Logo] Department of the Treasury Internal Revenue Service	Notice	CP501
	Tax Year	2014
	Notice date	December 16, 2016
	Social Security number	
	To contact us	Phone
	Your Caller ID	
	Page 1 of 5	

You have unpaid taxes for 2014

Amount due:

Our records show you have unpaid taxes for the tax year ending December 31, 2014 (Form 1040).

Billing Summary

Amount you owed
Failure-to-pay penalty
Interest charges
Amount due by January 26, 2015

What you need to do immediately

Pay immediately

- Pay the amount due of ▮ by January 26, 2015, to avoid additional penalty and interest charges. **You can pay online now at www.irs.gov/directpay.**

Continued on back...

![IRS Logo]

Payment

	Notice	CP501
	Notice date	December 16, 2016
	Social Security Number	

- Make your check or money order payable to the United States Treasury.
- Write your Social Security number ▮, the tax year (2014), and the form number (1040) on your payment and any correspondence.

Amount due by
January 26, 2015

INTERNAL REVENUE SERVICE

Exhibit 2

Notice	CP501
Tax Year	2014
Notice date	December 16, 2016
Social Security number	

What you need to do immediately—continued

Pay immediately—**continued**

- If you can't pay the amount due, pay as much as you can now and make payment arrangements that allow you to pay off the rest over time. Visit www.irs.gov/payments for more information about:
  -- Credit and debit card payments
  -- Electronic payments
  -- Installment and payment plans:
    - Automatic deductions from your bank account
    - Payroll deductions

    - [Apply online or mail Form 9465, Installment Agreement Request.]

  -- Offer in Compromise- To see if you qualify for an offer, visit the Offer in Compromise Pre-Qualifier tool at www.irs.gov/Individuals/Offer-in-Compromise-1

Or, call us at 1-800-XXX-XXXX to discuss your options

If you need to pay your tax debt over time, we encourage you to apply for
a Direct Debit Installment Agreement. These agreements save you time
and money by having your monthly payment automatically withdrawn from your bank account. There are no checks to write and mail and these agreements have a reduced user fee.

[Apply for a payment plan using the Online Payment Agreement application at: www.irs.gov and search "online-payment.".]

Apply for a payment plan by completing Form 433-F prior to calling us at 1-800-XXX-XXXX. This will assist us in handling your call more efficiently.]

[By setting up an agreement online now, you may be able to avoid the filing of a Notice of Federal Tax Lien, if one hasn't already been filed. If a
Notice of Federal Tax Lien has been filed, certain taxpayers may request
the notice be withdrawn after establishing a Direct Debit Installment Agreement. For more information on liens, visit: www.irs.gov and search
"federal tax lien"].

If you already paid your balance in full within the past 14 days or made payment arrangements, please disregard this notice.

Notice	CP501
Tax Year	2014
Notice date	December 16, 2016
Social Security number	

If we don't hear from you

- If you don't pay ▮▮▮▮ by January 26, 2015, interest will increase and additional penalties may apply.
- If you don't pay the amount due or call us to make payment arrangements, we can file a Notice of Federal Tax Lien on your property at any time, if we haven't already done so.
- If the lien is in place, you may find it difficult to sell or borrow against your property. The tax lien would also appear on your credit report—which may harm your credit rating--and your creditors would also be publicly notified that the IRS has priority to seize your property.
- If you don't pay your tax debt, we have the right to seize ("levy") your property.

Penalties

We are required by law to charge any applicable penalties.

Failure-to-pay

Description	Amount
Total failure-to-pay	

When you pay your taxes after the due date, we charge a penalty of 0.5% of the unpaid amount due per month, up to 25% of the amount due. We count part of a month as a full month. (Internal Revenue Code Section 6651)

For a detailed calculation of your penalty charges, call 1-800-829-0922.

IRS

Notice	CP501
Notice date	December 16, 2016
Social Security Number	

Contact information

If your address has changed, please call 1-800-829-0922 or visit www.irs.gov.

☐ Please check here if you've included any correspondence. Write your Social Security number (▮▮▮▮▮▮▮), the tax year (2014), and the form number (1040) on any correspondence.

☐ a.m. ☐ p.m.		☐ a.m. ☐ p.m.	
Primary phone	Best time to call	Secondary phone	Best time to call

Notice	CP501
Tax Year	2014
Notice date	December 16, 2016
Social Security number	

Removal of penalties due to erroneous written advice from the IRS

If you were penalized based on written advice from the IRS, we will remove the penalty if you meet the following criteria:
- If you sent a written request to the IRS for written advice on a specific issue
- You gave us complete and accurate information
- You received written advice from us
- You reasonably relied on our written advice and were penalized based on that advice

To request removal of penalties based on erroneous written advice from us, submit a completed Claim for Refund and Request for Abatement (Form 843) to the IRS service center where you filed your tax return. For a copy of the form or to find your IRS service center, go to www.irs.gov or call 1-800-829-0922.

Removal or reduction of penalties

We understand that circumstances—such as serious illness or injury, a family member's death, or loss of financial records due to natural disaster—may make it difficult for you to meet your taxpayer responsibility in a timely manner.

If you would like us to consider removing or reducing any of your penalty charges, please do the following:
- Identify which penalty charges you would like us to remove or reduce (e.g., 2005 late filing penalty).
- For each penalty charge, explain why you believe removal or reduction is appropriate.
- Sign your statement, and mail it to us along with any supporting documents.

We will review your statement and let you know whether we accept your explanation as reasonable cause to reduce or remove the penalty charge(s).

Notice	CP501
Tax Year	2014
Notice date	December 16, 2016
Social Security number	

Interest charges

We are required by law to charge interest on unpaid tax from the date the tax return was due to the date the tax is paid in full. The interest is charged as long as there is an unpaid amount due, including penalties, if applicable. (Internal Revenue Code section 6601)

Description	Amount
Total interest	

The table below shows the rates used to calculate the interest on your unpaid amount due. For a detailed calculation of your interest, call 1-800-829-0922.

Period	Interest rate
July 1, 2013–December 31, 2013	8%
January 1, 2014–March 31, 2014	7%
April 1, 2014–June 30, 2014	6%
July 1, 2014–September 30, 2014	5%
October 1, 2014–December 31, 2014	6%
Beginning January 1, 2015	5%

Additional information

- Visit www.irs.gov/cp501
- For tax forms, instructions, and publications, visit www.irs.gov or call 1-800-TAX-FORM (1-800-829-3676).
- Paying online is convenient, secure, and ensures timely receipt of your payment. To pay your taxes online or for more information, go to www.irs.gov/directpay.
- Keep this notice for your records.

We're required to send a copy of this notice to both you and your spouse. Each copy contains the same information about your joint account. Please note: Only pay the amount due once.
If you need assistance, please don't hesitate to contact us.

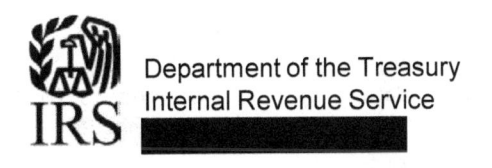

Notice	CP503
Tax Year	2014
Notice date	December 16, 2016
Social Security number	
To contact us	Phone
Your Caller ID	|️
Page 1 of 5	

Department of the Treasury
Internal Revenue Service

Second reminder: You have unpaid taxes for 2014

Amount due:

As we notified you before, our records show you have unpaid taxes for the tax year ending December 31, 2014 (Form 1040). If you don't pay ▮▮▮▮▮ by February 26, 2006, interest will increase and additional penalties may apply.

Billing Summary

Amount you owed
Failure-to-pay penalty
Interest charges
Amount due by January 26, 2015

What you need to do immediately

Pay immediately

- Pay the amount due of ▮▮▮▮▮ by January 26, 2015 to avoid additional penalty and interest charges. **You can pay online now at www.irs.gov/directpay.**

Continued on back...

Notice	CP503
Notice date	December 16, 2016
Social Security Number	

Payment

- Make your check or money order payable to the United States Treasury.
- Write your Social Security number ▮▮▮▮▮, the tax year (2014), and the form number (1040) on your payment and any correspondence.

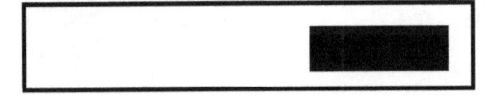

Amount due by January 26, 2015

INTERNAL REVENUE SERVICE

Exhibit 3

Notice	CP503
Tax Year	2014
Notice date	December 16, 2016
Social Security number	

What you need to do immediately—continued

Pay immediately—**continued**

- If you can't pay the amount due, pay as much as you can now and make payment arrangements that allow you to pay off the rest over time. Visit www.irs.gov/payments for more information about:
  -- Credit and debit card payments
  -- Electronic payments
  -- Installment and payment plans:
     - Automatic deductions from your bank account
     - Payroll deductions

     - [Apply online or mail Form 9465, Installment Agreement Request.]

  -- Offer in Compromise- To see if you qualify for an offer, visit the Offer in Compromise Pre-Qualifier tool at www.irs.gov/Individuals/Offer-in-Compromise-1

  Or, call us at 1-800-XXX-XXXX to discuss your options

If you need to pay your tax debt over time, we encourage you to apply for
a Direct Debit Installment Agreement. These agreements save you time
and money by having your monthly payment automatically withdrawn from your bank account. There are no checks to write and mail and these agreements have a reduced user fee.

[Apply for a payment plan using the Online Payment Agreement application at: www.irs.gov and search "online-payment.".]
Apply for a payment plan by completing Form 433-F prior to calling us at 1-800-XXX-XXXX. This will assist us in handling your call more efficiently.]

[By setting up an agreement online now, you may be able to avoid the
filing of a Notice of Federal Tax Lien, if one hasn't already been filed. If a
Notice of Federal Tax Lien has been filed, certain taxpayers may request
the notice be withdrawn after establishing a Direct Debit Installment Agreement. For more information on liens, visit: www.irs.gov and search
"federal tax lien"].

If you already paid your balance in full within the past 14 days or made payment arrangements, please disregard this notice.

Notice	CP503
Tax Year	2014
Notice date	December 16, 2016
Social Security number	

Page 3 of 5

If we don't hear from you

- If you don't pay ▓▓▓▓ by January 26, 2015, interest will increase and additional penalties may apply.
- If you don't pay the amount due or call us to make payment arrangements, we can file a Notice of Federal Tax Lien on your property at any time, if we haven't already done so.
- If the lien is in place, you may find it difficult to sell or borrow against your property. The tax lien would also appear on your credit report—which may harm your credit rating--and your creditors would also be publicly notified that the IRS has priority to seize your property.
- If you don't pay your tax debt, we have the right to seize ("levy") your property.

Penalties

We are required by law to charge any applicable penalties.

Failure-to-pay

Description	Amount
Total failure-to-pay	▓▓▓▓

When you pay your taxes after the due date, we charge a penalty of 0.5% of the unpaid amount due per month, up to 25% of the amount due. We count part of a month as a full month. (Internal Revenue Code Section 6651)

For a detailed calculation of your penalty charges, call 1-800-829-0922.

IRS

Notice	CP503
Notice date	December 16, 2016
Social Security Number	

Contact information

If your address has changed, please call 1-800-829-0922 or visit www.irs.gov.

☐ Please check here if you've included any correspondence. Write your Social Security number ▓▓▓▓, the tax year (2014), and the form number (1040) on any correspondence.

	☐ a.m. ☐ p.m.		☐ a.m. ☐ p.m.
Primary phone	Best time to call	Secondary phone	Best time to call

Notice	CP503
Tax Year	2014
Notice date	December 16, 2016
Social Security number	

Removal of penalties due to erroneous written advice from the IRS

If you were penalized based on written advice from the IRS, we will remove the penalty if you meet the following criteria:

- If you sent a written request to the IRS for written advice on a specific issue
- You gave us complete and accurate information
- You received written advice from us
- You reasonably relied on our written advice and were penalized based on that advice

To request removal of penalties based on erroneous written advice from us, submit a completed Claim for Refund and Request for Abatement (Form 843) to the IRS service center where you filed your tax return. For a copy of the form or to find your IRS service center, go to www.irs.gov or call 1-800-829-0922.

Removal or reduction of penalties

We understand that circumstances—such as serious illness or injury, a family member's death, or loss of financial records due to natural disaster—may make it difficult for you to meet your taxpayer responsibility in a timely manner.

If you would like us to consider removing or reducing any of your penalty charges, please do the following:

- Identify which penalty charges you would like us to remove or reduce (e.g., 2005 late filing penalty).
- For each penalty charge, explain why you believe removal or reduction is appropriate.
- Sign your statement, and mail it to us along with any supporting documents.

We will review your statement and let you know whether we accept your explanation as reasonable cause to reduce or remove the penalty charge(s).

Notice	CP503
Tax Year	2014
Notice date	December 16, 2016
Social Security number	

Interest charges

We are required by law to charge interest on unpaid tax from the date the tax return was due to the date the tax is paid in full. The interest is charged as long as there is an unpaid amount due, including penalties, if applicable. (Internal Revenue Code section 6601)

Description	Amount
Total interest	

The table below shows the rates used to calculate the interest on your unpaid amount due. For a detailed calculation of your interest, call 1-800-829-0922.

Period	Interest rate
July 1, 2013–December 31, 2013	8%
January 1, 2014–March 31, 2014	7%
April 1, 2014–June 30, 2014	6%
July 1, 2014–September 30, 2014	5%
October 1, 2014 December 31, 2014	6%
Beginning January 1, 2015	5%

Additional information

- Visit www.irs.gov/cp503.
- For tax forms, instructions, and publications, visit www.irs.gov or call 1-800-TAX-FORM (1-800-829-3676).
- Paying online is convenient, secure, and ensures timely receipt of your payment. To pay your taxes online or for more information, go to www.irs.gov/directpay.
- Keep this notice for your records.

We're required to send a copy of this notice to both you and your spouse. Each copy contains the same information about your joint account. Please note: Only pay the amount due once.
If you need assistance, please don't hesitate to contact us.

Notice	CP504
Tax Year	2014
Notice date	December 16, 2016
Social Security number	
To contact us	Phone
Your Caller ID	
Page 1 of 5	

Department of Treasury
Internal Revenue Service

Notice of Intent to Levy

Amount due immediately:

This is a notice of intent to seize ("levy") your state tax refund or other property. As we notified you before, our records show you have unpaid taxes for the tax year ending December 31, 2014 (Form 1040). If you don't call us immediately or pay the amount due, we may seize ("levy") your property or rights to property (including any state tax refunds) and apply it to the ▇▇▇ you owe.

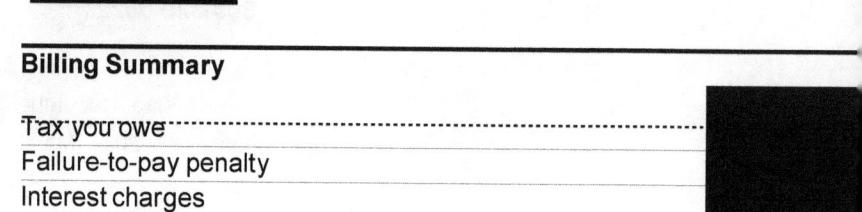

Billing Summary

Tax you owe
Failure-to-pay penalty
Interest charges
Amount due immediately

What you need to do immediately

Pay immediately

- Pay the amount due of ▇▇▇. If you fail to pay by January 26, 2015, interest will increase and additional penalties may apply. If you don't pay by January 26, 2015, we may seize ("levy") your property or rights to property (including any state tax refunds). **You can pay online now at www.irs.gov/directpay.**

Continued on back...

Notice	CP504
Notice date	December 16, 2016
Social Security Number	

- Make your check or money order payable to the United States Treasury.
- Write your Social Security number ▇▇▇, the tax year (2014), and the form number (1040) on your payment and any correspondence.

Payment

Amount due immediately

INTERNAL REVENUE SERVICE

Exhibit 4

Notice	CP504
Tax Year	2014
Notice date	December 16, 2016
Social Security number	

What you need to do immediately—continued

Pay immediately—**continued**

- If you can't pay the amount due, pay as much as you can now and make payment arrangements that allow you to pay off the rest over time. Visit www.irs.gov/Payments for more information about:
  -- Credit and debit card payments
  -- Electronic payments
  -- Installment and payment plans:
    - Automatic deductions from your bank account
    - Payroll deductions
    - [Apply online or mail Form 9465, Installment Agreement Request.]

  -- Offer in Compromise- To see if you qualify for an offer, visit the Offer in Compromise Pre-Qualifier tool at www.irs.gov/Individuals/Offer-in-Compromise-1.

Or, call us at 1-800-XXX-XXXX to discuss your options.]

If you need to pay your tax debt over time, we encourage you to apply for a Direct Debit Installment Agreement. These agreements save you time and money by having your monthly payment automatically withdrawn from your bank account. There are no checks to write and mail and these agreements have a reduced user fee.

[Apply for a payment plan using the Online Payment Agreement application at:www.irs.gov and search "online-payment.".

[Apply for a payment plan by completing Form 433-F prior to calling us at 1-800-XXX-XXXX. This will assist us in handling your call more efficiently.]

[By setting up an agreement online now, you may be able to avoid the filing of a Notice of Federal Tax Lien, if one hasn't already been filed. If a Notice of Federal Tax Lien has been filed, certain taxpayers may request the notice be withdrawn after establishing a Direct Debit Installment Agreement. For more information on liens, visit: www.irs.gov and search "federal tax lien".]

If you already paid your balance in full or believe we haven't credited a payment to your account, please call 1-800-XXX-XXXX, and have your payment information available to review with us. You can also contact us by mail. Fill out the Contact information section, detach, and send it to us with any correspondence or documentation, including proof of payment.

Notice	CP504
Tax Year	2014
Notice date	December 16, 2016
Social Security number	
Page 3 of 5	

If we don't hear from you	• If you don't pay or make payment arrangements by ▇ we may seize ("levy") your property (including any state tax refund).
	• Property and your rights to property include:
	  -Wages, real estate commissions, and other income
	  -Bank Accounts
	  -Personal assets (e.g., your car and home)
	  -Social Security Benefits
	• This is your **Notice of Intent to Levy**. (Internal Revenue Code section 6331(d)).
	• If you don't pay the amount due or call us to make payment arrangements, we may file a notice of Federal Tax Lien in your property at any time, if we haven't already done so.
	• If the lien is filed, you may find it difficult to sell or borrow against your property. The Notice of federal Tax Lien would also appear on your credit report—which may harm your credit rating—and your creditors would also be publicly notified that the IRS has priority to seize your property.

Penalties	We are required by law to charge any applicable penalties.
Failure-to-pay	Description Amount **Total failure-to-pay** When you pay your taxes after the due date, we charge a penalty of 0.5% of the unpaid amount due per month, up to 25% of the amount due. Beginning 10 days after we issue this notice, the penalty increases to 1.0% for each month the amount remains unpaid. We count part of a month as a full month. (Internal Revenue Code section 6651) For a detailed calculation of your penalty charges, call 1-800-829-0922.

	Notice CP504
	Notice date December 16, 2016
	Social Security Number

Contact information	If your address has changed, please call 1-800-829-0922 or visit www.irs.gov.
	☐ Please check here if you've included any correspondence. Write your Social Security number ▇, the tax year (2014), and the form number (1040) on any correspondence.
	
	                               ☐ a.m. ☐ a.m.
	                               ☐ p.m. ☐ p.m.
	Primary phone Best time to call Secondary phone Best time to call

Notice	CP504
Tax Year	2014
Notice date	December 16, 2016
Social Security number	

Removal or reduction of penalties

We understand that circumstances—such as serious illness or injury, a family member's death, or loss of financial records due to natural disaster—may make it difficult for you to meet your taxpayer responsibility in a timely manner.

If you would like us to consider removing or reducing any of your penalty charges, please do the following:

- Identify which penalty charges you would like us to remove or reduce (e.g., 2005 late filing penalty).
- For each penalty charge, explain why you believe removal or reduction is appropriate.
- Sign your statement, and mail it to us with any supporting documents. We will review your statement and let you know whether we accept your explanation as reasonable cause to reduce or remove the penalty charge(s).

Removal of penalties due to erroneous written advice from the IRS

If you were penalized based on written advice from the IRS, we will remove the penalty if you meet the following criteria:

- If you sent a written request to the IRS for written advice on a specific issue
- You gave us complete and accurate information
- You received written advice from us
- You reasonably relied on our written advice and were penalized based on that advice

To request removal of penalties based on erroneous written advice from us, submit a completed Claim for Refund and Request for Abatement (Form 843) to the IRS service center where you filed your tax return. For a copy of the form or to find your IRS service center, go to www.irs.gov or call 1-800-829-8374.

Notice	CP504
Tax Year	2014
Notice date	December 16, 2016
Social Security number	

Page 5 of 5

Interest charges

We are required by law to charge interest on unpaid tax from the date the tax return was due to the date the tax is paid in full. The interest is charged as long as there is an unpaid amount due, including penalties, if applicable. (Internal Revenue Code section 6601)

Description	Amount
Total interest	

The table below shows the rates used to calculate the interest on your unpaid amount due. For a detailed calculation of your interest, call 1-800-829-0922.

Period	Interest rate
October 1, 2013–June 30, 2013	7%
July 1, 2013–December 31, 2013	8%
January 1, 2014–March 31, 2014	7%
April 1, 2014–June 30, 2014	6%
July 1, 2014–September 30, 2014	5%
October 1, 2014–December 31, 2014	6%
Beginning January 1, 2015	5%

Additional information

- Visit www.irs.gov/cp504.
- For tax forms, instructions, and publications, visit www.irs.gov or call 1-800-TAX-FORM (1-800-829-3676).
- Paying online is convenient, secure, and ensures timely receipt of your payment. To pay your taxes online or for more information, go to www.irs.gov/directpay.
- Review the enclosed document: IRS Collection Process (Publication 594)
- Generally, we deal directly with taxpayers or their authorized representatives. Sometimes, however, it's necessary for us to speak with other people, such as employees, employers, banks, or neighbors to gather the information we need about a taxpayer's account. You have the right to request a list of individuals we've contacted in connection with your account at any time.
- Keep this notice for your records.

[We're required to send a copy of this notice to both you and your spouse. Each copy contains the same information about your joint account. Please note: Only pay the amount due once.]
If you need assistance, please don't hesitate to contact us.

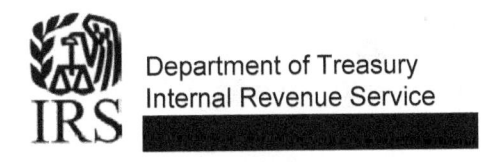

Notice	LT11
Notice date	March 2, 2009
Taxpayer ID number	
To contact us	
Your caller ID	
Page 1 of 5	

Department of Treasury
Internal Revenue Service

Notice of intent to levy

Intent to seize your property or rights to property
Amount due immediately: $

We haven't received a payment despite sending you several notices about your overdue taxes. The IRS may seize (levy) your property or your rights to property on or after April 1, 2009.
Property includes:
- Wages and other income
- Bank accounts
- Business assets
- Personal assets (including your car and home)
- Alaska Permanent Fund Dividend and state tax refund
- Social Security benefits

Billing Summary

Amount you owed	$
Additional penalty charges	
Additional interest charges	
Amount due immediately	$

Continued on back...

Payment

Notice	LT11
Notice date	March 2, 2009
Taxpayer ID number	

- Make your check or money order payable to the United States Treasury.
- Write your Social Security number ( ) on your payment and any correspondence.

Amount due immediately $

INTERNAL REVENUE SERVICE

Exhibit 5

Notice	LT11
Notice date	March 2, 2009
Taxpayer ID number	

What you need to do immediately

Pay immediately

- Send us the amount due of $ or we may seize (levy) your property on or after April 1, 2009.
- If you can't pay the amount due, pay as much as you can now and ma payment arrangements that allow you to pay off the rest over time. Vis www.irs.gov/payments for more information about:
  - Installment and payment agreements—download required forms or save time and money by applying online if you qualify
  - Automatic deductions from your bank account
  - Payroll deductions
  - Credit card payments

  Or, call us at to discuss your options.
- If you've already paid your balance in full or think we haven't credited a payment to your account, please send proof of that payment.

Right to request a Collection Due Process hearing
If you wish to appeal this proposed levy action, complete and mail the enclosed Form 12153, Request for a Collection Due Process or Equivale Hearing, by April 1, 2009. Send the form to us at the address listed at th top of page 1. Be sure to include the reason you are requesting a hearin (see section 8 of, and the instructions to, Form 12153) as well as other information requested by the form. If you don't file Form 12153 by April 2009, you will lose the ability to contest Appeals' decision in the U.S. Ta Court.

IRS

Contact information

Notice	LT11
Notice date	March 2, 2009
Taxpayer ID number	

If your address has changed, please call or visit www.irs.gov.

☐ Please check here if you've included any correspondence. Write your Social Security number (on any correspondence.

	☐ a.m. ☐ p.m.		☐ a.m. ☐ p.m.
Primary phone	Best time to call	Secondary phone	Best time to call

Notice	LT11
Notice date	March 2, 2009
Taxpayer ID number	

What you need to do immediately - continued

About Federal Tax Liens

If you don't pay the amount due or call us to make payment arrangements, we can file a Notice of Federal Tax Lien at any time, if we haven't already done so. The Notice of Federal Tax Lien publically notifies your creditors that the IRS has a lien (or claim) against all your property, including property acquired by you after the Notice of Federal Tax Lien is filed. Once the lien's notice to creditors has been filed, it may appear on your credit report and may harm your credit rating. The lien itself arises once you have not paid your bill. It cannot be released until your bill, including interest, penalties, and fees, is paid in full or until we may no longer legally collect your debt. The lien's notice to creditors may be withdrawn under certain circumstances. You can find additional information about tax liens, including helpful videos, at http://www.irs.gov/Businesses/Small-Businesses-&-Self-Employed/Understanding-a-Federal-Tax-Lien or by typing lien in the IRS.gov search box.

If we don't hear from you

If you don't call us immediately, pay the amount due, or request a hearing by April 1, 2009, we may seize (levy) your property or your rights to property. Property includes:
- Wages and other income
- Bank accounts
- Business assets
- Personal assets (including your car and home)
- Social security benefits

Your billing details

Tax period ending	Form number	Amount you owed	Additional interest	Additional penalty	Total
MM/DD/YYYY		$	$	$	$
MM/DD/YYYY		$	$	$	$
MM/DD/YYYY		$	$	$	$
MM/DD/YYYY		$	$	$	$

Penalties

We are required by law to charge any applicable penalties.

Failure-to-pay

When you pay your taxes after the due date, we charge a penalty of 0.5% of the unpaid amount due per month, up to 25% of the amount due. Beginning 10 days after we issue a notice of intent to levy, the penalty increases to 1.0% for each month the amount remains unpaid. We count part of a month as a full month. (Internal Revenue Code Section 6651)

For a detailed calculation of your penalty charges, call 1-866-829-7650.

Penalties-continued

Removal or reduction of penalties

We understand that circumstances—such as serious illness or injury, a family member's death, or loss of financial records due to natural disaster—may make it difficult for you to meet your taxpayer responsibility in a timely manner.

If you would like us to consider removing or reducing any of your penalty charges, please do the following:
- Identify which penalty charges you would like us to remove or reduce (e.g., 2005 late filing penalty).
- For each penalty charge, explain why you believe removal or reduction is appropriate.
- Sign your statement, and mail it to us with any supporting documents.

We will review your statement and let you know whether we accept your explanation as reasonable cause to reduce or remove the penalty charge(s).

Removal of penalties due to erroneous written advice from the IRS

If you were penalized based on written advice from the IRS, we will remove the penalty if you meet the following criteria:

- If you sent a written request to the IRS for written advice on a specific issue
- You gave us complete and accurate information
- You received written advice from us
- You reasonably relied on our written advice and were penalized based on that advice

To request removal of penalties based on erroneous written advice from us, submit a completed Claim for Refund and Request for Abatement (Form 843) to the IRS service center where you filed your tax return. For a copy of the form or to find your IRS service center, go to www.irs.gov or call ██████.

Interest charges

We are required by law to charge interest on unpaid tax from the date the tax return was due to the date the tax is paid in full. The interest is charged as long as there is an unpaid amount due, including penalties, if applicable. (Internal Revenue Code Section 6601) For a detailed calculation of your interest, call ██████.

Notice	LT11
Notice date	March 2, 2009
Taxpayer ID number	

Additional information

- Visit www.irs.gov/lt11
- For tax forms, instructions, and publications, visit www.irs.gov or call 1-800-TAX-FORM (1-800-829-3676).
- Review the enclosed documents:
  - IRS Collection Process (Publication 594)
  - Collection Appeal Rights (Publication 1660)
  - Request for a Collection Due Process Hearing (Form 12153)
- Keep this notice for your records.

We're required to send a copy of this notice to both you and your spouse. Each copy contains the information you are authorized to receive. Please note: Only pay the amount due once.

If you need assistance, please don't hesitate to contact us

Form 12153 (Rev. 12-2013)

Request for a Collection Due Process or Equivalent Hearing

Use this form to request a Collection Due Process (CDP) or equivalent hearing with the IRS Office of Appeals if you have been issued one of the following lien or levy notices:

- Notice of Federal Tax Lien Filing and Your Right to a Hearing under IRC 6320,
- Notice of Intent to Levy and Notice of Your Right to a Hearing,
- Notice of Jeopardy Levy and Right of Appeal,
- Notice of Levy on Your State Tax Refund,
- Notice of Levy and Notice of Your Right to a Hearing.

Complete this form and send it to the address shown on your lien or levy notice. Include a copy of your lien or levy notice to ensure proper handling of your request.

Call the phone number on the notice or 1-800-829-1040 if you are not sure about the correct address or if you want to fax your request.

You can find a section explaining the deadline for requesting a Collection Due Process hearing in this form's instructions. If you've missed the deadline for requesting a CDP hearing, you must check line 7 (Equivalent Hearing) to request an equivalent hearing.

1. Taxpayer Name: (Taxpayer 1) _____
   Taxpayer Identification Number _____
   Current Address _____
   City _____ State _____ Zip Code _____

2. Telephone Number and Best Time to Call During Normal Business Hours
   Home (___) ___ - _____ ☐ am. ☐ pm.
   Work (___) ___ - _____ ☐ am. ☐ pm.
   Cell (___) ___ - _____ ☐ am. ☐ pm.

3. Taxpayer Name: (Taxpayer 2) _____
   Taxpayer Identification Number _____
   Current Address _____
   (If Different from Address Above)
   City _____ State _____ Zip Code _____

4. Telephone Number and Best Time to Call During Normal Business Hours
   Home (___) ___ - _____ ☐ am. ☐ pm.
   Work (___) ___ - _____ ☐ am. ☐ pm.
   Cell (___) ___ - _____ ☐ am. ☐ pm.

5. Tax Information as Shown on the Lien or Levy Notice *(If possible, attach a copy of the notice)*

Type of Tax (Income, Employment, Excise, etc. or Civil Penalty)	Tax Form Number (1040, 941, 720, etc)	Tax Period or Periods

Form **12153** (Rev. 12-2013) Catalog Number 26685D **Exhibit 6** www.irs.gov Department of the Treasury - **Internal Revenue Service**

Form **12153**	
(Rev. 12-2013)	**Request for a Collection Due Process or Equivalent Hearing**

6. Basis for Hearing Request (Both boxes can be checked if you have received both a lien and levy notice)

☐ Filed Notice of Federal Tax Lien   ☐ Proposed Levy or Actual Levy

7. Equivalent Hearing (See the instructions for more information on Equivalent Hearings)

☐ I would like an Equivalent Hearing - I would like a hearing equivalent to a CDP Hearing if my request for a CDP hearing does not meet the requirements for a timely CDP Hearing.

8. Check the most appropriate box for the reason you disagree with the filing of the lien or the levy. **See page 4 of this form for examples.** You can add more pages if you don't have enough space. If, during your CDP Hearing, you think you would like to discuss a Collection Alternative to the action proposed by the Collection function it is recommended you submit a completed Form 433A (Individual) and/or Form 433B (Business), as appropriate, with this form. See www.irs.gov for copies of the forms. Generally, the Office of Appeals will ask the Collection Function to review, verify and provide their opinion on any new information you submit. We will share their comments with you and give you the opportunity to respond.

Collection Alternative   ☐ Installment Agreement   ☐ Offer in Compromise   ☐ I Cannot Pay Balance

Lien   ☐ Subordination   ☐ Discharge   ☐ Withdrawal

Please explain:

My Spouse Is Responsible   ☐ Innocent Spouse Relief (Please attach Form 8857, *Request for Innocent Spouse Relief,* to your request.)

Other (*For examples, see page 4*)   ☐

Reason (*You must provide a reason for the dispute or your request for a CDP hearing will not be honored. Use as much space as you need to explain the reason for your request. Attach extra pages if necessary.*):

9. Signatures   I understand the CDP hearing and any subsequent judicial review will suspend the statutory period of limitations for collection action. I also understand my representative or I must sign and date this request before the IRS Office of Appeals can accept it. If you are signing as an officer of a company add your title (*president, secretary, etc.*) behind your signature.

SIGN HERE

Taxpayer 1's Signature	Date
Taxpayer 2's Signature (*if a joint request, both must sign*)	Date

☐ I request my CDP hearing be held with my authorized representative (*attach a copy of Form 2848*)

Authorized Representative's Signature	Authorized Representative's Name	Telephone Number

IRS Use Only

IRS Employee (Print)	Employee Telephone Number	IRS Received Date

Form **12153** (Rev. 12-2013)   Catalog Number 26685D   www.irs.gov   Department of the Treasury - **Internal Revenue Service**

Internal Revenue Service
United States Department of the Treasury

This Product Contains Sensitive Taxpayer Data

Account Transcript

Request Date: 04-08-2014
Response Date: 04-08-2014
Tracking Number: 200191107146

FORM NUMBER: 1040
TAX PERIOD: Dec. 31, 2011

TAXPAYER IDENTIFICATION NUMBER: 999-99-9999
SPOUSE TAXPAYER IDENTIFICATION NUMBER: 888-88-8888

SANTA & JESSICA CLAUS

<<<<POWER OF ATTORNEY/TAX INFORMATION AUTHORIZATION (POA/TIA) ON FILE>>>>

--- ANY MINUS SIGN SHOWN BELOW SIGNIFIES A CREDIT AMOUNT ---

ACCOUNT BALANCE:	0.00	
ACCRUED INTEREST:	0.00	AS OF: Jul. 01, 2013
ACCRUED PENALTY:	0.00	AS OF: Jul. 01, 2013

ACCOUNT BALANCE PLUS ACCRUALS
(this is not a payoff amount): 0.00

** INFORMATION FROM THE RETURN OR AS ADJUSTED **

EXEMPTIONS:	04
FILING STATUS:	Married Filing Joint
ADJUSTED GROSS INCOME:	63,328.00
TAXABLE INCOME:	26,844.00
TAX PER RETURN:	1,915.00
SE TAXABLE INCOME TAXPAYER:	0.00
SE TAXABLE INCOME SPOUSE:	0.00
TOTAL SELF EMPLOYMENT TAX:	0.00

RETURN DUE DATE OR RETURN RECEIVED DATE (WHICHEVER IS LATER)   May 02, 2012
PROCESSING DATE   May 21, 2012

TRANSACTIONS

CODE	EXPLANATION OF TRANSACTION	CYCLE	DATE	AMOUNT
150	Tax return filed	20121905	05-21-2012	$1,956.00
n/a	30221-123-00588-2			
806	W-2 or 1099 withholding		04-15-2012	-$6,691.00
960	Appointed representative		07-05-2011	$0.00
961	Removed appointed representative		01-16-2012	$0.00
960	Appointed representative		04-02-2012	$0.00

Exhibit 7

460	Extension of time to file ext. Date 10-15-2012	04-15-2012	$0.00
846	Refund issued	05-21-2012	$4,775.00
960	Appointed representative	07-18-2012	$0.00
960	Appointed representative	01-21-2013	$0.00
291	Prior tax abated	02-11-2013	-$891.00
n/a	45254-761-07170-2		
971	Notice issued CP 0021	02-11-2013	$0.00
846	Refund issued	02-11-2013	$809.42
776	Interest credited to your account	02-11-2013	-$17.42

This Product Contains Sensitive Taxpayer Data

IRS Department of the Treasury
Internal Revenue Service

CCP-LU ACS CORRESPONDENCE
P.O. BOX 145566, STOP 813G CSC
CINCINNATI, OH 45250-5566

CERTIFIED MAIL

9307110756602784308405

Letter Date: 08/23/2016
Taxpayer Identification Number:
XXX-XX-XXXX
Person to Contact:
P.A. BELTON
Contact Telephone Number:
(800) 829-3903
Employee Identification Number:

TAXPAYER NAME
PO BOX
HARTFORD, CT XXXXX

000342

Notice of Federal Tax Lien Filing and Your Right to a Hearing Under IRC 6320

Dear TAXPAYER NAME

We filed a Notice of Federal Tax Lien on ███████.

Type of Tax	Tax Period	Assessment Date	Amount on Lien
CIVP	12/31/2011	12/29/2014	38428.87

NOTE: Please contact the person whose name and telephone number appears on this notice to obtain the current amount you owe. Additional interest and penalties may be increasing the amount on the lien shown above.

A lien attaches to all property you currently own and to all property you may acquire in the future. It also may damage your credit rating and hinder your ability to obtain additional credit.

You have the right to a hearing with us to appeal this collection action and to discuss your payment method options. To explain the different collection appeal procedures available to you, we have enclosed Publication 1660, Collection Appeal Rights.

You must request your hearing by 09/29/2016. Please complete the enclosed Form 12153, *Request for a Collection Due Process or Equivalent Hearing*, and mail it to:

Internal Revenue Service
IRS-ACS/CDP
P.O. BOX 42346
PHILADELPHIA, PA 19101-2346

Letter 3172 (DO) rev. (3-2000)
Catalog No. 267671

Exhibit 8

COURT RECORDING DATA

```
-------------------------------------------+----------------------------------
                                           | Lien Recorded      :        - 16:30PM
       INTERNAL REVENUE SERVICE            | Recording Number:
    FACSIMILE FEDERAL TAX LIEN DOCUMENT    | UCC Number         :
                                           | Liber              :
                                           | Page               :
-------------------------------------------+----------------------------------
 Area: SMALL BUSINESS/SELF EMPLOYED #1     | IRS Serial Number:
 Lien Unit Phone: (800) 829-3903           |
-------------------------------------------+----------------------------------
```

This Lien Has Been Filed in Accordance with
Internal Revenue Regulation 301.6323(f)-1.

Name of Taxpayer :

Residence :
  PO BOX
  HARTFORD, CT

With respect to each assessment below, unless notice of lien
is refiled by the date in column(e), this notice shall constitute
the certificate of release of lien as defined in IRC 6325(a).

Form (a)	Period (b)	ID Number (c)	Assessed (d)	Refile Deadline (e)	Unpaid Balance (f)
CIVP	12/31/2011	XXX-XX-	12/29/2014	01/28/2025	38428.87

Filed at: SECRETARY OF STATE
           state   Total | $ 38428.87
           HARTFORD, CT 06115

This notice was prepared and executed at MANHATTAN, NY
on this, the 11th day of August, 2016.

Authorizing Official: | Title:
    P.A. BELTON | ACS SBSE

Form 668 (Y)(c)
(Rev. February 2004)

1872

Department of the Treasury - Internal Revenue Service

Notice of Federal Tax Lien

Area: SMALL BUSINESS/SELF EMPLOYED AREA #1
(800) 829-3903

Serial Number: ███

For Optional Use by Recording Office

- This Notice of Federal Tax Lien has been filed as a matter of public record.
- IRS will continue to charge penalty and interest until you satisfy the amount you owe.
- Contact the Area Office Collection Function for information on the amount you must pay before we can release this lien.
- See the back of this page for an explanation of your Administrative Appeal rights.

As provided by section 6321, 6322, and 6323 of the Internal Revenue Code, we are giving a notice that taxes (including interest and penalties) have been assessed against the following-named taxpayer. We have made a demand for payment of this liability, but it remains unpaid. Therefore, there is a lien in favor of the United States on all property and rights to property belonging to this taxpayer for the amount of these taxes, and additional penalties, interest, and costs that may accrue.

000343

Name of Taxpayer ███

Residence
PO BOX ███
HARTFORD, CT ███

IMPORTANT RELEASE INFORMATION: For each assessment listed below, unless notice of the lien is refiled by the date given in column (e), this notice shall, on the day following such date, operate as a certificate of release as defined in IRC 6325(a).

Kind of Tax (a)	Tax Period Ending (b)	Identifying Number (c)	Date of Assessment (d)	Last Day for Refiling (e)	Unpaid Balance of Assessment (f)
CIVP	12/31/2011	XXX-XX-████	12/29/2014	01/28/2025	38428.87

Place of Filing
TOWN CLERK
HARTFORD City of
HARTFORD, CT 06103

Total 38428.87

This notice was prepared and signed at __MANHATTAN, NY__, on this, the ███ day of ███, 2016.

Signature: *Cheryl Cordero* for P.A. BELTON

Title: ACS SBSE
(800) 829-3903

(NOTE: Certificate of officer authorized by law to take acknowledgment is not essential to the validity of Notice of Federal Tax Lien Rev. Rul. 71-466, 1971 - 2 C.B. 409)

Part 3 - Taxpayer's Copy

CAT. NO 60025X
Form 668 (Y)(c) (Rev. 02-04)

Form **668-A(c)(DO)**
(Rev. July 2002)

Department of the Treasury – Internal Revenue Service
Notice of Levy

DATE:

REPLY TO:

TELEPHONE NUMBER
OF IRS OFFICE:

NAME AND ADDRESS OF TAXPAYER:

TO:

IDENTIFYING NUMBER(S):

THIS ISN'T A BILL FOR TAXES YOU OWE. THIS IS A NOTICE OF LEVY WE ARE USING TO COLLECT MONEY OWED BY THE TAXPAYER NAMED ABOVE.

Kind of Tax	Tax Period Ended	Unpaid Balance of Assessment	Statutory Additions	Total

THIS LEVY WON'T ATTACH FUNDS IN IRAs, SELF-EMPLOYED INDIVIDUALS' RETIREMENT PLANS, OR ANY OTHER RETIREMENT PLANS IN YOUR POSSESSION OR CONTROL, UNLESS IT IS SIGNED IN THE BLOCK TO THE RIGHT. ⟶

Total Amount Due ▶

We figured the interest and late payment penalty to _____

The Internal Revenue Code provides that there is a lien for the amount that is owed. Although we have given the notice and demand required by the Code, the amount owed hasn't been paid. This levy requires you to turn over to us this person's property and rights to property *(such as money, credits, and bank deposits)* that you have or which you are already obligated to pay this person. However, don't send us more than the "Total Amount Due."

Money in banks, credit unions, savings and loans, and similar institutions described in section 408(n) of the Internal Revenue Code must be held for 21 calendar days from the day you receive this levy before you send us the money. Include any interest the person earns during the 21 days. Turn over any other money, property, credits, etc. that you have or are already obligated to pay the taxpayer, when you would have paid it if this person asked for payment.

Make a reasonable effort to identify all property and rights to property belonging to this person. At a minimum, search your records using the taxpayer's name, address, and identifying numbers*(s)* shown on this form. Don't offset money this person owes you without contacting us at the telephone number shown above for instructions. You may not subtract a processing fee from the amount you send us.

To respond to this levy —
1. Make your check or money order payable to **United States Treasury**.
2. Write the taxpayer's name, identifying number*(s)*, kind of tax and tax period shown on this form, and "LEVY PROCEEDS" on your check or money order *(not on a detachable stub.)*.
3. Complete the back of Part 3 of this form and mail it to us with your payment in the enclosed envelope.
4. Keep Part 1 of this form for your records and give the taxpayer Part 2 within 2 days.

If you don't owe any money to the taxpayer, please complete the back of Part 3, and mail that part back to us in the enclosed envelope.

Signature of Service Representative

Exhibit 9

Title

Part 1— For Addressee   Catalog No. 15704T   www.irs.gov   Form **668-A(c)(DO)** (Rev. 7-2002)

Excerpts from the Internal Revenue Code

* * * * * * * * *

SEC. 6331. LEVY AND DISTRAINT.

(b) Seizure and Sale of Property.—The term "levy" as used in this title includes the power of distraint and seizure by any means. Except as otherwise provided in subsection (e), a levy shall extend only to property possessed and obligations existing at the time thereof. In any case in which the Secretary may levy upon property or rights to property, he may seize and sell such property or rights to property (whether real or personal, tangible or intangible).

(c) Successive Seizures.—Whenever any property or right to property upon which levy has been made by virtue of subsection (a) is not sufficient to satisfy the claim of the United States for which levy is made, the Secretary may, thereafter, and as often as may be necessary, proceed to levy in like manner upon any other property liable to levy of the person against whom such claim exists, until the amount due from him, together with all expenses, is fully paid.

SEC. 6332. SURRENDER OF PROPERTY SUBJECT TO LEVY.

(a) Requirement.—Except as otherwise provided in this section, any person in possession of (or obligated with respect to) property or rights to property subject to levy upon which a levy has been made shall, upon demand of the Secretary, surrender such property or rights (or discharge such obligation) to the Secretary, except such part of the property or rights as is, at the time of such demand, subject to an attachment or execution under any judicial process.

(b) Special rule for Life Insurance and Endowment Contracts

(1) In general.—A levy on an organization with respect to a life insurance or endowment contract issued by such organization shall, without necessity for the surrender of the contract document, constitute a demand by the Secretary for payment of the amount described in paragraph (2) and the exercise of the right of the person against whom the tax is assessed to the advance of such amount. Such organization shall pay over such amount 90 days after service of notice of levy. Such notice shall include a certification by the Secretary that a copy of such notice has been mailed to the person against whom the tax is assessed at his last known address.

(2) Satisfaction of levy.—Such levy shall be deemed to be satisfied if such organization pays over to the Secretary the amount which the person against whom the tax is assessed could have had advanced to him by such organization on the date prescribed in paragraph (1) for the satisfaction of such levy, increased by the amount of any advance (including contractual interest thereon) made to such person on or after the date such organization had actual notice or knowledge (within the meaning of section 6323 (i)(1)) of the existence of the lien with respect to which such levy is made, other than an advance (including contractual interest thereon) made automatically to maintain such contract in force under an agreement entered into before such organization had such notice or knowledge.

(3) Enforcement proceedings.—The satisfaction of a levy under paragraph (2) shall be without prejudice to any civil action for the enforcement of any lien imposed by this title with respect to such contract.

(c) Special Rule for Banks.—Any bank (as defined in section 408(n)) shall surrender (subject to an attachment or execution under judicial process) any deposits (including interest thereon) in such bank only after 21 days after service of levy.

(d) Enforcement of Levy.

(1) Extent of personal liability.—Any person who fails or refuses to surrender any property or rights to property, subject to levy, upon demand by the Secretary, shall be liable in his own person and estate to the United States in a sum equal to the value of the property or rights not so surrendered, but not exceeding the amount of taxes for the collection of which such levy has been made, together with costs and interest on such sum at the underpayment rate established under section 6621 from the date of such levy (or, in the case of a levy described in section 6331 (d)(3), from the date such person would otherwise have been obligated to pay over such amounts to the taxpayer). Any amount (other than costs) recovered under this paragraph shall be credited against the tax liability for the collection of which such levy was made.

(2) Penalty for violation.—In addition to the personal liability imposed by paragraph (1), if any person required to surrender property or rights to property fails or refuses to surrender such property or rights to property without reasonable cause, such person shall be liable for a penalty equal to 50 percent of the amount recoverable under paragraph (1). No part of such penalty shall be credited against the tax liability for the collection of which such levy was made.

(e) Effect of honoring levy.—Any person in possession of (or obligated with respect to) property or rights to property subject to levy upon which a levy has been made who, upon demand by the Secretary, surrenders such property or rights to property (or discharges such obligation) to the Secretary (or who pays a liability under subsection (d)(1)), shall be discharged from any obligation or liability to the delinquent taxpayer and any other person with respect to such property or rights to property arising from such surrender or payment.

SEC. 6333. PRODUCTION OF BOOKS.

If a levy has been made or is about to be made on any property, or right to property, any person having custody or control of any books or records, containing evidence or statements relating to the property or right to property subject to levy, shall, upon demand of the Secretary, exhibit such books or records to the Secretary.

SEC. 6343. AUTHORITY TO RELEASE LEVY AND RETURN PROPERTY.

(a) Release of Levy and Notice of Release.—

(1) In general.—Under regulations prescribed by the Secretary, the Secretary shall release the levy upon all, or part of, the property or rights to property levied upon and shall promptly notify the person upon whom such levy was made (if any) that such levy has been released if—

(A) the liability for which such levy was made is satisfied or becomes unenforceable by reason of lapse of time,

(B) release of such levy will facilitate the collection of such liability,

(C) the taxpayer has entered into an agreement under section 6159 to satisfy such liability by means of installment payments, unless such agreement provides otherwise,

(D) the Secretary has determined that such levy is creating an economic hardship due to the financial condition of the taxpayer, or

(E) the fair market value of the property exceeds such liability and release of the levy on a part of such property could be made without hindering the collection of such liability.

For purposes of subparagraph (C), the Secretary is not required to release such levy if such release would jeopardize the secured creditor status of the Secretary.

(2) Expedited determination on certain business property.—In the case of any tangible personal property essential in carrying on the trade or business of the taxpayer, the Secretary shall provide for an expedited determination under paragraph (1) if levy on such tangible personal property would prevent the taxpayer from carrying on such trade or business.

(3) Subsequent levy.—The release of levy on any property under paragraph (1) shall not prevent any subsequent levy on such property.

(b) Return of Property.—If the Secretary determines that property has been wrongfully levied upon, it shall be lawful for the Secretary to return—

(1) the specific property levied upon,
(2) an amount of money equal to the amount of money levied upon, or
(3) an amount of money equal to the amount of money received by the United States from a sale of such property.

Property may be returned at any time. An amount equal to the amount of money levied upon or received from such sale may be returned at any time before the expiration of 9 months from the date of such levy. For purposes of paragraph (3), if property is declared purchased by the United States at a sale pursuant to section 6335(e) (relating to manner and conditions of sale), the United States shall be treated as having received an amount of money equal to the minimum price determined pursuant to such section or (if larger) the amount received by the United States from the resale of such property.

(d) Return of Property in Certain Cases.—If—

(1) any property has been levied upon, and
(2) the Secretary determines that—

(A) the levy on such property was premature or otherwise not in accordance with administrative procedures of the Secretary,

(B) the taxpayer has entered into an agreement under section 6159 to satisfy the tax liability for which the levy was imposed by means of installment payments, unless such agreement provides otherwise,

(C) the return of such property will facilitate the collection of the tax liability, or

(D) with the consent of the taxpayer or the National Taxpayer Advocate, the return of such property would be in the best interests of the taxpayer (as determined by the National Taxpayer Advocate) and the United States,

the provisions of subsection (b) shall apply in the same manner as if such property had been wrongly levied upon, except that no interest shall be allowed under subsection (c).

* * * * * * * * *

Applicable Sections of Internal Revenue Code

6321. LIEN FOR TAXES.
6322. PERIOD OF LIEN.
6325. RELEASE OF LIEN OR DISCHARGE OF PROPERTY.
6331. LEVY AND DISTRAINT.
6332. SURRENDER OF PROPERTY SUBJECT TO LEVY.
6333. PRODUCTION OF BOOKS.
6334. PROPERTY EXEMPT FROM LEVY.
6343. AUTHORITY TO RELEASE LEVY AND RETURN PROPERTY.
7426. CIVIL ACTIONS BY PERSONS OTHER THAN TAXPAYERS.
7429. REVIEW OF JEOPARDY LEVY OR ASSESSMENT PROCEDURES.

For more information about this notice, please call the phone number on the front of this form.

Form **668-A(c)(DO)** (Rev. 7-2002)

Form 1040-ES
**Department of the Treasury
Internal Revenue Service**

2017 Estimated Tax

Payment Voucher 3

OMB No. 1545-0074

Calendar year—Due Sept. 15, 2017

File only if you are making a payment of estimated tax by check or money order. Mail this voucher with your check or money order payable to **"United States Treasury."** Write your social security number and "2017 Form 1040-ES" on your check or money order. Do not send cash. Enclose, but do not staple or attach, your payment with this voucher.

Amount of estimated tax you are paying by check or money order. | Dollars | Cents

Print or type

Your first name and initial	Your last name	Your social security number
If joint payment, complete for spouse		
Spouse's first name and initial	Spouse's last name	Spouse's social security number
Address (number, street, and apt. no.)		
City, state, and ZIP code. (If a foreign address, enter city, also complete spaces below.)		
Foreign country name	Foreign province/county	Foreign postal code

For Privacy Act and Paperwork Reduction Act Notice, see instructions.

Tear off here

Form 1040-ES
**Department of the Treasury
Internal Revenue Service**

2017 Estimated Tax

Payment Voucher 2

OMB No. 1545-0074

Calendar year—Due June 15, 2017

File only if you are making a payment of estimated tax by check or money order. Mail this voucher with your check or money order payable to **"United States Treasury."** Write your social security number and "2017 Form 1040-ES" on your check or money order. Do not send cash. Enclose, but do not staple or attach, your payment with this voucher.

Amount of estimated tax you are paying by check or money order. | Dollars | Cents

Print or type

Your first name and initial	Your last name	Your social security number
If joint payment, complete for spouse		
Spouse's first name and initial	Spouse's last name	Spouse's social security number
Address (number, street, and apt. no.)		
City, state, and ZIP code. (If a foreign address, enter city, also complete spaces below.)		
Foreign country name	Foreign province/county	Foreign postal code

For Privacy Act and Paperwork Reduction Act Notice, see instructions.

Tear off here

Form 1040-ES
**Department of the Treasury
Internal Revenue Service**

2017 Estimated Tax

Payment Voucher 1

OMB No. 1545-0074

Calendar year—Due April 18, 2017

File only if you are making a payment of estimated tax by check or money order. Mail this voucher with your check or money order payable to **"United States Treasury."** Write your social security number and "2017 Form 1040-ES" on your check or money order. Do not send cash. Enclose, but do not staple or attach, your payment with this voucher.

Amount of estimated tax you are paying by check or money order. | Dollars | Cents

Print or type

Your first name and initial	Your last name	Your social security number
If joint payment, complete for spouse		
Spouse's first name and initial	Spouse's last name	Spouse's social security number
Address (number, street, and apt. no.)		
City, state, and ZIP code. (If a foreign address, enter city, also complete spaces below.)		
Foreign country name	Foreign province/county	Foreign postal code

For Privacy Act and Paperwork Reduction Act Notice, see instructions.

Form 1040-ES (2017)

EXHIBIT 10

Form 9465 (Rev. December 2013)
Department of the Treasury
Internal Revenue Service

Installment Agreement Request

▶ Information about Form 9465 and its separate instructions is at *www.irs.gov/form9465*.
▶ If you are filing this form with your tax return, attach it to the front of the return.
▶ See separate instructions.

OMB No. 1545-0074

Tip: If you owe $50,000 or less, you may be able to establish an installment agreement online, even if you have not yet received a bill for your taxes. Go to IRS.gov to apply to pay online. **Caution:** *Do not file this form if you are currently making payments on an installment agreement or can pay your balance in full within 120 days. Instead, call 1-800-829-1040. Do not file if your business is still operating and owes employment or unemployment taxes. Instead, call the telephone number on your most recent notice. If you are in bankruptcy or we have accepted your offer-in-compromise, see* **Bankruptcy or offer-in-compromise,** *in the instructions.*

Part I

This request is for Form(s) (for example, Form 1040 or Form 941) ▶ _____ and for tax year(s) (for example, 2012 and 2013) ▶ _____

1a Your first name and initial | Last name | Your social security number

If a joint return, spouse's first name and initial | Last name | Spouse's social security number

Current address (number and street). If you have a P.O. box and no home delivery, enter your box number. | Apt. number

City, town or post office, state, and ZIP code. If a foreign address, also complete the spaces below (see instructions)

Foreign country name | Foreign province/state/county | Foreign postal code

1b If this address is new since you filed your last tax return, check here . . . . ▶ ☐

2 Name of your business (must be no longer operating) | Employer identification number (EIN)

3 Your home phone number | Best time for us to call | **4** Your work phone number | Ext. | Best time for us to call

5 Name of your bank or other financial institution:

Address

City, state, and ZIP code

6 Your employer's name:

Address

City, state, and ZIP code

7 Enter the total amount you owe as shown on your tax return(s) (or notice(s)) . . . . | **7**
8 Enter the amount of any payment you are making with your tax return(s) (or notice(s)). See instructions | **8**
9 Subtract line 8 from line 7 and enter the result . . . . | **9**
10 Enter the amount you can pay each month. Make your payments as large as possible to limit interest and penalty charges. **The charges will continue until you pay in full. If no payment amount is listed on line 10, a payment will be determined for you by dividing the balance due by 72 months** . . | **10**
11 Divide the amount on line 9 by 72 and enter the result . . . . | **11**

• If the amount on line 10 is less than the amount on line 11 and you are unable to increase your payment to the amount on line 11, complete and attach Form 433-F, Collection Information Statement.

• If the amount on line 10 is equal to or greater than the amount on line 11 but the amount you owe is greater than $25,000 but not more than $50,000, you must complete either line 13 or 14, if you do not wish to complete Form 433-F.

• If the amount on line 9 is greater than $50,000, complete and attach Form 433-F, Collection Information Statement.

12 Enter the date you want to make your payment each month. **Do not** enter a date later than the 28th ▶

13 If you want to make your payments by direct debit from your checking account, see the instructions and fill in lines 13a and 13b. This is the most convenient way to make your payments and it will ensure that they are made on time.

▶ **a** Routing number ☐☐☐☐☐☐☐☐☐

▶ **b** Account number ☐☐☐☐☐☐☐☐☐☐☐☐☐☐☐☐☐

I authorize the U.S. Treasury and its designated Financial Agent to initiate a monthly ACH debit (electronic withdrawal) entry to the financial institution account indicated for payments of my Federal taxes owed, and the financial institution to debit the entry to this account. This authorization is to remain in full force and effect until I notify the U.S. Treasury Financial Agent to terminate the authorization. To revoke payment, I must contact the U.S. Treasury Financial Agent at **1-800-829-1040** no later than 14 business days prior to the payment (settlement) date. I also authorize the financial institutions involved in the processing of the electronic payments of taxes to receive confidential information necessary to answer inquiries and resolve issues related to the payments.

14 If you want to make your payments by payroll deduction, check this box and attach a completed Form 2159, Payroll Deduction Agreement . . . . ☐

Your signature | Date | Spouse's signature. If a joint return, **both** must sign. | Date

For Privacy Act and Paperwork Reduction Act Notice, see instructions. | Cat. No. 14842Y | Form **9465** (Rev. 12-2013)

Exhibit 11

Form 9465 (Rev. 12-2013) Page **2**

Part II **Additional information.** Complete this part only if you have defaulted on an installment agreement within the past 12 months and the amount you owe is greater than $25,000 but not more $50,000 and the amount on line 10 is equal to or greater than the amount on line 11. If you owe more than $50,000, complete and attach Form 433-F, Collection Information Statement.

15 In which county is your primary residence? ☐

16a Marital status:
    ☐ Single. Skip question 16b and go to question 17.
    ☐ Married. Go to question 16b.
  b Do you share household expenses with your spouse?
    ☐ Yes.
    ☐ No.

17 How many dependents will you be able to claim on this year's tax return? . . . . **17** |

18 How many people in your household are 65 or older? . . . . **18** |

19 How often are you paid?
    ☐ Once a week.
    ☐ Once every two weeks.
    ☐ Once a month.
    ☐ Twice a month.

20 What is your net income per pay period (take home pay)? . . . . **20** $

21 How often is your spouse paid?
    ☐ Once a week.
    ☐ Once every two weeks.
    ☐ Once a month.
    ☐ Twice a month.

22 What is your spouse's net income per pay period (take home pay)? . . . . **22** $

23 How many vehicles do you own? . . . . **23** |

24 How many car payments do you have each month? . . . . **24** |

25a Do you have health insurance?
    ☐ Yes. Go to question 25b.
    ☐ No. Skip question 25b and go to question 26a.
  b Are your premiums deducted from your paycheck?
    ☐ Yes. Skip question 25c and go to question 26a.
    ☐ No. Go to question 25c.
  c How much are your monthly premiums? . . . . **25c** $

26a Do you make court-ordered payments?
    ☐ Yes. Go to question 26b.
    ☐ No. Go to question 27.
  b Are your court-ordered payments deducted from your paycheck?
    ☐ Yes. Go to question 27.
    ☐ No. Go to question 26c.
  c How much are your court-ordered payments each month? . . . . **26c** $

27 Not including any court-ordered payments for child and dependent support, how much do you pay for child or dependent care each month? . . . . **27** $

Form **9465** (Rev. 12-2013)

Form 433-A
(Rev. December 2012)
Department of the Treasury
Internal Revenue Service

Collection Information Statement for Wage Earners and Self-Employed Individuals

Wage Earners Complete Sections 1, 2, 3, 4, and 5 including the signature line on page 4. *Answer all questions or write N/A if the question is not applicable.*
Self-Employed Individuals Complete Sections 1, 3, 4, 5, 6 and 7 and the signature line on page 4. *Answer all questions or write N/A if the question is not applicable.*
For Additional Information, refer to Publication 1854, "How To Prepare a Collection Information Statement."
Include attachments if additional space is needed to respond completely to any question.

Name on Internal Revenue Service (IRS) Account	Social Security Number *SSN* on IRS Account	Employer Identification Number *EIN*

Section 1: Personal Information

1a Full Name of Taxpayer and Spouse *(if applicable)* | **1c** Home Phone ( ) | **1d** Cell Phone ( )

1b Address *(Street, City, State, ZIP code) (County of Residence)* | **1e** Business Phone ( ) | **1f** Business Cell Phone ( )

2b Name, Age, and Relationship of dependent(s)

2a Marital Status: ☐ Married ☐ Unmarried *(Single, Divorced, Widowed)*

	Social Security No. *(SSN)*	Date of Birth *(mmddyyyy)*	Driver's License Number and State
3a Taxpayer			
3b Spouse			

Section 2: Employment Information for Wage Earners

If you or your spouse have self-employment income instead of, or in addition to wage income, complete Business Information in Sections 6 and 7.

Taxpayer	Spouse
4a Taxpayer's Employer Name	**5a** Spouse's Employer Name
4b Address *(Street, City, State, and ZIP code)*	**5b** Address *(Street, City, State, and ZIP code)*
4c Work Telephone Number ( )	**4d** Does employer allow contact at work ☐ Yes ☐ No	**5c** Work Telephone Number ( )	**5d** Does employer allow contact at work ☐ Yes ☐ No
4e How long with this employer (years) (months)	**4f** Occupation	**5e** How long with this employer (years) (months)	**5f** Occupation
4g Number of withholding allowances claimed on Form W-4	**4h** Pay Period: ☐ Weekly ☐ Bi-weekly ☐ Monthly ☐ Other	**5g** Number of withholding allowances claimed on Form W-4	**5h** Pay Period: ☐ Weekly ☐ Bi-weekly ☐ Monthly ☐ Other

Section 3: Other Financial Information *(Attach copies of applicable documentation)*

6 Are you a party to a lawsuit *(If yes, answer the following)* ☐ Yes ☐ No

☐ Plaintiff ☐ Defendant | Location of Filing | Represented by | Docket/Case No.

Amount of Suit $ | Possible Completion Date *(mmddyyyy)* | Subject of Suit

7 Have you ever filed bankruptcy *(If yes, answer the following)* ☐ Yes ☐ No

Date Filed *(mmddyyyy)* | Date Dismissed *(mmddyyyy)* | Date Discharged *(mmddyyyy)* | Petition No. | Location Filed

8 In the past 10 years, have you lived outside of the U.S for 6 months or longer *(If yes, answer the following)* ☐ Yes ☐ No

Dates lived abroad: from *(mmddyyyy)* | To *(mmddyyyy)*

9a Are you the beneficiary of a trust, estate, or life insurance policy *(If yes, answer the following)* ☐ Yes ☐ No

Place where recorded: | EIN:

Name of the trust, estate, or policy | Anticipated amount to be received $ | When will the amount be received

9b Are you a trustee, fiduciary, or contributor of a trust ☐ Yes ☐ No

Name of the trust: | EIN:

10 Do you have a safe deposit box (business or personal) *(If yes, answer the following)* ☐ Yes ☐ No

Location *(Name, address and box number(s))* | Contents | Value $

11 In the past 10 years, have you transferred any assets for less than their full value *(If yes, answer the following)* ☐ Yes ☐ No

List Asset(s) | Value at Time of Transfer $ | Date Transferred *(mmddyyyy)* | To Whom or Where was it Transferred

www.irs.gov | Cat. No. 20312N | Exhibit 12 | Form **433-A** (Rev.12-2012)

Form 433-A (Rev. 12-2012) Page **2**

Section 4: Personal Asset Information for All Individuals

12 CASH ON HAND Include cash that is not in a bank   **Total Cash on Hand** $

PERSONAL BANK ACCOUNTS Include all checking, online and mobile (*e.g., PayPal*) accounts, money market accounts, savings accounts, and stored value cards (*e.g., payroll cards, government benefit cards, etc.*).

Type of Account	Full Name & Address (*Street, City, State, ZIP code*) of Bank, Savings & Loan, Credit Union, or Financial Institution	Account Number	Account Balance As of _____ *mmddyyyy*
13a			$
13b			$
13c			$
13d Total Cash (*Add lines 13a through 13c, and amounts from any attachments*)			$

INVESTMENTS Include stocks, bonds, mutual funds, stock options, certificates of deposit, and retirement assets such as IRAs, Keogh, and 401(k) plans. Include all corporations, partnerships, limited liability companies, or other business entities in which you are an officer, director, owner, member, or otherwise have a financial interest.

Type of Investment or Financial Interest	Full Name & Address (*Street, City, State, ZIP code*) of Company	Current Value	Loan Balance (*if applicable*) As of _____ *mmddyyyy*	**Equity** Value minus Loan
14a	Phone	$	$	$
14b	Phone	$	$	$
14c	Phone	$	$	$
14d Total Equity (*Add lines 14a through 14c and amounts from any attachments*)				$

AVAILABLE CREDIT Include all lines of credit and bank issued credit cards. Full Name & Address (*Street, City, State, ZIP code*) of Credit Institution	Credit Limit	Amount Owed As of _____ *mmddyyyy*	**Available Credit** As of _____ *mmddyyyy*
15a Acct. No	$	$	$
15b Acct. No	$	$	$
15c Total Available Credit (*Add lines 15a, 15b and amounts from any attachments*)			$

16a LIFE INSURANCE Do you own or have any interest in any life insurance policies with cash value (*Term Life insurance does not have a cash value*)
☐ Yes   ☐ No   If yes, complete blocks 16b through 16f for each policy.

16b	Name and Address of Insurance Company(ies):			
16c	Policy Number(s)			
16d	Owner of Policy			
16e	Current Cash Value	$	$	$
16f	Outstanding Loan Balance	$	$	$

16g Total Available Cash (*Subtract amounts on line 16f from line 16e and include amounts from any attachments*) $

Form **433-A** (Rev. 12-2012)

Form 433-A (Rev. 12-2012) Page 3

REAL PROPERTY Include all real property owned or being purchased

	Purchase Date (mmddyyyy)	Current Fair Market Value (FMV)	Current Loan Balance	Amount of Monthly Payment	Date of Final Payment (mmddyyyy)	Equity FMV Minus Loan
17a Property Description		$	$	$		$
Location (Street, City, State, ZIP code) and County		Lender/Contract Holder Name, Address (Street, City, State, ZIP code), and Phone				
		Phone				
17b Property Description		$	$	$		$
Location (Street, City, State, ZIP code) and County		Lender/Contract Holder Name, Address (Street, City, State, ZIP code), and Phone				
		Phone				

17c Total Equity (Add lines 17a, 17b and amounts from any attachments) $

PERSONAL VEHICLES LEASED AND PURCHASED Include boats, RVs, motorcycles, all-terrain and off-road vehicles, trailers, etc.

Description (Year, Mileage, Make/Model, Tag Number, Vehicle Identification Number)		Purchase/ Lease Date (mmddyyyy)	Current Fair Market Value (FMV)	Current Loan Balance	Amount of Monthly Payment	Date of Final Payment (mmddyyyy)	Equity FMV Minus Loan
18a Year	Make/Model		$	$	$		$
Mileage	License/Tag Number	Lender/Lessor Name, Address (Street, City, State, ZIP code), and Phone					
Vehicle Identification Number						Phone	
18b Year	Make/Model		$	$	$		$
Mileage	License/Tag Number	Lender/Lessor Name, Address (Street, City, State, ZIP code), and Phone					
Vehicle Identification Number						Phone	

18c Total Equity (Add lines 18a, 18b and amounts from any attachments) $

PERSONAL ASSETS Include all furniture, personal effects, artwork, jewelry, collections (coins, guns, etc.), antiques or other assets. Include intangible assets such as licenses, domain names, patents, copyrights, mining claims, etc.

	Purchase/ Lease Date (mmddyyyy)	Current Fair Market Value (FMV)	Current Loan Balance	Amount of Monthly Payment	Date of Final Payment (mmddyyyy)	Equity FMV Minus Loan
19a Property Description		$	$	$		$
Location (Street, City, State, ZIP code) and County		Lender/Lessor Name, Address (Street, City, State, ZIP code), and Phone				
		Phone				
19b Property Description		$	$	$		$
Location (Street, City, State, ZIP code) and County		Lender/Lessor Name, Address (Street, City, State, ZIP code), and Phone				
		Phone				

19c Total Equity (Add lines 19a, 19b and amounts from any attachments) $

Form **433-A** (Rev. 12-2012)

Form 433-A (Rev. 12-2012) Page 4

If you are self-employed, sections 6 and 7 must be completed before continuing.

Section 5: Monthly Income and Expenses

Monthly Income/Expense Statement *(For additional information, refer to Publication 1854.)*

Total Income		Total Living Expenses		IRS USE ONLY
Source	Gross Monthly	Expense Items [6]	Actual Monthly	Allowable Expenses
20 Wages (Taxpayer) [1]	$	35 Food, Clothing and Misc. [7]	$	
21 Wages (Spouse) [1]	$	36 Housing and Utilities [8]	$	
22 Interest - Dividends	$	37 Vehicle Ownership Costs [9]	$	
23 Net Business Income [2]	$	38 Vehicle Operating Costs [10]	$	
24 Net Rental Income [3]	$	39 Public Transportation [11]	$	
25 Distributions (K-1, IRA, etc.) [4]	$	40 Health Insurance	$	
26 Pension (Taxpayer)	$	41 Out of Pocket Health Care Costs [12]	$	
27 Pension (Spouse)	$	42 Court Ordered Payments	$	
28 Social Security (Taxpayer)	$	43 Child/Dependent Care	$	
29 Social Security (Spouse)	$	44 Life Insurance	$	
30 Child Support	$	45 Current year taxes (Income/FICA) [13]	$	
31 Alimony	$	46 Secured Debts (Attach list)	$	
Other Income (Specify below) [5]		47 Delinquent State or Local Taxes	$	
32	$	48 Other Expenses (Attach list)	$	
33	$	49 Total Living Expenses (add lines 35-48)	$	
34 Total Income (add lines 20-33)	$	50 Net difference (Line 34 minus 49)	$	

1 **Wages, salaries, pensions, and social security:** Enter gross monthly wages and/or salaries. Do not deduct tax withholding or allotments taken out of pay, such as insurance payments, credit union deductions, car payments, etc. To calculate the gross monthly wages and/or salaries:

If paid weekly - multiply weekly gross wages by 4.3. Example: $425.89 x 4.3 = $1,831.33

If paid biweekly (every 2 weeks) - multiply biweekly gross wages by 2.17. Example: $972.45 x 2.17 = $2,110.22

If paid semimonthly (twice each month) - multiply semimonthly gross wages by 2. Example: $856.23 x 2 = $1,712.46

2 **Net Income from Business:** Enter monthly net business income. This is the amount earned after ordinary and necessary monthly business expenses are paid. **This figure is the amount from page 6, line 89.** If the net business income is a loss, enter "0". Do not enter a negative number. If this amount is more or less than previous years, attach an explanation.

3 **Net Rental Income:** Enter monthly net rental income. This is the amount earned after ordinary and necessary monthly rental expenses are paid. Do not include deductions for depreciation or depletion. If the net rental income is a loss, enter "0." Do not enter a negative number.

4 **Distributions:** Enter the total distributions from partnerships and subchapter S corporations reported on Schedule K-1, and from limited liability companies reported on Form 1040, Schedule C, D or E. Enter total distributions from IRAs if not included under pension income.

5 **Other Income:** Include agricultural subsidies, unemployment compensation, gambling income, oil credits, rent subsidies, etc.

6 **Expenses not generally allowed:** We generally do not allow tuition for private schools, public or private college expenses, charitable contributions, voluntary retirement contributions or payments on unsecured debts. However, we may allow the expenses if proven that they are necessary for the health and welfare of the individual or family or the production of income. See Publication 1854 for exceptions.

7 **Food, Clothing and Miscellaneous:** Total of food, clothing, housekeeping supplies, and personal care products for one month. The miscellaneous allowance is for expenses incurred that are not included in any other allowable living expense items. Examples are credit card payments, bank fees and charges, reading material, and school supplies.

8 **Housing and Utilities:** For principal residence: Total of rent or mortgage payment. Add the average monthly expenses for the following: property taxes, homeowner's or renter's insurance, maintenance, dues, fees, and utilities. Utilities include gas, electricity, water, fuel, oil, other fuels, trash collection, telephone, cell phone, cable television and internet services.

9 **Vehicle Ownership Costs:** Total of monthly lease or purchase/loan payments.

10 **Vehicle Operating Costs:** Total of maintenance, repairs, insurance, fuel, registrations, licenses, inspections, parking, and tolls for one month.

11 **Public Transportation:** Total of monthly fares for mass transit *(e.g., bus, train, ferry, taxi, etc.)*

12 **Out of Pocket Health Care Costs:** Monthly total of medical services, prescription drugs and medical supplies *(e.g., eyeglasses, hearing aids, etc.)*

13 **Current Year Taxes:** Include state and Federal taxes withheld from salary or wages, or paid as estimated taxes.

Certification: *Under penalties of perjury, I declare that to the best of my knowledge and belief this statement of assets, liabilities, and other information is true, correct, and complete.*

Taxpayer's Signature	Spouse's signature	Date

After we review the completed Form 433-A, you may be asked to provide verification for the assets, encumbrances, income and expenses reported. Documentation may include previously filed income tax returns, pay statements, self-employment records, bank and investment statements, loan statements, bills or statements for recurring expenses, etc.

IRS USE ONLY *(Notes)*

Form 433-A (Rev. 12-2012) Page **5**

Sections 6 and 7 must be completed only if you are SELF-EMPLOYED.

Section 6: Business Information

51 Is the business a sole proprietorship *(filing Schedule C)* ☐ **Yes**, Continue with Sections 6 and 7. ☐ **No**, Complete Form 433-B.
All other business entities, including limited liability companies, partnerships or corporations, must complete Form 433-B.

52 Business Name & Address *(if different than 1b)*

53 Employer Identification Number	54 Type of Business	55 Is the business a Federal Contractor ☐ Yes ☐ No
56 Business Website (web address)	57 Total Number of Employees	58 Average Gross Monthly Payroll
59 Frequency of Tax Deposits	60 Does the business engage in e-Commerce *(Internet sales)* If yes, complete *lines 61a and 61b*	☐ Yes ☐ No

PAYMENT PROCESSOR *(e.g., PayPal, Authorize.net, Google Checkout, etc.)* Name & Address *(Street, City, State, ZIP code)* | Payment Processor Account Number

61a

61b

CREDIT CARDS ACCEPTED BY THE BUSINESS

	Credit Card	Merchant Account Number	Issuing Bank Name & Address *(Street, City, State, ZIP code)*
62a			
62b			
62c			

63 **BUSINESS CASH ON HAND** Include cash that is not in a bank. | **Total Cash on Hand** $

BUSINESS BANK ACCOUNTS Include checking accounts, online and mobile *(e.g., PayPal)* accounts, money market accounts, savings accounts, and stored value cards *(e.g., payroll cards, government benefit cards, etc.)*. Report Personal Accounts in Section 4.

Type of Account	Full name & Address *(Street, City, State, ZIP code)* of Bank, Savings & Loan, Credit Union or Financial Institution.	Account Number	Account Balance As of _____ *mmddyyyy*
64a			$
64b			$

64c **Total Cash in Banks** *(Add lines 64a, 64b and amounts from any attachments)* | $

ACCOUNTS/NOTES RECEIVABLE Include e-payment accounts receivable and factoring companies, and any bartering or online auction accounts. *(List all contracts separately, including contracts awarded, but not started.)* Include Federal, state and local government grants and contracts.

Accounts/Notes Receivable & Address *(Street, City, State, ZIP code)*	Status *(e.g., age, factored, other)*	Date Due *(mmddyyyy)*	Invoice Number or Government Grant or Contract Number	Amount Due
65a				$
65b				$
65c				$
65d				$
65e				$

65f **Total Outstanding Balance** *(Add lines 65a through 65e and amounts from any attachments)* | $

Form **433-A** (Rev. 12-2012)

Form 433-A (Rev. 12-2012) — Page 6

BUSINESS ASSETS Include all tools, books, machinery, equipment, inventory or other assets used in trade or business. Include a list and show the value of all intangible assets such as licenses, patents, domain names, copyrights, trademarks, mining claims, etc.

	Purchase/Lease Date (mmddyyyy)	Current Fair Market Value (FMV)	Current Loan Balance	Amount of Monthly Payment	Date of Final Payment (mmddyyyy)	Equity FMV Minus Loan
66a Property Description		$	$	$		$
Location (Street, City, State, ZIP code) and Country			Lender/Lessor/Landlord Name, Address (Street, City, State, ZIP code), and Phone			
			Phone			
66b Property Description		$	$	$		$
Location (Street, City, State, ZIP code) and Country			Lender/Lessor/Landlord Name, Address (Street, City, State, ZIP code), and Phone			
			Phone			

66c **Total Equity** (Add lines 66a, 66b and amounts from any attachments) $

Section 7 should be completed only if you are SELF-EMPLOYED

Section 7: Sole Proprietorship Information (lines 67 through 87 should reconcile with business Profit and Loss Statement)

Accounting Method Used: ☐ Cash ☐ Accrual
Use the prior 3, 6, 9 or 12 month period to determine your typical business income and expenses.

Income and Expenses during the period (mmddyyyy) _____ to (mmddyyyy) _____
Provide a breakdown below of your average monthly income and expenses, based on the period of time used above.

Total Monthly Business Income		Total Monthly Business Expenses (Use attachments as needed)	
Source	Gross Monthly	Expense Items	Actual Monthly
67 Gross Receipts	$	77 Materials Purchased [1]	$
68 Gross Rental Income	$	78 Inventory Purchased [2]	$
69 Interest	$	79 Gross Wages & Salaries	$
70 Dividends	$	80 Rent	$
71 Cash Receipts not included in lines 67-70	$	81 Supplies [3]	$
Other Income (Specify below)		82 Utilities/Telephone [4]	$
72	$	83 Vehicle Gasoline/Oil	$
73	$	84 Repairs & Maintenance	$
74	$	85 Insurance	$
75	$	86 Current Taxes [5]	$
76 Total Income (Add lines 67 through 75)	$	87 Other Expenses, including installment payments (Specify)	$
		88 Total Expenses (Add lines 77 through 87)	$
		89 Net Business Income (Line 76 minus 88) [6]	$

Enter the monthly net income amount from line 89 on line 23, section 5. If line 89 is a loss, enter "0" on line 23, section 5.
Self-employed taxpayers must return to page 4 to sign the certification.

---

1 Materials Purchased: Materials are items directly related to the production of a product or service.
2 Inventory Purchased: Goods bought for resale.
3 Supplies: Supplies are items used in the business that are consumed or used up within one year. This could be the cost of books, office supplies, professional equipment, etc.
4 Utilities/Telephone: Utilities include gas, electricity, water, oil, other fuels, trash collection, telephone, cell phone and business internet.

5 Current Taxes: Real estate, excise, franchise, occupational, personal property, sales and employer's portion of employment taxes.
6 Net Business Income: Net profit from Form 1040, Schedule C may be used if duplicated deductions are eliminated (e.g., expenses for business use of home already included in housing and utility expenses on page 4). Deductions for depreciation and depletion on Schedule C are not cash expenses and must be added back to the net income figure. In addition, interest cannot be deducted if it is already included in any other installment payments allowed.

IRS USE ONLY (Notes)

Form **433-A** (Rev. 12-2012)

Form 433-F (February 2019)

Department of the Treasury - Internal Revenue Service

Collection Information Statement

Name(s) and Address

Your Social Security Number or Individual Taxpayer Identification Number

Your Spouse's Social Security Number or Individual Taxpayer Identification Number

☐ If address provided above is different than last return filed, please check here

County of Residence

Your telephone numbers
Home:
Work:
Cell:

Spouse's telephone numbers
Home:
Work:
Cell:

Enter the number of people in the household who can be claimed on this year's tax return including you and your spouse. Under 65 _____ 65 and Over _____

If you or your spouse are self employed or have self employment income, provide the following information:

Name of Business	Business EIN	Type of Business	Number of Employees *(not counting owner)*

A. ACCOUNTS / LINES OF CREDIT

PERSONAL BANK ACCOUNTS Include checking, online, mobile (e.g., PayPal), savings accounts, money market accounts. (Use additional sheets if necessary.)

Name and Address of Institution	Account Number	Type of Account	Current Balance/Value	Check if Business Account
				☐
				☐

INVESTMENTS Include Certificates of Deposit, Trusts, Individual Retirement Accounts (IRAs), Keogh Plans, Simplified Employee Pensions, 401(k) Plans, Profit Sharing Plans, Mutual Funds, Stocks, Bonds, Commodities (Silver, Gold, etc.), and other investments. If applicable, include business accounts. *(Use additional sheets if necessary.)*

Name and Address of Institution	Account Number	Type of Account	Current Balance/Value	Check if Business Account
				☐
				☐

VIRTUAL CURRENCY (CRYPTOCURRENCY) List all virtual currency you own or in which you have a financial interest (e.g., Bitcoin, Ethereum, Litecoin, Ripple, etc.). *(Use additional sheets if necessary.)*

Type of Virtual Currency	Name of Virtual Currency Wallet, Exchange or Digital Currency Exchange (DCE)	Email Address Used to Set-up With the Virtual Currency Exchange or DCE	Location(s) of Virtual Currency *(Mobile Wallet, Online, and/or External Hardware storage)*	Virtual Currency Amount and Value in US dollars as of today *(e.g., 10 Bitcoins $64,600 USD)*

B. REAL ESTATE
Include home, vacation property, timeshares, vacant land and other real estate. *(Use additional sheets if necessary.)*

Description/Location/County	Monthly Payment(s)	Financing		Current Value	Balance Owed	Equity
☐ Primary Residence ☐ Other		Year Purchased	Purchase Price			
		Year Refinanced	Refinance Amount			
☐ Primary Residence ☐ Other		Year Purchased	Purchase Price			
		Year Refinanced	Refinance Amount			

C. OTHER ASSETS
Include cars, boats, recreational vehicles, whole life policies, etc. Include make, model and year of vehicles and name of Life Insurance company in Description. If applicable, include business assets such as tools, equipment, inventory, etc. *(Use additional sheets if necessary.)*

Description	Monthly Payment	Year Purchased	Final Payment (mo/yr)	Current Value	Balance Owed	Equity
			/			
			/			

D. CREDIT CARDS *(Visa, MasterCard, American Express, Department Stores, etc.)*

Type	Credit Limit	Balance Owed	Minimum Monthly Payment

TURN PAGE TO CONTINUE

Catalog Number 62053J   www.irs.gov   Form **433-F** (Rev. 2-2019)

Exhibit 13

E. BUSINESS INFORMATION Complete E1 for Accounts Receivable owed to you or your business. *(Use additional sheets if necessary.)* Complete E2 if you or your business accepts credit card payments. Include virtual currency wallet, exchange or digital currency exchange.

E1. Accounts Receivable owed to you or your business

Name	Address	Amount Owed
	List total amount owed from additional sheets	
	Total amount of accounts receivable available to pay to IRS now	

E2. Name of individual or business on account

Credit Card *(Visa, Master Card, etc.)*	Issuing Bank Name and Address	Merchant Account Number

F. EMPLOYMENT INFORMATION If you have more than one employer, include the information on another sheet of paper. *(If attaching a copy of current pay stub, you do not need to complete this section.)*

Your current Employer *(name and address)* | Spouse's current Employer *(name and address)*

How often are you paid *(check one)*
☐ Weekly ☐ Biweekly ☐ Semi-monthly ☐ Monthly
Gross per pay period _____
Taxes per pay period *(Fed)* _____ *(State)* _____ *(Local)* _____
How long at current employer _____

How often are you paid *(check one)*
☐ Weekly ☐ Biweekly ☐ Semi-monthly ☐ Monthly
Gross per pay period _____
Taxes per pay period *(Fed)* _____ *(State)* _____ *(Local)* _____
How long at current employer _____

G. NON-WAGE HOUSEHOLD INCOME List monthly amounts. For Self-Employment and Rental Income, list the monthly amount received after expenses or taxes and attach a copy of your current year profit and loss statement.

Alimony Income		Net Rental Income		Interest/Dividends Income	
Child Support Income		Unemployment Income		Social Security Income	
Net Self Employment Income		Pension Income		Other:	

H. MONTHLY NECESSARY LIVING EXPENSES List monthly amounts. (For expenses paid other than monthly, see instructions.)

1. Food / Personal Care *See instructions. If you do not spend more than the standard allowable amount for your family size, fill in the Total amount only.*

	Actual Monthly Expenses	IRS Allowed
Food		
Housekeeping Supplies		
Clothing and Clothing Services		
Personal Care Products & Services		
Miscellaneous		
Total		

2. Transportation

	Actual Monthly Expenses	IRS Allowed
Gas / Insurance / Licenses / Parking / Maintenance etc.		
Public Transportation		
Total		

3. Housing & Utilities

	Actual Monthly Expenses	IRS Allowed
Rent		
Electric, Oil/Gas, Water/Trash		
Telephone/Cell/Cable/Internet		
Real Estate Taxes and Insurance *(if not included in B above)*		
Maintenance and Repairs		
Total		

4. Medical

	Actual Monthly Expenses	IRS Allowed
Health Insurance		
Out of Pocket Health Care Expenses		
Total		

5. Other

	Actual Monthly Expenses	IRS Allowed
Child / Dependent Care		
Estimated Tax Payments		
Term Life Insurance		
Retirement *(Employer Required)*		
Retirement *(Voluntary)*		
Union Dues		
Delinquent State & Local Taxes *(minimum payment)*		
Student Loans *(minimum payment)*		
Court Ordered Child Support		
Court Ordered Alimony		
Other Court Ordered Payments		
Other *(specify)*		
Other *(specify)*		
Other *(specify)*		
Total		

Under penalty of perjury, I declare to the best of my knowledge and belief this statement of assets, liabilities and other information is true, correct and complete.

Your signature | Spouse's signature | Date

Catalog Number 62053J | www.irs.gov | Form **433-F** (Rev. 2-2019)

Instructions for Form 433-F, Collection Information Statement

What is the purpose of Form 433F?

Form 433-F is used to obtain current financial information necessary for determining how a wage earner or self-employed individual can satisfy an outstanding tax liability.

Note: You may be able to establish an Online Payment Agreement on the IRS web site. To apply online, go to https://www.irs.gov, click on "I need to pay my taxes," and select "Installment Agreement" under the heading "What if I can't pay now?"

If you are requesting an Installment Agreement, you should submit Form 9465, *Installment Agreement Request*, along with Form 433-F. (A large down payment may streamline the installment agreement process, pay your balance faster and reduce the amount of penalties and interest.

Please retain a copy of your completed form and supporting documentation. After we review your completed form, we may contact you for additional information. For example, we may ask you to send supporting documentation of your current income or substantiation of your stated expenditures.

If any section on this form is too small for the information you need to supply, please use a separate sheet.

Section A – Accounts / Lines of Credit

List all accounts, even if they currently have no balance. However, do not enter bank loans in this section. Include business accounts, if applicable. If you are entering information for a stock or bond, etc. and a question does not apply, enter N/A.

Section B – Real Estate

List all real estate you own or are purchasing including your home. Include insurance and taxes if they are included in your monthly payment. The county/description is needed if different than the address and county you listed above. To determine equity, subtract the amount owed for each piece of real estate from its current market value.

Section C – Other Assets

List all cars, boats and recreational vehicles with their make, model and year. If a vehicle is leased, write "lease" in the "year purchased" column. List whole life insurance policies with the name of the insurance company. List other assets with a description such as "paintings", "coin collection", or "antiques". If applicable, include business assets, such as tools, equipment, inventory, and intangible assets such as domain names, patents, copyrights, etc. To determine equity, subtract the amount owed from its current market value. If you are entering information for an asset and a question does not apply, enter N/A.

Section D – Credit Cards

List all credit cards and lines of credit, even if there is no balance owed.

Section E – Business Information

Complete this section if you or your spouse are self-employed, or have self-employment income. This includes self-employment income from online sales.

E1: List all Accounts Receivable owed to you or your business. Include federal, state and local grants and contracts.

E2: Complete if you or your business accepts credit card payments (e.g., Visa, MasterCard, etc.) and/or virtual currency wallet, exchange or digital currency exchange.

Section F – Employment Information

Complete this section if you or your spouse are wage earners.

If attaching a copy of current pay stub, you do not need to complete this section.

Section G – Non-Wage Household Income

List all non-wage income received monthly.

Net Self-Employment Income is the amount you or your spouse earns after you pay ordinary and necessary monthly business expenses. This figure should relate to the yearly net profit from Schedule C on your Form 1040 or your current year profit and loss statement. Please attach a copy of Schedule C or your current year profit and loss statement. If net income is a loss, enter "0".

Net Rental Income is the amount you earn after you pay ordinary and necessary monthly rental expenses. This figure should relate to the amount reported on Schedule E of your Form 1040.

Do not include depreciation expenses. Depreciation is a non-cash expense. Only cash expenses are used to determine ability to pay).

If net rental income is a loss, enter "0".

Other Income includes distributions from partnerships and subchapter S corporations reported on Schedule K-1, and from limited liability companies reported on Form 1040, Schedule C, D or E. It also includes agricultural subsidies, gambling income, oil credits, and rent subsidies. Enter total distributions from IRAs if not included under Pension Income.

Section H – Monthly Necessary Living Expenses

Enter monthly amounts for expenses. For any expenses not paid monthly, convert as follows:

If a bill is paid ...	Calculate the monthly amount by ...
Quarterly	Dividing by 3
Weekly	Multiplying by 4.3
Biweekly (every two weeks)	Multiplying by 2.17
Semimonthly (twice each month)	Multiplying by 2

For expenses claimed in boxes 1 and 4, you should provide the IRS allowable standards, or the actual amount you pay if the amount exceeds the IRS allowable standards. IRS allowable standards can be found by accessing https://www.irs.gov/businesses/small-businesses-self-employed/collection-financial-standards.

Substantiation may be required for any expenses over the standard once the financial analysis is completed.

The amount claimed for Miscellaneous cannot exceed the standard amount for the number of people in your family. The miscellaneous allowance is for expenses incurred that are not included in any other allowable living expense items. Examples are credit card payments, bank fees and charges, reading material and school supplies.

If you do not have access to the IRS web site, itemize your actual expenses and we will ask you for additional proof, if required. Documentation may include pay statements, bank and investment statements, loan statements and bills for recurring expenses, etc.

Housing and Utilities — Includes expenses for your primary residence. You should only list amounts for utilities, taxes and insurance that are not included in your mortgage or rent payments.

Rent — Do not enter mortgage payment here. Mortgage payment is listed in Section B.

Transportation — Include the total of maintenance, repairs, insurance, fuel, registrations, licenses, inspections, parking, and tolls for one month.

Public Transportation — Include the total you spend for public transportation if you do not own a vehicle or if you have public transportation costs in addition to vehicle expenses.

Medical — You are allowed expenses for health insurance and out-of-pocket health care costs.

Health insurance — Enter the monthly amount you pay for yourself or your family.

Out-of-Pocket health care expenses — are costs not covered by health insurance, and include:

- Medical services
- Prescription drugs
- Dental expenses
- Medical supplies, including eyeglasses and contact lenses. Medical procedures of a purely cosmetic nature, such as plastic surgery or elective dental work are generally not allowed.

Child / Dependent Care — Enter the monthly amount you pay for the care of dependents that can be claimed on your Form 1040.

Estimated Tax Payments — Calculate the monthly amount you pay for estimated taxes by dividing the quarterly amount due on your Form 1040ES by 3.

Life Insurance — Enter the amount you pay for term life insurance only. Whole life insurance has cash value and should be listed in Section C.

Delinquent State & Local Taxes — Enter the minimum amount you are required to pay monthly. Be prepared to provide a copy of the statement showing the amount you owe and if applicable, any agreement you have for monthly payments.

Student Loans — Minimum payments on student loans for the taxpayer's post-secondary education may be allowed if they are guaranteed by the federal government. Be prepared to provide proof of loan balance and payments.

Court Ordered Payments — For any court ordered payments, be prepared to submit a copy of the court order portion showing the amount you are ordered to pay, the signatures, and proof you are making the payments. Acceptable forms of proof are copies of cancelled checks or copies of bank or pay statements.

Other Expenses not listed above — We may allow other expenses in certain circumstances. For example, if the expenses are necessary for the health and welfare of the taxpayer or family, or for the production of income. Specify the expense and list the minimum monthly payment you are billed.

Form **433-B**
(February 2019)
Department of the Treasury
Internal Revenue Service

Collection Information Statement for Businesses

Note: *Complete all entry spaces with the current data available or "N/A" (not applicable). Failure to complete all entry spaces may result in rejection of your request or significant delay in account resolution.* **Include attachments if additional space is needed to respond completely to any question.**

Section 1: Business Information

1a Business Name _____

1b Business Street Address _____
   Mailing Address _____
   City _____ State _____ ZIP _____
1c County _____
1d Business Telephone (_____) _____
1e Type of Business _____
1f Business Website (web address) _____

2a Employer Identification No. (EIN) _____
2b Type of entity *(Check appropriate box below)*
   ☐ Partnership ☐ Corporation ☐ Other _____
   ☐ Limited Liability Company (LLC) classified as a corporation
   ☐ Other LLC - Include number of members _____
2c Date Incorporated/Established _____
   mmddyyyy

3a Number of Employees _____
3b Monthly Gross Payroll _____
3c Frequency of Tax Deposits _____
3d Is the business enrolled in Electronic Federal Tax Payment System (EFTPS)   ☐ Yes   ☐ No

4 Does the business engage in e-Commerce *(Internet sales)* If yes, complete 5a and 5b.   ☐ Yes   ☐ No

PAYMENT PROCESSOR *(e.g., PayPal, Authorize.net, Google Checkout, etc.)* Include virtual currency wallet, exchange or digital currency exchange.

	Name and Address *(Street, City, State, ZIP code)*	Payment Processor Account Number
5a		
5b		

CREDIT CARDS ACCEPTED BY THE BUSINESS

	Type of Credit Card *(e.g., Visa, Mastercard, etc.)*	Merchant Account Number	Issuing Bank Name and Address *(Street, City, State, ZIP code)*
6a			Phone
6b			Phone
6c			Phone

Section 2: Business Personnel and Contacts

PARTNERS, OFFICERS, LLC MEMBERS, MAJOR SHAREHOLDERS *(Foreign and Domestic),* **ETC.**

7a Full Name _____
   Title _____
   Home Address _____
   City _____ State _____ ZIP _____
   Responsible for Depositing Payroll Taxes ☐ Yes ☐ No
   Taxpayer Identification Number _____
   Home Telephone (_____) _____
   Work/Cell Phone (_____) _____
   Ownership Percentage & Shares or Interest _____
   Annual Salary/Draw _____

7b Full Name _____
   Title _____
   Home Address _____
   City _____ State _____ ZIP _____
   Responsible for Depositing Payroll Taxes ☐ Yes ☐ No
   Taxpayer Identification Number _____
   Home Telephone (_____) _____
   Work/Cell Phone (_____) _____
   Ownership Percentage & Shares or Interest _____
   Annual Salary/Draw _____

7c Full Name _____
   Title _____
   Home Address _____
   City _____ State _____ ZIP _____
   Responsible for Depositing Payroll Taxes ☐ Yes ☐ No
   Taxpayer Identification Number _____
   Home Telephone (_____) _____
   Work/Cell Phone (_____) _____
   Ownership Percentage & Shares or Interest _____
   Annual Salary/Draw _____

7d Full Name _____
   Title _____
   Home Address _____
   City _____ State _____ ZIP _____
   Responsible for Depositing Payroll Taxes ☐ Yes ☐ No
   Taxpayer Identification Number _____
   Home Telephone (_____) _____
   Work/Cell Phone (_____) _____
   Ownership Percentage & Shares or Interest _____
   Annual Salary/Draw _____

Catalog Number 16649P   www.irs.gov   Form **433-B** (Rev. 2-2019)

Exhibit 14

Form 433-B (Rev. 2-2019) Page **2**

Section 3: Other Financial Information *(Attach copies of all applicable documents)*

8 Does the business use a Payroll Service Provider or Reporting Agent *(If yes, answer the following)* ☐ Yes ☐ No

Name and Address *(Street, City, State, ZIP code)* | Effective dates *(mmddyyyy)*

9 Is the business a party to a lawsuit *(If yes, answer the following)* ☐ Yes ☐ No

☐ Plaintiff ☐ Defendant | Location of Filing | Represented by | Docket/Case No.

Amount of Suit $ | Possible Completion Date *(mmddyyyy)* | Subject of Suit

10 Has the business ever filed bankruptcy *(If yes, answer the following)* ☐ Yes ☐ No

Date Filed *(mmddyyyy)* | Date Dismissed *(mmddyyyy)* | Date Discharged *(mmddyyyy)* | Petition No. | District of Filing

11 Do any related parties *(e.g., officers, partners, employees)* have outstanding amounts owed to the business *(If yes, answer the following)* ☐ Yes ☐ No

Name and Address *(Street, City, State, ZIP code)* | Date of Loan | Current Balance As of _____ *mmddyyyy* $ | Payment Date | Payment Amount $

12 Have any assets been transferred, in the last 10 years, from this business for less than full value *(If yes, answer the following)* ☐ Yes ☐ No

List Asset | Value at Time of Transfer $ | Date Transferred *(mmddyyyy)* | To Whom or Where Transferred

13 Does this business have other business affiliations *(e.g., subsidiary or parent companies)* *(If yes, answer the following)* ☐ Yes ☐ No

Related Business Name and Address *(Street, City, State, ZIP code)* | Related Business EIN:

14 Any increase/decrease in income anticipated *(If yes, answer the following)* ☐ Yes ☐ No

Explain *(Use attachment if needed)* | How much will it increase/decrease $ | When will it increase/decrease

15 Is the business a Federal Government Contractor *(Include Federal Government contracts in #18, Accounts/Notes Receivable)* ☐ Yes ☐ No

Section 4: Business Asset and Liability Information (Foreign and Domestic)

16a CASH ON HAND *Include cash that is not in the bank* | Total Cash on Hand $

16b Is there a safe on the business premises ☐ Yes ☐ No | Contents

BUSINESS BANK ACOUNTS Include online and mobile accounts *(e.g., PayPal)*, money market accounts, savings accounts, checking accounts and stored value cards *(e.g., payroll cards, government benefit cards, etc.)*
List safe deposit boxes including location, box number and value of contents. Attach list of contents.

	Type of Account	Full Name and Address *(Street, City, State, ZIP code)* of Bank, Savings & Loan, Credit Union or Financial Institution	Account Number	Account Balance As of _____ *mmddyyyy*
17a				$
17b				$
17c				$
17d	Total Cash in Banks *(Add lines 17a through 17c and amounts from any attachments)*			$

Catalog Number 16649P | www.irs.gov | Form **433-B** (Rev. 2-2019)

Form 433-B (Rev. 2-2019) Page **3**

ACCOUNTS/NOTES RECEIVABLE Include e-payment accounts receivable and factoring companies, and any bartering or online auction accounts.
(List all contracts separately including contracts awarded, but not started). **Include Federal, state and local government grants and contracts.**

Name & Address *(Street, City, State, ZIP code)*	Status *(e.g., age, factored, other)*	Date Due *(mmddyyyy)*	Invoice Number or Government Grant or Contract Number	Amount Due
18a Contact Name Phone				$
18b Contact Name Phone				$
18c Contact Name Phone				$
18d Contact Name Phone				$
18e Contact Name Phone				$

18f **Outstanding Balance** *(Add lines 18a through 18e and amounts from any attachments)* $

INVESTMENTS List all investment assets below. Include stocks, bonds, mutual funds, stock options, certificates of deposit, commodities (e.g., gold, silver, copper, etc.) and virtual currency (e.g., Bitcoin, Ripple and Litecoin).

Name of Company & Address *(Street, City, State, ZIP code)*	Used as collateral on loan	Current Value	Loan Balance	**Equity** Value Minus Loan
19a Phone	☐ Yes ☐ No	$	$	$
19b Phone	☐ Yes ☐ No	$	$	$

19c **Total Investments** *(Add lines 19a, 19b, and amounts from any attachments)* $

AVAILABLE CREDIT Include all lines of credit and credit cards.

Full Name & Address *(Street, City, State, ZIP code)*	Credit Limit	Amount Owed As of _____ *mmddyyyy*	**Available Credit** As of _____ *mmddyyyy*
20a Account No.	$	$	$
20b Account No.	$	$	$

20c **Total Credit Available** *(Add lines 20a, 20b, and amounts from any attachments)* $

Catalog Number 16649P www.irs.gov Form **433-B** (Rev. 2-2019)

Form 433-B (Rev. 2-2019) Page **4**

REAL PROPERTY Include all real property and land contracts the business owns/leases/rents.

	Purchase/ Lease Date (mmddyyyy)	Current Fair Market Value (FMV)	Current Loan Balance	Amount of Monthly Payment	Date of Final Payment (mmddyyyy)	**Equity** FMV Minus Loan
21a Property Description		$	$	$		$
Location (Street, City, State, ZIP code) and County		Lender/Lessor/Landlord Name, Address, (Street, City, State, ZIP code) and Phone				
		Phone				
21b Property Description		$	$	$		$
Location (Street, City, State, ZIP code) and County		Lender/Lessor/Landlord Name, Address, (Street, City, State, ZIP code) and Phone				
		Phone				
21c Property Description		$	$	$		$
Location (Street, City, State, ZIP code) and County		Lender/Lessor/Landlord Name, Address, (Street, City, State, ZIP code) and Phone				
		Phone				
21d Property Description		$	$	$		$
Location (Street, City, State, ZIP code) and County		Lender/Lessor/Landlord Name, Address, (Street, City, State, ZIP code) and Phone				
		Phone				

21e Total Equity (Add lines 21a through 21d and amounts from any attachments) $

VEHICLES, LEASED AND PURCHASED Include boats, RVs, motorcycles, all-terrain and off-road vehicles, trailers, mobile homes, etc.

			Purchase/ Lease Date (mmddyyyy)	Current Fair Market Value (FMV)	Current Loan Balance	Amount of Monthly Payment	Date of Final Payment (mmddyyyy)	**Equity** FMV Minus Loan
22a Year		Make/Model		$	$	$		$
Mileage		License/Tag Number	Lender/Lessor Name, Address, (Street, City, State, ZIP code) and Phone					
Vehicle Identification Number (VIN)			Phone					
22b Year		Make/Model		$	$	$		$
Mileage		License/Tag Number	Lender/Lessor Name, Address, (Street, City, State, ZIP code) and Phone					
Vehicle Identification Number (VIN)			Phone					
22c Year		Make/Model		$	$	$		$
Mileage		License/Tag Number	Lender/Lessor Name, Address, (Street, City, State, ZIP code) and Phone					
Vehicle Identification Number (VIN)			Phone					
22d Year		Make/Model		$	$	$		$
Mileage		License/Tag Number	Lender/Lessor Name, Address, (Street, City, State, ZIP code) and Phone					
Vehicle Identification Number (VIN)			Phone					

22e Total Equity (Add lines 22a through 22d and amounts from any attachments) $

Catalog Number 16649P　　　　www.irs.gov　　　　Form **433-B** (Rev. 2-2019)

Form 433-B (Rev. 2-2019) Page **5**

BUSINESS EQUIPMENT AND INTANGIBLE ASSETS Include all machinery, equipment, merchandise inventory, and other assets in 23a through 23d. List intangible assets in 23e through 23g *(licenses, patents, logos, domain names, trademarks, copyrights, software, mining claims, goodwill and trade secrets.)*

	Purchase/Lease Date *(mmddyyyy)*	Current Fair Market Value (FMV)	Current Loan Balance	Amount of Monthly Payment	Date of Final Payment *(mmddyyyy)*	**Equity** FMV Minus Loan
23a Asset Description		$	$	$		$
Location of asset *(Street, City, State, ZIP code)* and County			Lender/Lessor Name, Address, *(Street, City, State, ZIP code)* and Phone			
			Phone			
23b Asset Description		$	$	$		$
Location of asset *(Street, City, State, ZIP code)* and County			Lender/Lessor Name, Address, *(Street, City, State, ZIP code)* and Phone			
			Phone			
23c Asset Description		$	$	$		$
Location of asset *(Street, City, State, ZIP code)* and County			Lender/Lessor Name, Address, *(Street, City, State, ZIP code)* and Phone			
			Phone			
23d Asset Description		$	$	$		$
Location of asset *(Street, City, State, ZIP code)* and County			Lender/Lessor Name, Address, *(Street, City, State, ZIP code)* and Phone			
			Phone			
23e Intangible Asset Description						$
23f Intangible Asset Description						$
23g Intangible Asset Description						$
23h Total Equity *(Add lines 23a through 23g and amounts from any attachments)*						$

BUSINESS LIABILITIES Include notes and judgements not listed previously on this form.

Business Liabilities	Secured/Unsecured	Date Pledged *(mmddyyyy)*	Balance Owed	Date of Final Payment *(mmddyyyy)*	Payment Amount
24a Description:	☐ Secured ☐ Unsecured		$		$
Name Street Address City/State/ZIP code			Phone		
24b Description:	☐ Secured ☐ Unsecured		$		$
Name Street Address City/State/ZIP code			Phone		
24c Total Payments *(Add lines 24a and 24b and amounts from any attachments)*					$

Catalog Number 16649P www.irs.gov Form **433-B** (Rev. 2-2019)

Form 433-B (Rev. 2-2019)   Page **6**

Section 5: Monthly Income/Expenses Statement for Business

Accounting Method Used: ☐ Cash   ☐ Accrual

Use the prior 3, 6, 9 or 12 month period to determine your typical business income and expenses.

Income and Expenses during the period (mmddyyyy) _____ to (mmddyyyy) _____

Provide a breakdown below of your average monthly income and expenses, based on the period of time used above.

Total Monthly Business Income			Total Monthly Business Expenses	
Income Source	Gross Monthly		Expense items	Actual Monthly
25 Gross Receipts from Sales/Services	$	36	Materials Purchased [1]	$
26 Gross Rental Income	$	37	Inventory Purchased [2]	$
27 Interest Income	$	38	Gross Wages & Salaries	$
28 Dividends	$	39	Rent	$
29 Cash Receipts (Not included in lines 25-28)	$	40	Supplies [3]	$
Other Income (Specify below)		41	Utilities/Telephone [4]	$
30	$	42	Vehicle Gasoline/Oil	$
31	$	43	Repairs & Maintenance	$
32	$	44	Insurance	$
33	$	45	Current Taxes [5]	$
34	$	46	Other Expenses (Specify)	$
35 **Total Income** (Add lines 25 through 34)	$	47	IRS Use Only-Allowable Installment Payments	$
		48	**Total Expenses** (Add lines 36 through 47)	$
		49	**Net Income** (Line 35 minus Line 48)	$

1. **Materials Purchased:** Materials are items directly related to the production of a product or service.
2. **Inventory Purchased:** Goods bought for resale.
3. **Supplies:** Supplies are items used to conduct business and are consumed or used up within one year. This could be the cost of books, office supplies, professional equipment, etc.
4. **Utilities/Telephone:** Utilities include gas, electricity, water, oil, other fuels, trash collection, telephone, cell phone and business internet.
5. **Current Taxes:** Real estate, state, and local income tax, excise, franchise, occupational, personal property, sales and the employer's portion of employment taxes.

Certification: *Under penalties of perjury, I declare that to the best of my knowledge and belief this statement of assets, liabilities, and other information is true, correct, and complete.*

Signature	Title	Date

Print Name of Officer, Partner or LLC Member

After we review the completed Form 433-B, you may be asked to provide verification for the assets, encumbrances, income and expenses reported. Documentation may include previously filed income tax returns, profit and loss statements, bank and investment statements, loan statements, financing statements, bills or statements for recurring expenses, etc.

IRS USE ONLY (Notes)

Privacy Act: The information requested on this Form is covered under Privacy Acts and Paperwork Reduction Notices which have already been provided to the taxpayer.

Catalog Number 16649P   www.irs.gov   Form **433-B** (Rev. 2-2019)

Form **433-H**
(May 2019)

Department of the Treasury - Internal Revenue Service

Installment Agreement Request and Collection Information Statement

Use Form 433-H if you earn wages, you are requesting an installment agreement, and your liability is either greater than $50,000 or cannot be paid within 72 months.

Tip If you can pay your liability within 72 months or less and owe $50,000 or less, you may be able to establish an installment agreement online, even if you have not yet received a bill for your taxes. Go to IRS.gov to apply to pay online.

Caution Don't file this form if you can pay your balance in full within 120 days. Instead, call the number on your most recent notice. If you are in bankruptcy or we have accepted your offer-in-compromise, see Bankruptcy or Offer-in-Compromise, in the instructions.

Name(s) and address	Your Social Security Number or Individual Taxpayer Identification Number
	Your Spouse's Social Security Number or Individual Taxpayer Identification Number

☐ If address provided above is different than last return filed, please check here

County of Residence

Your Telephone Numbers
Home:
Work:
Cell:

Spouse's Telephone Numbers
Home:
Work:
Cell:

Enter the number of people in the household who can be claimed on this year's tax return including you and your spouse. Under 65 ___ 65 and Over ___

Part 1 - INSTALLMENT AGREEMENT REQUEST Complete to request an installment agreement

1. Enter the total amount you owe as shown on your tax return(s) (or notices(s)) Form ___ Tax Period ___
2. If you have additional balances due that are not reflected on Line 1, list the total here *(even if they are included in an existing installment agreement)* Form ___ Tax Period(s) ___
3. Add lines 1 & 2 and enter the result
4. Enter the amount of any payment you are making with this request *(See instructions.)*
5. Subtract line 4 from line 3 and enter the result
6. Enter the amount you can pay each month. Make your payments as large as possible to limit interest and penalty charges, since these charges will continue to accrue until you pay in full. *(If you have an existing installment agreement, this amount should represent your total proposed monthly payment amount for all your liabilities.)* If no payment amount is listed on line 6, a payment will be determined for you by analyzing the information you provided on your financial statement.
7. Enter the date you want to make your payment each month. Do not enter a date later than the 28th
8. If you want to make your payments by direct debit from your checking account, see the instructions and fill in lines 8a and 8b. This is the most convenient way to make your payments and it will ensure that they are made on time.

    a. Routing number
    b. Account number

I authorize the U.S. Treasury and its designated Financial Agent to initiate a monthly ACH debit *(electronic withdrawal)* entry to the financial institution account indicated for payments of my federal taxes owed, and the financial institution to debit the entry to this account. This authorization is to remain in full force and effect until I notify the U.S. Treasury Financial Agent to terminate the authorization. To revoke payment, I must contact the U.S. Treasury Financial Agent at 1-800-829-1040 no later than 14 business days prior to the payment *(settlement)* date. I also authorize the financial institutions involved in the processing of the electronic payments of taxes to receive confidential information necessary to answer inquiries and resolve issues related to the payments.

   c. If you are unable to make electronic payments through a debit instrument (debit payments) by entering into a direct debit installment agreement (DDIA) in Sections 8. a. and b. above, please check the box below:

   I am unable to make debit payments. ☐

   Note: Not checking this box indicates that you are able but choosing not to make debit payments. See Instructions for line 8c. for details.

9. If you want to make your payments by payroll deduction, check this box and attach a completed Form 2159, Payroll Deduction Agreement ☐

Part 2 - COLLECTION INFORMATION STATEMENT Complete Sections A through G below to provide financial information

A. ACCOUNTS / LINES OF CREDIT

PERSONAL BANK ACCOUNTS Include checking, online, mobile (e.g., PayPal), savings accounts, money market accounts. (Use additional sheets if necessary.)

Name and Address of Institution	Account Number	Type of Account	Current Balance/Value	Check if Business Account
				☐
				☐

Catalog Number 71232U   www.irs.gov   Form **433-H** (5-2019)

Exhibit 15

Part 2 - COLLECTION INFORMATION STATEMENT (Continued)

INVESTMENTS Include Certificates of Deposit, Trusts, Individual Retirement Accounts (IRAs), Keogh Plans, Simplified Employee Pensions, 401(k) Plans, Profit Sharing Plans, Mutual Funds, Stocks, Bonds, Commodities (Silver, Gold, etc.), and other investments. If applicable, include business accounts. *(Use additional sheets if necessary.)*

Name and Address of Institution	Account Number	Type of Account	Current Balance/Value	Check if Business Account
				☐
				☐

VIRTUAL CURRENCY (CRYPTOCURRENCY) List all virtual currency you own or in which you have a financial interest (e.g., Bitcoin, Ethereum, Litecoin, Ripple, etc.). *(Use additional sheets if necessary.)*

Type of Virtual Currency	Name of Virtual Currency Wallet, Exchange or Digital Currency Exchange (DCE)	Email Address Used to Set-up With the Virtual Currency Exchange or DCE	Location(s) of Virtual Currency *(Mobile Wallet, Online, and/or External Hardware storage)*	Virtual Currency Amount and Value in US dollars as of today *(e.g., 10 Bitcoins $64,600 USD)*

B. REAL ESTATE Include home, vacation property, timeshares, vacant land and other real estate. *(Use additional sheets if necessary.)*

Description/Location/County	Monthly Payment(s)	Financing		Current Value	Balance Owed	Equity
☐ Primary Residence ☐ Other		Year Purchased	Purchase Price			
		Year Refinanced	Refinance Amount			
☐ Primary Residence ☐ Other		Year Purchased	Purchase Price			
		Year Refinanced	Refinance Amount			
☐ Primary Residence ☐ Other		Year Purchased	Purchase Price			
		Year Refinanced	Refinance Amount			
☐ Primary Residence ☐ Other		Year Purchased	Purchase Price			
		Year Refinanced	Refinance Amount			

C. OTHER ASSETS Include cars, boats, recreational vehicles, whole life policies, etc. Include make, model and year of vehicles and name of Life Insurance company in Description. *(Use additional sheets if necessary.)*

Description	Monthly Payment	Year Purchased	Final Payment *(mo/yr)*	Current Value	Balance Owed	Equity
			/			
			/			
			/			
			/			
			/			
			/			
			/			

D. CREDIT CARDS *(Visa, MasterCard, American Express, Department Stores, etc.)*

Type	Credit Limit	Balance Owed	Minimum Monthly Payment

Catalog Number 71232U   www.irs.gov   Form **433-H** (5-2019)

Page 3

Part 2 - COLLECTION INFORMATION STATEMENT *(Continued)*

E. EMPLOYMENT INFORMATION
If you have more than one employer, include the information on another sheet of paper. *(If attaching a copy of current pay stub, you do not need to complete the lines regarding gross pay and taxes.)*

Your current employer (name and address)	Spouse's current employer (name and address)

How often are you paid *(Check one)*: ☐ Weekly ☐ Biweekly ☐ Semi-monthly ☐ Monthly
Gross per pay period _____
Taxes per pay period *(Fed)* _____ *(State)* _____ *(Local)* _____
How long at current employer _____

How often are you paid *(Check one)*: ☐ Weekly ☐ Biweekly ☐ Semi-monthly ☐ Monthly
Gross per pay period _____
Taxes per pay period *(Fed)* _____ *(State)* _____ *(Local)* _____
How long at current employer _____

F. NON-WAGE HOUSEHOLD INCOME List monthly amounts.

Alimony Income	_____	Net Rental Income	_____	Interest/Dividends Income	_____
Child Support Income	_____	Unemployment Income	_____	Social Security Income	_____
Net Self Employment Income	_____	Pension Income	_____	Other	_____

G. MONTHLY NECESSARY LIVING EXPENSES
List monthly amounts. *(For expenses paid other than monthly, see instructions.)*

1. Food / Personal Care See instructions. National Standards for food, clothing and other items apply nationwide. For expenses claimed in box 1, you should provide the IRS allowable standards *(found by accessing IRS.gov and entering "Collection Financial Standards" in the search box)* or your actual expenses. If you claim a higher amount for a specific expense, you must be able to verify that amount.

	Actual Monthly Expenses	IRS Allowed
Food		
Housekeeping Supplies		
Clothing and Clothing Services		
Personal Care Products & Services		
Miscellaneous		
Total		

2. Transportation

	Actual Monthly Expenses	IRS Allowed
Gas / Insurance / Licenses / Parking / Maintenance etc.		
Public Transportation		
Total		

3. Housing & Utilities

	Actual Monthly Expenses	IRS Allowed
Rent		
Electric, Oil/Gas, Water/Trash		
Telephone/Cell/Cable/Internet		
Real Estate Taxes and Insurance *(if not included in B above)*		
Maintenance and Repairs		
Total		

4. Medical See instructions. National Standards for out of pocket health case expenses. For expenses claimed in box 4, you should provide the IRS allowable standards *(found by accessing IRS.gov and entering "Collection Financial Standards" in the search box)* or your actual expenses. If you claim a higher amount for a specific expense, you must be able to verify that amount.

	Actual Monthly Expenses	IRS Allowed
Health Insurance		
Out of Pocket Health Care Expenses		
Total		

5. Other

	Actual Monthly Expenses	IRS Allowed
Child / Dependent Care		
Estimated Tax Payments		
Term Life Insurance		
Retirement *(Employer Required)*		
Retirement *(Voluntary)*		
Union Dues		
Delinquent State & Local Taxes *(minimum payment)*		
Student Loans *(minimum payment)*		
Court Ordered Child Support		
Court Ordered Alimony		
Other Court Ordered Payments		
Other *(specify)*		
Other *(specify)*		
Total		

Notes

Under penalty of perjury, I declare to the best of my knowledge and belief this request for installment agreement, statement of assets, liabilities and income, and all other information is true, correct and complete.

Your Signature	Spouse's Signature	Date

Catalog Number 71232U   www.irs.gov   Form **433-H** (5-2019)

Instructions for Form 433-H, Installment Agreement Request and Collection Information Statement

What is the purpose of Form 433-H?

Form 433-H, *Installment Agreement Request and Collection Information Statement*, is used by wage earners to provide current financial information and request an installment agreement, allowing the Service to determine how best to satisfy outstanding tax liabilities.

However, before requesting an installment agreement, you should consider other payment options, which may be less costly, such as getting a bank loan or using available credit on a credit card.

You must submit all required returns that have not been filed. Your request for an installment agreement will be denied if all required tax returns have not been filed.

Use Form 433-H if you earn wages and are requesting an installment agreement and either:
- You cannot pay your outstanding liability within 72 months, or
- Your outstanding liability exceeds $50,000.

Do not use Form 433-H if:
- Your outstanding liability is $50,000 or less and you can pay within 72 months. Instead, use Form 9465, Installment Agreement Request. See the tip below.
- You are self-employed. Instead, use Form 433-D, *Installment Agreement*.
- You operate a business. Instead, use Form 433-D, *Installment Agreement*.

TIP If you can pay your outstanding liability within 120 days, there is no user fee for this type of agreement, and you may be able to establish an Online Payment Agreement (OPA). To apply online, go to http://www.irs.gov, and enter "Online Payment Agreement" in the "Search" box.

TIP If you owe $50,000 or less in combined tax, penalties and interest and filed all required returns, you may be able to establish an installment agreement online. Go to IRS.gov to pay online. You may owe a lower user fee if you establish your agreement through the OPA application.

A large down payment to reduce your liability to $50,000 or less may streamline the installment agreement process, pay your balance faster and reduce the amount of penalties and interest charged.

Bankruptcy or offer-in-compromise. If you are in bankruptcy or we have accepted your offer-in-compromise, do not file this form. Instead, call 1-800-829-1040 to get the number of your local IRS Insolvency function for bankruptcy or Technical Support function for offer-incompromise.

Please retain a copy of your completed form and supporting documentation. After we review your completed form, we may contact you for additional information. For example, we may ask you to send supporting documentation of your current income or substantiation of your stated expenditures.

Instructions

Part 1 – Installment Agreement Request

We will usually let you know within 30 days after we receive your request whether it is approved or denied. However, if this request is for tax due on a return you filed after March 31, it may take us longer than 30 days to reply.

We will review the financial information provided in Sections A through G, determine your ability to pay and compare it with the monthly payment amount you proposed in Part 1, Line 6. We will contact you if we have questions or believe you can pay your liability more quickly.

If we approve your request, we will send you a notice detailing the terms of your agreement and requesting a fee of $225 ($107 if you make your payments by direct debit).

Low income taxpayer. You are a low income taxpayer if your adjusted gross income, as determined for the most recent year for which such information is available, is at or below 250% of the federal poverty rate. However, you may qualify to pay a reduced fee of $43 if your income is below a certain level. The IRS will let you know whether you have low income taxpayer status.

If the IRS does not say you qualify for low income taxpayer status, you can request reconsideration by using Form 13844, Application For Reduced User Fee For Installment Agreements. The user fee for low income taxpayers is $43, which may be waived or reimbursed if certain conditions are met. See the instructions for line 8c. for details.

You will also be charged interest and may be charged a late payment penalty on any tax not paid by its due date, even if your request to pay in installments is granted. Interest and any applicable penalties will be charged until the balance is paid in full. To limit interest and penalty charges, file your return on time and pay as much of the tax as possible with your return *(or notice)*.

By approving your request, we agree to let you pay the tax you owe in monthly installments instead of immediately paying the amount in full. In return, you agree to make your monthly payments on time.

You also agree to meet all your future tax obligations. This means that you must have enough withholding or estimated tax payments so that your tax obligation for future years is paid in full when you timely file your return.

Part 1 – Installment Agreement Request *(Continued)*

Any refund you are due in a future year will be applied against the amount you owe. If your refund is applied to your balance, you are still required to make your regular monthly installment payment.

Payment methods. You can make your payments by check, money order, credit card, or one of the other payment methods shown next. The fee for setting up an installment agreement for each payment method is also shown.

Payment Method	Applicable User Fee
Check, money order, credit card or payroll deduction installment agreement	$225
Direct debit installment agreement	$107

Your specific tax situation will determine which payment options are available to you. You may owe a lower user fee if you establish your agreement through the OPA application on the IRS web site; however, not all taxpayers qualify to apply for an installment agreement online to pay off their balance over time. Go to IRS.gov, and enter "Online Payment Agreement" in the "Search" box for more information.

After we receive each payment, we will send you a notice showing the remaining amount you owe, and the due date and amount of your next payment. But if you choose to have your payments automatically withdrawn from your checking account, you will not receive a notice. Your bank statement is your record of payment.

We will also send you an annual statement showing the amount you owed at the beginning of the year, all payments made during the year, and the amount you owe at the end of the year. If you do not make your payments on time or do not pay any balance due on a return you file later, you will be in default on your agreement and we may take enforcement actions, such as the filing of a Notice of Federal Tax Lien or initiating an IRS levy action, to collect the entire amount you owe.

For additional information on the IRS collection process, see Pub. 594, *The IRS Collection Process*, or Pub. 1, *Know Your Rights as a Taxpayer*. You may also visit IRS.gov and put "collection process" into the "Search" box. To ensure that your payments are made timely, you should consider making them by direct debit. See the instructions for lines 8a and 8b on page 5.

⚠ CAUTION: An installment agreement may be terminated if you provide materially incomplete or inaccurate information in response to an IRS request for a financial update.

Notice of Federal Tax Lien. A Notice of Federal Tax Lien (NFTL) may be filed to protect the government's interests until you pay in full. If you meet certain criteria, you may be able to get the NFTL withdrawn. To learn more about NFTL withdrawals and to see if you qualify, visit **www.irs.gov** and enter "lien" in the "Search" box.

Where To File

Send Form 433-H, *Installment Agreement Request and Collection Information Statement*, with any attachments, to the Internal Revenue Service Center at the address in the table below that applies to you.

IF you live in . . .	THEN use this address . . .
Alaska, Arizona, Colorado, Connecticut, Delaware, District of Columbia, Hawaii, Idaho, Illinois, Maine, Maryland, Massachusetts, Montana, New Hampshire, New Jersey, New Mexico, Nevada, North Dakota, Oregon, Rhode Island, South Dakota, Tennessee, Utah, Vermont, Washington, Wisconsin, Wyoming	Internal Revenue Service PO Box 9041 CSCO Bal Due Andover, MA 01810-9041
Alabama, Florida, Georgia, Kentucky, Louisiana, Mississippi, North Carolina, South Carolina, Texas, Virginia	Internal Revenue Service PO Box 47421, Stop 74 Doraville, GA 30362
Arkansas, California, Iowa, Indiana, Kansas, Michigan, Minnesota, Missouri, Nebraska, New York, Ohio, Oklahoma, Pennsylvania, West Virginia	Internal Revenue Service Stop P-4 5000 PO Box 219236 Kansas City, MO 64121-9236
A foreign country, American Samoa, or Puerto Rico (or are excluding income under Internal Revenue Code section 933), Guam, the U.S. Virgin Islands, or use an APO or FPO address, or file Form 2555, 2555-EZ, or 4563, or are a dual-status alien	Internal Revenue Service CSCO Stop 4-N31.142 2970 Market St. Philadelphia, PA 19104
For all taxpayers who are bona fide residents of Guam, the U.S. Virgin Islands, or the Commonwealth of the Northern Mariana Islands, See Pub. 570, Tax Guide for Income From U.S. Possessions.	

Catalog Number 71232U   www.irs.gov   Form **433-H** (5-2019)

Part 1 – Installment Agreement Request *(Continued)*

Line 1
Enter the tax form, tax period, and the total amount you owe as shown on your tax return(s) (or notice(s)).

Line 2
List additional tax forms, tax periods, and balances due that are not reflected on Line 1 (even if they are included in an existing installment agreement).

Line 3
Add lines 1 & 2 and enter the result.

Line 4
Enter the amount of any payment you are making with this request.

Even if you cannot pay the full amount you owe now, you should pay as much as possible to limit penalty and interest charges. If you are filing this form with your tax return, make the payment with your return. For details on how to pay, see your tax return instructions.

Attach a check or money order payable to "United States Treasury." Do not send cash. Be sure to include:

- Your name, address, SSN/ITN, and daytime phone number.
- The tax year and tax return (for example, "2012 Form 1040") for which you are making this request.

Line 5
Subtract line 4 from line 3 and enter the result.

Line 6
Enter the amount you can pay each month. Make your payments as large as possible to limit interest and penalty charges. The charges will continue until you pay in full. (If you have an existing installment agreement, this amount should represent your total proposed monthly payment amount for all your liabilities.)

If no payment amount is listed on line 6, a payment will be determined for you by analyzing the information provided on your financial statement.

Line 7
You can choose the day of each month your payment is due. This can be on or after the 1st of the month, but no later than the 28th of the month. For example, if your rent or mortgage payment is due on the 1st of the month, you may want to make your installment payments on the 15th. If we approve your request, we will tell you the month and day that your first payment is due.

If we have not replied by the date you chose for your first payment, you can send the first payment to the Internal Revenue Service Center at the address shown earlier that applies to you. See the instructions for line 4 for details on what to write on your payment.

Line 8a, 8b, and 8c

TIP: Making your payments by direct debit will help ensure that your payments are made timely and that you are not in default of this agreement.

To pay by direct debit from your checking account at a bank or other financial institution (such as a mutual fund, brokerage firm, or credit union), fill in lines 8a and 8b. Check with your financial institution to make sure that a direct debit is allowed and to get the correct routing and account numbers.

Line 8a. The routing number must be nine digits. The first two digits of the routing number must be 01 through 12 or 21 through 32. Use a check to verify the routing number. On the following sample check, the routing number is 250250025. But if your check is payable through
a financial institution different from the one at which you have your checking account, do not use the routing number on that check. Instead, contact your financial institution for the correct routing number.

Line 8b. The account number can be up to 17 characters (both numbers and letters). Include hyphens but omit spaces and special symbols. Enter the number from left to right and leave any unused boxes blank. On the following sample check, the account number is 20202086. Do not include the check number.

CAUTION: We may file a Notice of Federal Tax Lien (NFTL) against you, or may have previously filed one. If you meet certain criteria, you may be able to get the NFTL withdrawn. To learn more about NFTL withdrawals and to see if you qualify, visit IRS gov and enter "lien" in the "Search" box.

If you qualify as a low income taxpayer, you will receive a waiver of the installment agreement user fees if you agree to make electronic payments through a debit instrument (debit payments) by following the direct debit instructions in lines 8 a. and b.

Line 8c. If you are a low income taxpayer that is unable to make debit payments, please indicate by checking the box in line 8c. to receive a reimbursement of the reduced user fees upon completion of your agreement.

If you do not check the box in line 8c. and you do not provide your checking account information in lines 8a. and b., then you will be treated as being able to but choosing not to make debit payments and your user fees will not be reimbursed upon completion of your installment agreement.

Catalog Number 71232U   www.irs.gov   Form **433-H** (5-2019)

Part 1 – Installment Agreement Request *(Continued)*

Sample Check - Lines 8a and 8b

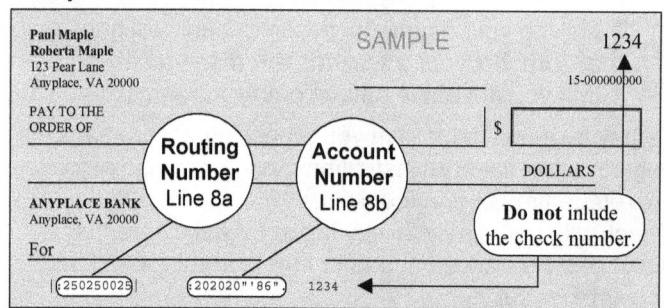

The routing and account numbers may be in different places on your check.

Line 9

If you want to make your payments by payroll deduction, check the box on line 9 and attach a completed and signed Form 2159, *Payroll Deduction Agreement,* with your request. Ask your employer to complete and sign their portion of Form 2159, *Payroll Deduction Agreement.*

Part 2 – Collection Information Statement

Section A – Accounts/Lines of Credit

List all accounts, even if they currently have no balance. However, do not enter bank loans in this section. Include business accounts, if applicable. If you are entering information for a stock or bond, etc. and a column box does not apply, enter N/A.

Section B – Real Estate

List all real estate you own or are purchasing including your home. Include insurance, taxes and homeowner's association dues if they are included in your monthly payment. The county/description is needed if different than the address and county you listed above. To determine equity, subtract the amount owed for each piece of real estate from its current market value.

Section C – Other Assets

List all cars, boats and recreational vehicles with their make, model and year. If a vehicle is leased, write "lease" in the "year purchased" column. List whole life insurance policies with the name of the insurance company. List other assets with a description such as "paintings", "coin collection", or "antiques". If applicable, include business assets, such as tools, equipment, inventory, and intangible assets such as domain names, patents, copyrights, etc. To determine equity, subtract the amount owed from its current market value. If you are entering information for an asset and a column box does not apply, enter N/A.

Section D – Credit Cards

List all credit cards and lines of credit, even if there is no balance owed.

Section E – Employment Information

Enter wage information for you or your spouse as applicable. If attaching a copy of current pay stub(s), you do not need to complete this section.

Section F – Non-Wage Household Income

List all non-wage income received monthly.

Other Income includes distributions from partnerships and subchapter S corporations reported on Schedule K-1, and from limited liability companies reported on Form 1040, Schedule C, D or E. It also includes agricultural subsidies, gambling income, and oil credits. Enter total distributions from RAs if not included under Pension Income.

Section G – Monthly Necessary Living Expenses

Enter monthly amounts for expenses. For any expenses not paid monthly, convert as follows:

If a bill is paid	Calculate the monthly amount by
Quarterly	Dividing by 3
Weekly	Multiplying by 4 3
Biweekly (every two weeks)	Multiplying by 2.17
Semimonthly (twice each month)	Multiplying by 2

National Standards for food, clothing and other items apply nationwide. For expenses claimed in boxes 1 and 4 you should provide the IRS allowable standards that can be found by accessing IRS.gov and entering "Collection Financial Standards" in the search box.

If you claim a higher amount for a specific expense, you must verify and substantiate that amount.

The amount claimed for Miscellaneous cannot exceed the standard amount for the number of people in your family. The miscellaneous allowance is for expenses incurred that are not included in any other allowable living expense items. Examples are credit card payments, bank fees and charges, reading material and school supplies.

If you do not have access to the IRS web site, itemize your actual expenses and we will ask you for additional proof, if required. Documentation may include pay statements, bank and investment statements, loan statements and bills for recurring expenses, etc.

Housing and Utilities – Includes expenses for your primary residence. You should only list amounts for utilities, taxes, insurance and homeowner's association dues that are not included in your mortgage or rent payments.

Rent – Do not enter mortgage payment here. Mortgage payment is listed in Section B.

Transportation – Include the total of maintenance, repairs, insurance, fuel, registrations, licenses, inspections, parking, and tolls for one month.

Public Transportation – Include the total you spend for public transportation if you do not own a vehicle or if you have public transportation costs in addition to vehicle expenses.

Medical – You are allowed expenses for health insurance and out-of-pocket health care costs.

Health insurance – Enter the monthly amount you pay for yourself or your family.

Out-of-Pocket health care expenses – Are costs not covered by health insurance, and include:

- Medical services
- Prescription drugs
- Dental expenses
- Medical supplies, including eyeglasses and contact lenses. Medical procedures of a purely cosmetic nature, such as plastic surgery or elective dental work are generally not allowed.

Child / Dependent Care – Enter the monthly amount you pay for the care of dependents that can be claimed on your Form 1040.

Estimated Tax Payments – Calculate the monthly amount you pay for estimated taxes by dividing the quarterly amount due on your Form 1040ES by 3.

Life Insurance – Enter the amount you pay for term life insurance only. Whole life insurance has cash value and should be listed in Section C.

Delinquent State & Local Taxes – Enter the minimum amount you are required to pay monthly. Be prepared to provide a copy of the statement showing the amount you owe and if applicable, any agreement you have for monthly payments.

Student Loans – Minimum payments on student loans for the taxpayer's post-secondary education may be allowed if they are guaranteed by the federal government. Be prepared to provide proof of loan balance and payments.

Court Ordered Payments – For any court ordered payments, be prepared to submit a copy of the court order portion showing the amount you are ordered to pay, the signatures, and proof you are making the payments. Acceptable forms of proof are copies of cancelled checks or copies of bank or pay statements.

Other Expenses (not listed above) – We may allow other expenses in certain circumstances. For example, if the expenses are necessary for the health and welfare of the taxpayer or family, or for the production of income. Specify the expense and list the minimum monthly payment you are billed.

Signature(s) & Date - Review the terms of this agreement and financial information entered. Please sign and date this completed agreement form. Then, return it to IRS at the address shown on page 5.

Privacy Act and Paperwork Reduction Act Notice.

Our legal right to ask for the information on this form is sections 6001, 6011, 6012(a), 6109, and 6159 and their regulations. We will use the information to process your request for an installment agreement. The reason we need your name and social security number is to secure proper identification. We require this information to gain access to the tax information in our files and properly respond to your request. You are not required to request an installment agreement. If you do request an installment agreement, you are required to provide the information requested on this form. Failure to provide this information may prevent processing your request; providing false information may subject you to fines or penalties.

You are not required to provide the information requested on a form that is subject to the Paperwork Reduction Act unless the form displays a valid OMB control number. Books or records relating to a form or its instructions must be retained as long as their contents may become material in the administration of any Internal Revenue law. Generally, tax returns and return information are confidential, as required by section 6103. However, we may give this information to the Department of Justice for civil and criminal litigation, and to cities, states, the District of Columbia, and U.S. commonwealths and possessions to carry out their tax laws. We may also disclose this information to other countries under a tax treaty, to federal and state agencies to enforce federal nontax criminal laws, or to federal law enforcement and intelligence agencies to combat terrorism.

The average time and expenses required to complete and file this form will vary depending on individual circumstances. For the estimated averages, see the instructions for your income tax return.

If you have suggestions for making this form simpler, we would be happy to hear from you. See the instructions for your income tax return.

Form 433-D (July 2018)

Department of the Treasury - Internal Revenue Service

Installment Agreement
(See Instructions on the back of this page)

Name and address of taxpayer(s)	Social Security or Employer Identification Number (SSN/EIN)
	(Taxpayer) / *(Spouse)*
	Your telephone numbers *(including area code)*
	(Home) / *(Work, cell or business)*

For assistance, call: 1-800-829-0115 (Business), or
1-800-829-8374 (Individual – Self-Employed/Business Owners)
1-800-829-0922 (Individuals – Wage Earners)

☐ Submit a new Form W-4 to your employer to increase your withholding.

Or write _____
(City, State, and ZIP Code)

Kinds of taxes *(form numbers)*	Tax periods	Amount owed as of _____ $

I / We agree to pay the federal taxes shown above, PLUS PENALTIES AND INTEREST PROVIDED BY LAW, as follows

$ _____ on _____ and $ _____ on the _____ of each month thereafter

I / We also agree to increase or decrease the above installment payments as follows:

Date of increase *(or decrease)*	Amount of increase *(or decrease)*	New installment payment amount

The terms of this agreement are provided on the back of this page. Please review them thoroughly.

☐ Please initial this box after you've reviewed all terms and any additional conditions.

Additional Conditions / Terms *(To be completed by IRS)*

Note: Internal Revenue Service employees may contact third parties in order to process and maintain this agreement.

DIRECT DEBIT — Attach a voided check or complete this part only if you choose to make payments by direct debit. Read the instructions on the back of this page.

a. Routing number ☐☐☐☐☐☐☐☐☐
b. Account number ☐☐☐☐☐☐☐☐☐☐☐☐☐☐☐☐☐

I authorize the U.S. Treasury and its designated Financial Agent to initiate a monthly ACH debit (electronic withdrawal) entry to the financial institution account indicated for payments of my federal taxes owed, and the financial institution to debit the entry to this account. This authorization is to remain in full force and effect until I notify the Internal Revenue Service to terminate the authorization. To revoke payment, I must contact the Internal Revenue Service at the applicable toll free number listed above no later than 14 business days prior to the payment (settlement) date. I also authorize the financial institutions involved in the processing of the electronic payments of taxes to receive confidential information necessary to answer inquiries and resolve issues related to the payments.

Debit Payments Self-Identifier

If you are unable to make electronic payments through a debit instrument (debit payments) by providing your banking information in a. and b. above, please check the box below:

☐ I am unable to make debit payments

Note: Not checking this box indicates that you are able but choosing not to make debit payments. See Instructions to Taxpayer below for more details.

Your signature	Date	Title *(if Corporate Officer or Partner)*	Spouse's signature *(if a joint liability)*	Date

FOR IRS USE ONLY

AGREEMENT LOCATOR NUMBER: __ __ __ __ __

Check the appropriate boxes:
☐ RSI "1" no further review
☐ RSI "5" PPIA IMF 2 year review
☐ RSI "6" PPIA BMF 2 year review

☐ AI "0" Not a PPIA
☐ AI "1" Field Asset PPIA
☐ AI "2" All other PPIAs

Agreement Review Cycle __ __ __ Earliest CSED _____
☐ Check box if pre-assessed modules included

Originator's ID number _____ Originator Code _____
Name _____ Title _____

A NOTICE OF FEDERAL TAX LIEN *(Check one box below)*
☐ HAS ALREADY BEEN FILED
☐ WILL BE FILED IMMEDIATELY
☐ WILL BE FILED WHEN TAX IS ASSESSED
☐ MAY BE FILED IF THIS AGREEMENT DEFAULTS

NOTE: A NOTICE OF FEDERAL TAX LIEN WILL NOT BE FILED ON ANY PORTION OF YOUR LIABILITY WHICH REPRESENTS AN INDIVIDUAL SHARED RESPONSIBILITY PAYMENT UNDER THE AFFORDABLE CARE ACT.

Agreement examined or approved by *(Signature, title, function)* _____ Date _____

Catalog Number 16644M   www.irs.gov   Form **433-D** (Rev. 7-2018)

Part 1 — IRS Copy   Exhibit 16

Form **433-D**
(July 2018)

Department of the Treasury - Internal Revenue Service

Installment Agreement
(See Instructions on the back of this page)

Name and address of taxpayer(s)

Social Security or Employer Identification Number (SSN/EIN)
(Taxpayer) _____ *(Spouse)* _____

Your telephone numbers *(including area code)*
(Home) _____ *(Work, cell or business)* _____

For assistance, call: **1-800-829-0115** (Business), or
1-800-829-8374 (Individual – Self-Employed/Business Owners), or
1-800-829-0922 (Individuals – Wage Earners)

Submit a new Form W-4 to your employer to increase your withholding.

Or write _____
(City, State, and ZIP Code)

Kinds of taxes *(form numbers)*	Tax periods	Amount owed as of _____ $

We agree to pay the federal taxes shown above, PLUS PENALTIES AND INTEREST PROVIDED BY LAW, as follows
$ _____ on _____ and $ _____ on the _____ of each month thereafter

We also agree to increase or decrease the above installment payments as follows:

Date of increase *(or decrease)*	Amount of increase *(or decrease)*	New installment payment amount

The terms of this agreement are provided on the back of this page. Please review them thoroughly.

☐ Please initial this box after you've reviewed all terms and any additional conditions.

Additional Conditions / Terms *(To be completed by IRS)*

Note: Internal Revenue Service employees may contact third parties in order to process and maintain this agreement.

DIRECT DEBIT — Attach a voided check or complete this part only if you choose to make payments by direct debit. Read the instructions on the back of this page.

a. Routing number ☐☐☐☐☐☐☐☐☐
b. Account number ☐☐☐☐☐☐☐☐☐☐☐☐☐☐☐☐☐

I authorize the U.S. Treasury and its designated Financial Agent to initiate a monthly ACH debit (electronic withdrawal) entry to the financial institution account indicated for payments of my federal taxes owed, and the financial institution to debit the entry to this account. This authorization is to remain in full force and effect until I notify the Internal Revenue Service to terminate the authorization. To revoke payment, I must contact the Internal Revenue Service at the applicable toll free number listed above no later than 14 business days prior to the payment (settlement) date. I also authorize the financial institutions involved in the processing of the electronic payments of taxes to receive confidential information necessary to answer inquiries and resolve issues related to the payments.

Debit Payments Self-Identifier

If you are unable to make electronic payments through a debit instrument (debit payments) by providing your banking information in a. and b. above, please check the box below:

☐ I am unable to make debit payments

Note: Not checking this box indicates that you are able but choosing not to make debit payments. See Instructions to Taxpayer below for more details.

Your signature	Date	Title *(if Corporate Officer or Partner)*	Spouse's signature *(if a joint liability)*	Date

FOR IRS USE ONLY

AGREEMENT LOCATOR NUMBER: __ __ __ __ __

Check the appropriate boxes:
☐ RSI "1" no further review
☐ RSI "5" PPIA IMF 2 year review
☐ RSI "6" PPIA BMF 2 year review

☐ AI "0" Not a PPIA
☐ AI "1" Field Asset PPIA
☐ AI "2" All other PPIAs

Agreement Review Cycle __ __ __ __ Earliest CSED _____

☐ Check box if pre-assessed modules included

Originator's ID number _____ Originator Code _____
Name _____ Title _____

A NOTICE OF FEDERAL TAX LIEN *(Check one box below)*
☐ HAS ALREADY BEEN FILED
☐ WILL BE FILED IMMEDIATELY
☐ WILL BE FILED WHEN TAX IS ASSESSED
☐ MAY BE FILED IF THIS AGREEMENT DEFAULTS

NOTE: A NOTICE OF FEDERAL TAX LIEN WILL NOT BE FILED ON ANY PORTION OF YOUR LIABILITY WHICH REPRESENTS AN INDIVIDUAL SHARED RESPONSIBILITY PAYMENT UNDER THE AFFORDABLE CARE ACT.

Agreement examined or approved by *(Signature, title, function)* _____ Date _____

Catalog Number 16644M www.irs.gov Form **433-D** (Rev. 7-2018)

Part 2 — Taxpayer's Copy

INSTRUCTIONS TO TAXPAYER

If not already completed by an IRS employee, please fill in the information in the spaces provided on the front of this form for:

- Your name *(include spouse's name if a joint return)* and current address; Your social security number and/or employer identification number *(whichever applies to your tax liability)*; Your home and work, cell or business telephone numbers;
- The amount you can pay now as a partial payment;
- The amount you can pay each month *(or the amount determined by IRS personnel)*; and
- The date you prefer to make this payment *(This must be the same day for each month, from the 1st to the 28th)*. We must receive your payment by this date. If you elect the direct debit option, this is the day you want your payment electronically withdrawn from your financial institution account.

Review the terms of this agreement.
When you've completed this agreement form, please sign and date it. Then, return Part 1 to IRS at the address on the letter that came with it or the address shown in the "For assistance" box on the front of the form.

Terms of this agreement

By completing and submitting this agreement, you *(the taxpayer)* agree to the following terms:

- This agreement will remain in effect until your liabilities *(including penalties and interest)* are paid in full, the statutory period for collection has expired, or the agreement is terminated. You will receive a notice from us prior to termination of your agreement.
- You will make each payment so that we *(IRS)* receive it by the monthly due date stated on the front of this form. **If you cannot make a scheduled payment, contact us immediately.**
- This agreement is based on your current financial condition. We may modify or terminate the agreement if our information shows that your ability to pay has significantly changed. You must provide updated financial information when requested.
- While this agreement is in effect, you must file all federal tax returns and pay any *(federal)* taxes you owe on time.
- We will apply your federal tax refunds or overpayments *(if any)* to the entire amount you owe, including the shared responsibility payment under the Affordable Care Act, until it is fully paid or the statutory period for collection has expired.
- You must pay a $225 user fee, which we have authority to deduct from your first payment(s) ($107 for Direct Debit). For low-income taxpayers (at or below 250% of Federal poverty guidelines), the user fee is reduced to $43. The reduced user fee will be waived if you agree to make electronic payments through a debit instrument by providing your banking information in the Direct Debit section of this Form. For low-income taxpayers, unable to make electronic payments through a debit instrument, the reduced user fee will be reimbursed upon completion of the installment agreement. See Debit Payment Self-Identifier on page 1 and Form 13844 for qualifications and instructions.
- If you default on your installment agreement, you must pay a $89 reinstatement fee if we reinstate the agreement. We have the authority to deduct this fee from your first payment(s) after the agreement is reinstated.
- We will apply all payments on this agreement in the best interests of the United States. Generally we will apply the payment to the oldest collection statute, which is normally the oldest tax year or period.
- **We can terminate your installment agreement if:**
  - You do not make monthly installment payments as agreed. You do not pay any other federal tax debt when due. You do not provide financial information when requested.
- If we terminate your agreement, we may collect the entire amount you owe, EXCEPT the Individual Shared Responsibility Payment under the Affordable Care Act, by levy on your income, bank accounts or other assets, or by seizing your property.
- We may terminate this agreement at any time if we find that collection of the tax is in jeopardy.
- This agreement may require managerial approval. We'll notify you when we approve or don't approve the agreement.
- We may file a Notice of Federal Tax Lien if one has not been filed previously which, may negatively impact your credit rating, but we will not file a Notice of Federal Tax Lien with respect to the individual shared responsibility payment under the Affordable Care Act.

HOW TO PAY BY DIRECT DEBIT

Instead of sending us a check, you can pay by direct debit *(electronic withdrawal)* from your checking account at a financial institution *(such as a bank, mutual fund, brokerage firm, or credit union)*. To do so, fill in Lines a and b. Contact your financial institution to make sure that a direct debit is allowed and to get the correct routing and account numbers.

Line a. The first two digits of the routing number must be 01 through 12 or 21 through 32. Don't use a deposit slip to verify the number because it may contain internal routing numbers that are not part of the actual routing number.

Line b. The account number can be up to 17 characters. Include hyphens but omit spaces and special symbols. Enter the number from left to right and leave any unused boxes blank.

<u>**CHECKLIST FOR MAKING INSTALLMENT PAYMENTS:**</u>

1. Write your social security or employer identification number on each payment.
2. Make your check or money order payable to *"United States Treasury."*
3. Make each payment in an amount at least equal to the amount specified in this agreement.
4. Don't double one payment and skip the next without contacting us first.
5. Enclose a copy of the reminder notice, if you received one, with each payment using the envelope provided. Make a payment even if you do not receive a reminder notice, write the type of tax, the tax period and "Installment Agreement" on your payment. For example, "1040, 12/31/2014, Installment Agreement". You should choose the oldest unpaid tax period on your agreement. Mail the payment to the IRS address indicated on the front of this form.
6. If you didn't receive an envelope, call the number below.

This agreement will not affect your liability *(if any)* for backup withholding under Public Law 98-67, the Interest and Dividend Compliance Act of 1983

QUESTIONS? — If you have **any** questions, about the direct debit process or completing this form, please call the applicable telephone number below for assistance.

<u>**NOTE:** If you are unable to make your monthly payments or if you accrue additional liability, please contact us immediately.</u>

        1-800-829-0115 *(Business)*
        1-800-829-8374 *(Individuals – Self-Employed / Business Owners)*
        1-800-829-0922 *(Individuals – Wage Earners)*

Notice	CP523
Tax period	2014
Notice date	December 16, 2016
Social Security number	
To contact us	
Your Caller ID	
Page 1 of 5	

Department of Treasury
Internal Revenue Service

Notice of intent to levy

Intent to terminate your Installment Agreement
Amount due immediately:

The monthly payment for your installment agreement is overdue. Because we didn't receive one or more payments from you, as your installment agreement requires, we will terminate your installment agreement on [Month DD, YYYY].

In addition, we can seize (levy) any state tax refund you're entitled to and apply it to your ▮▮▮▮ in overdue taxes on or after [Month DD, YYYY].

Billing Summary

Amount you owed
Failure-to-pay penalty
Interest charges
Amount due immediately

Continued on back...

Notice	CP523
Notice date	December 16, 2016
Social Security number	

Payment

- Make your check or money order payable to the United States Treasury.
- Write your Social Security number ▮▮▮▮ the tax year (2014), and form number (1040) on your payment.

INTERNAL REVENUE SERVICE

- **Amount due immediately**

Exhibit 17

Notice	CP523
Tax Year	2014
Notice date	December 16, 2016
Social Security number	

What you need to do immediately

If you agree with the amount due
- Pay the past due amount or we will terminate your installment agreement under Internal Revenue Code Section 6159(b) and the full amount you owe will be due immediately.
- Pay online or send us a check or money order with the attached payment stub. **You can pay online now at www.irs.gov/payments.**

If you agree but can't pay the amount due
- Call 1-800-829-0922 to discuss the reason for default and provide us with your updated financial statement (Form 433-F). We may be able to restructure your installment agreement. If we agree, you'll have to pay an additional fee of $50.

If you disagree with the amount due
Call us at [1-800-xxx-xxx] to review your account with a representative. Be sure to have your account information available when you call.

We'll assume you agree with the information in this notice if we don't hear from you.

What you need to know

Notice of Intent to Levy
This notice is your Notice of Intent to Levy (Internal Revenue Code Section 6331(d)).

If you don't pay the amount due by [Month DD, YYYY], we can levy your state tax refund. If you still have an outstanding balance after we levy your state refund, we may send you a notice giving you the right to a hearing before the IRS Office of Appeals, if you have not already received one. At that time, we can (levy your other property or rights to property, which includes:

Notice	CP523
Tax Year	2014
Notice date	December 16, 2016
Social Security number	
Page 3 of 5	

What you need to know - continued

Notice of Intent to Levy - continued

- Wages, real estate commissions, and other income
- Bank accounts
- Business assets
- Personal assets (including your car and home)
- Social security benefits

Right to request an appeal
If you don't agree, you have the right to request an appeal under the Collection Appeals Program. Please call 1-800-829-0115 or send us a Collection Appeals Request (Form 9423) to the address at the top of the notice by [Month DD, YYYY].

Payment options

Pay now electronically or by phone
The Electronic Federal Tax Payment System (EFTPS) is a free payment service for paying taxes online or by phone. TO use EFTPS, you must enroll online at www.eftps.gov (registration may take up to 7 business days to take effect . When you use the EFTPS website, you can:

- Receive instant confirmation of your payment
- Access payment history to review previous payments
- Schedule payments up to 365 days in advance
- Cancel a payment before the scheduled date
- Make a payment 24 hours a day, 7 days a week
- Authorize your financial institution or authorized third party (such as an accountant or payroll provider) to schedule payments for you

You may also be able to pay by debit or credit card for a small fee, depending on the type of tax you owe. To see all of our payment options, visit www.irs.gov/payments.

Payment history
If you made payments through EFTPS, you can log on to your EFTPS account online to review payments you made by phone or online.

If you already paid your balance in full within the past 21 days or made payment arrangements, please disregard this notice.

If you think we made a mistake, call 1-[xxx-xxx-xxxx] to review your account.

If we don't hear from you

If you don't pay the amount due immediately or call us to make payment arrangements, we can file a Notice of Federal Tax Lien on your property at any time, if we haven't already done so.

If a lien is in place, it may be difficult to sell or borrow against your property. A tax lien will also appear on your credit report – which may harm your credit rating – and your creditors will be publicly notified that the IRS has priority to seize your property.

Notice		CP523
Tax Year		2014
Notice date		December 16, 2016
Social Security number		

Penalties

We are required by law to charge any applicable penalties.

Failure-to-pay

Description	Amount
Total failure-to-pay	

When you pay your taxes after the due date, we charge a penalty of 0.5% of the unpaid amount due per month, up to 25% of the amount due. We count part of a month as a full month. (Internal Revenue Code Section 6651)

For a detailed calculation of your penalty charges, call 1-800-829-0922.

Removal of penalties due to erroneous written advice from the IRS

If you were penalized based on written advice from the IRS, we will remove the penalty if you meet the following criteria:
- If you sent a written request to the IRS for written advice on a specific issue
- You gave us complete and accurate information
- You received written advice from us
- You reasonably relied on our written advice and were penalized based on that advice

To request removal of penalties based on erroneous written advice from us, submit a completed Claim for Refund and Request for Abatement (Form 843) to the IRS service center where you filed your tax return. For a copy of the form or to find your IRS service center, go to www.irs.gov or call 1-800-829-0922.

Removal or reduction of penalties

We understand that circumstances—such as serious illness or injury, a family member's death, or loss of financial records due to natural disaster—may make it difficult for you to meet your taxpayer responsibility in a timely manner.

If you would like us to consider removing or reducing any of your penalty charges, please do the following:
- Identify which penalty charges you would like us to remove or reduce (e.g., 2005 late filing penalty).
- For each penalty charge, explain why you believe removal or reduction is appropriate.
- Sign your statement, and mail it to us along with any supporting documents.

We will review your statement and let you know whether we accept your explanation as reasonable cause to reduce or remove the penalty charge(s).

Notice	CP523	
Tax Year	2014	
Notice date	December 16, 2016	
Social Security number		

Interest

We are required by law to charge interest on unpaid tax from the date the tax return was due to the date the tax is paid in full. The interest is charged as long as there is an unpaid amount due, including penalties, if applicable. (Internal Revenue Code section 6601)

Period	Interest rate
October 1, 2013 – December 31, 2013	3%
January 1, 2014 – March 31, 2014	3%
April 1, 2014 – June 30, 2014	3%
July 1, 2014 – September 30, 2014	3%
October 1, 2014 – December 31, 2014	3%
Beginning January 1, 2015	5%

Additional information

- Visit www.irs.gov/cp523.
- For tax forms, instructions, and publications, visit www.irs.gov or call 1-800-TAX-FORM (1-800-829-3676).
- Paying online is convenient, secure, and ensures timely receipt of your payment. To pay your taxes online or for more information, go to www.irs.gov/payments.
- You can contact us by mail at the address at the top of the first page of this notice. Be sure to include your social security number and the tax year and form number you are writing about.
- Review the enclosed IRS Collection Process (Publication 594).
- Generally, we deal directly with taxpayers or their authorized representatives. Sometimes, however, it's necessary for us to speak with other people, such as employees, employers, banks, or neighbors to gather the information we need about a taxpayer's account. You have the right to request a list of individuals we've contacted in connection with your account at any time.
- Keep this notice for your records.

If you need assistance, please don't hesitate to contact us.

Form **9423**
(August 2014)

Department of the Treasury - Internal Revenue Service

Collection Appeal Request

(Instructions are on the reverse side of this form)

1. Taxpayer's name	2. Representative *(Attach a copy of Form 2848, Power of Attorney)*

3. SSN/EIN	4. Taxpayer's business phone	5. Taxpayer's home phone	6. Representative's phone

7. Taxpayer's street address

8. City	9. State	10. ZIP code

11. Type of tax *(Tax form)*	12. Tax periods being appealed	13. Tax due

Collection Action(s) Appealed

14. Check the Collection action(s) you are appealing

☐ Federal Tax Lien ☐ Levy or Proposed Levy ☐ Seizure
☐ Rejection of Installment Agreement ☐ Termination of Installment Agreement ☐ Modification of Installment Agreement

Explanation

15. Explain why you disagree with the collection action(s) you checked above and explain how you would resolve your tax problem. Attach additional pages if needed. Attach copies of any documents that you think will support your position. Generally, the Office of Appeals will ask the Collection Function to review, verify and provide their opinion on any new information you submit. We will share their comments with you and give you the opportunity to respond.

Under penalties of perjury, I declare that I have examined this request and any accompanying documents, and to the best of my knowledge and belief, they are true, correct and complete. A submission by a representative, other than the taxpayer, is based on all information of which the representative has any knowledge.

16. ☐ Taxpayer's or ☐ Authorized Representative's signature *(Only check one box)*	17. Date signed

IRS USE ONLY

18. Revenue Officer's name	19. Revenue Officer's signature	20. Date signed
21. Revenue Officer's phone	22. Revenue Officer's email address	23. Date received
24. Collection Manager's name	25. Collection Manager's signature	26. Date signed
27. Collection Manager's phone	28. Collection Manager's email address	29. Date received

www.irs.gov

Form **9423** (Rev. 8-2014) Catalog Number 14169I Exhibit 18 Department of the Treasury - Internal Revenue Service

POA Copy

Internal Revenue Service　　　　　　　　　　**Department of the Treasury**

Date:
06/26/2013

Taxpayer Identification Number:

Person to Contact:

Contact Telephone Number:

Employee Identification Number:

Case Closed -- Currently Not Collectible

We have temporarily closed your collection case for the tax types and periods listed below. We have determined that you do not have the ability to pay the money you owe at this time.

Although we have temporarily closed your case, you still owe the money to the IRS. We may re-open your case in the future if your financial situation improves. Also, since you still owe money, we will continue to add penalties and interest to your account and it will be subject to other adjustments and offsets such as applying future tax refunds to the amount you owe.

You don't need to take any action at this time. However, it is very important that you file all future tax returns and pay any amounts you owe on time. Also, it is to your advantage to make voluntary payments towards the amount you owe, if possible, to minimize additional penalties and interest.

If you have any questions please call us at 1-800-829-1040 (individuals) or 1-800-829-4933 (businesses). For non-case-related questions, you can also check on our website at www.irs.gov.

Tax Type	Tax Period Ending	Tax Type	Tax Period Ending	Tax Type	Tax Period Ending
1040	12/31/2011	1040	12/31/2010	1040	12/31/2009
1040	12/31/2008	1040	12/31/2007	1040	12/31/2006
1040	12/31/2005	1040	12/31/2004	1040	12/31/2003
1040	12/31/2002				

Exhibit 19

Letter 4223 (Rev. 4-2007)
Catalog Number: 50072A

Form **656**
(Rev. March 2017)

Department of the Treasury — Internal Revenue Service

Offer in Compromise

IRS Received Date

▶ **To: Commissioner of Internal Revenue Service**

In the following agreement, the pronoun "we" may be assumed in place of "I" when there are joint liabilities and both parties are signing this agreement.

I submit this offer to compromise the tax liabilities plus any interest, penalties, additions to tax, and additional amounts required by law for the tax type and period(s) marked in Section 2 or Section 3 below.

Did you use the Pre-Qualifier tool located on our website at http://irs.treasury.gov/oic_pre_qualifier/ prior to filling out this form?
☐ Yes   ☐ No

Note: The use of the Pre-Qualifier tool is not mandatory before sending in your offer. However, it is recommended.

Include the $186 application fee and initial payment (personal check, cashier's check, or money order) with your Form 656. You must also include the completed Form 433-A (OIC) and/or 433-B (OIC) and supporting documentation. You should fill out either Section 1 or Section 2, but not both, depending on the tax debt you are offering to compromise.

Section 1	Individual Information (Form 1040 filers)

If you are a 1040 filer, an individual with personal liability for Excise tax, individual responsible for Trust Fund Recovery Penalty, self-employed individual, individual personally responsible for partnership liabilities, and/or an individual who operates as a single member LLC or a disregarded entity taxed as a sole proprietorship you should fill out Section 1. You must also include all required documentation including the Form 433-A (OIC), the $186 application fee, and initial payment.

Your First Name, Middle Initial, Last Name

Social Security Number (SSN)
— —

If a Joint Offer, Spouse's First Name, Middle Initial, Last Name

Social Security Number (SSN)
— —

Your Physical Home Address (Street, City, State, ZIP Code)

Your Home Mailing Address (if different from above or Post Office Box number)

Is this a new address?   ☐ Yes ☐ No
If yes, would you like us to update our records to this address?   ☐ Yes ☐ No

Employer Identification Number
—

Individual Tax Periods
If Your Offer is for Individual Tax Debt Only

☐ 1040 Income Tax-Year(s) _____

☐ Trust Fund Recovery Penalty as a responsible person of (enter business name) _____
for failure to pay withholding and Federal Insurance Contributions Act taxes (Social Security taxes), for period(s) ending

☐ 941 Employer's Quarterly Federal Tax Return - Quarterly period(s) _____

☐ 940 Employer's Annual Federal Unemployment (FUTA) Tax Return - Year(s) _____

☐ Other Federal Tax(es) [specify type(s) and period(s)] _____

Note: If you need more space, use attachment and title it "Attachment to Form 656 dated _____." Make sure to sign and date the attachment.

Catalog Number 16728N   Exhibit 20   www.irs.gov   Form **656** (Rev. 3-2017)

Low-Income Certification (Individuals and Sole Proprietors Only)

Do you qualify for Low-Income Certification? You qualify if your gross monthly household income is less than or equal to the amount shown in the chart below based on your family size and where you live. If you qualify, you are not required to submit any payments during the consideration of your offer. If your business is other than a sole proprietor or disregarded single member LLC taxed as a sole proprietor and you owe employment taxes after January 1, 2009, you cannot qualify for the waiver. IRS will determine whether the household income (at the time of the offer submission or at the time the offer is processed, whichever is lower) and family size support the decision not to pay the application fee.

☐ Check this box if your household's gross monthly income is equal to or less than the monthly income shown in the table below.

Size of family unit	48 contiguous states and D.C.	Hawaii	Alaska
1	$2,513	$2,888	$3,138
2	$3,383	$3,890	$4,227
3	$4,254	$4,892	$5,317
4	$5,125	$5,894	$6,406
5	$5,996	$6,896	$7,496
6	$6,867	$7,898	$8,585
7	$7,738	$8,900	$9,675
8	$8,608	$9,902	$10,765
For each additional person, add	$871	$1,002	$1,090

Section 2 — Business Information (Form 1120, 1065, etc., filers)

If your business is a Corporation, Partnership, LLC, or LLP and you want to compromise those tax debts, you must complete this section. You must also include all required documentation including the Form 433-B (OIC), and a separate $186 application fee, and initial payment.

Business Name

Business Physical Address *(Street, City, State, ZIP Code)*

Business Mailing Address *(Street, City, State, ZIP Code)*

Employer Identification Number (EIN)

Name and Title of Primary Contact

Telephone Number ( ) -

Business Tax Periods
If Your Offer is for Business Tax Debt Only

☐ 1120 Income Tax-Year(s) _____

☐ 941 Employer's Quarterly Federal Tax Return - Quarterly period(s) _____

☐ 940 Employer's Annual Federal Unemployment (FUTA) Tax Return - Year(s) _____

☐ Other Federal Tax(es) [specify type(s) and period(s)] _____

Note: If you need more space, use attachment and title it "Attachment to Form 656 dated _____." Make sure to sign and date the attachment.

Section 3 — Reason for Offer

☐ **Doubt as to Collectibility** - I do not have enough in assets and income to pay the full amount.

☐ **Exceptional Circumstances (Effective Tax Administration)** - I owe this amount and have enough assets to pay the full amount, but due to my exceptional circumstances, requiring full payment would cause an economic hardship or would be unfair and inequitable. I am submitting a written narrative explaining my circumstances.

Explanation of Circumstances *(Add additional pages, if needed)* — The IRS understands that there are unplanned events or special circumstances, such as serious illness, where paying the full amount or the minimum offer amount might impair your ability to provide for yourself and your family. If this is the case and you can provide documentation to prove your situation, then your offer may be accepted despite your financial profile. Describe your situation below and attach appropriate documents to this offer application.

Section 4 — Payment Terms

Check one of the payment options below to indicate how long it will take you to pay your offer in full. You must offer more than $0. The offer amount should be in whole dollars only.

Lump Sum Cash

☐ Check here if you will pay your offer in 5 or fewer payments within 5 or fewer months from the date of acceptance:

Enclose a check for 20% of the offer amount (waived if you are an individual or sole proprietor and met the requirements for Low Income Certification) and fill in the amount(s) of your future payment(s).

Total Offer Amount	-	20% Initial Payment	=	Remaining Balance
$	-	$	=	$

You may pay the remaining balance in one payment after acceptance of the offer or up to five payments, but cannot exceed 5 months.

Amount of payment	$	payable within	1	Month after acceptance
Amount of payment	$	payable within	2	Months after acceptance
Amount of payment	$	payable within	3	Months after acceptance
Amount of payment	$	payable within	4	Months after acceptance
Amount of payment	$	payable within	5	Months after acceptance

Periodic Payment

☐ Check here if you will pay your offer in full in 6 to 24 months.

Enter the amount of your offer $ _____

Note: The total amount must equal all of the proposed payments including the first and last payments.

Enclose a check for the first month's payment.

$ _____ is included with this offer then $ _____ will be sent in on the _____ day of each month thereafter for a total of _____ months with a final payment of $ _____ to be paid on the _____ day of the _____ month.

Note: The total months may not exceed a total of 24 months, including the first payment. Your first payment is considered to be month 1; therefore, the remainder of the payments must be made within 23 months for a total of 24.

You must continue to make these monthly payments while the IRS is considering the offer (waived if you met the requirements for Low Income Certification). Failure to make regular monthly payments will cause your offer to be returned with no appeal rights.

IRS Use Only

☐ Attached is an addendum dated (insert date) _____ setting forth the amended offer amount and payment terms.

Section 5 — Designation of Payment, Electronic Federal Transfer Payment System (EFTPS), and Deposit

Designation of Payment

If you want your payment to be applied to a specific tax year and a specific tax debt, such as a Trust Fund Recovery Penalty, please tell us the tax year/quarter _____. If you do not designate a preference, we will apply any money you send to the government's best interest. If you want to designate any payments not included with this offer, you must designate a preference for each payment at the time the payment is made. However, you cannot designate the $186 application fee or any payment after the IRS accepts the offer.

Note: Payments submitted with your offer cannot be designated as estimated tax payments for a current or past tax year.

Electronic Federal Transfer Payment System (EFTPS)

Did you make your payment through the Electronic Federal Tax Payment System (EFTPS)?

☐ Yes ☐ No

If yes, provide the amount of your payment(s) $ _____, the date paid _____, and the 15 digit Electronic Funds Transfer (EFT) Number _____.

Note: Any initial payments paid through the EFTPS system must be made the same date your offer is mailed.

Deposit

If you are paying **more than** the initial payment with your offer and you want any part of that payment treated as a deposit, check the box below and insert the amount.

☐ My payment of $ _____ includes the $186 application fee and $ _____ for my first month's payment. I am requesting the additional amount of $ _____ be held as a deposit.

If your offer is rejected, returned, or withdrawn please check one of the boxes below and let us know what you would like us to do with your deposit.

☐ Return it to you (Initial here _____)   ☐ Apply it to your tax debt (Initial here _____)

CAUTION: Do NOT designate the amounts sent in with your offer to cover the initial payment and application fee as "deposits." Doing so will result in the return of your offer with no right to appeal.

Section 6 — Source of Funds, Making Your Payment, Filing Requirements, and Tax Payment Requirements

Source of Funds

Tell us where you will obtain the funds to pay your offer. You may consider borrowing from friends and/or family, taking out a loan, or selling assets.

_____

_____

Making Your Payment

Include separate checks for the payment and application fee.

Make checks payable to the "United States Treasury" and attach to the front of your Form 656, Offer in Compromise. All payments must be in U.S. dollars. **Do not send cash.** Send a separate application fee with each offer; do not combine it with any other tax payments, as this may delay processing of your offer. You may also make payments through the Electronic Federal Tax Payment System (EFTPS). Your offer will be returned to you if the application fee and the required payment are not included, or if your check is returned for insufficient funds.

Filing Requirements

☐ I have filed all required tax returns.

☐ I was not required to file a tax return for the following years: _____

Note: Do not include original tax returns with your offer. You must either electronically file your tax return or mail it to the appropriate IRS processing office before sending in your offer.

Tax Payment Requirements *(check all that apply)*

☐ I have made all required estimated tax payments for the current tax year.

☐ I am not required to make any estimated tax payments for the current tax year.

☐ I have made all required federal tax deposits for the current quarter.

☐ I am not required to make any federal tax deposits for the current quarter.

Section 7 — Offer Terms

By submitting this offer, I have read, understand and agree to the following terms and conditions:

Terms, Conditions, and Legal Agreement

a) I request that the IRS accept the offer amount listed in this offer application as payment of my outstanding tax debt (including interest, penalties, and any additional amounts required by law) as of the date listed on this form. I authorize the IRS to amend Section 1 and/or Section 2 if I failed to list any of my assessed tax debt or tax debt assessed before acceptance of my offer. I also authorize the IRS to amend Section 1 and/or Section 2 by removing any tax years on which there is currently no outstanding liability. I understand that my offer will be accepted, by law, unless IRS notifies me otherwise, in writing, within 24 months of the date my offer was received by IRS. I also understand that if any tax debt that is included in the offer is in dispute in any judicial proceeding it/they will not be included in determining the expiration of the 24-month period.

IRS will keep my payments, fees, and some refunds.

b) I voluntarily submit the payments made on this offer and understand that they will not be returned even if I withdraw the offer or the IRS rejects or returns the offer. Unless I designate how to apply each required payment in Section 5, the IRS will apply my payment in the best interest of the government, choosing which tax years and tax debts to pay off. The IRS will also keep my application fee unless the offer is not accepted for processing.

c) The IRS will keep any refund, including interest, that I might be due for tax periods extending through the calendar year in which the IRS accepts my offer. I cannot designate that the refund be applied to estimated tax payments for the following year or the accepted offer amount. If I receive a refund after I submit this offer for any tax period extending through the calendar year in which the IRS accepts my offer, I will return the refund within 30 days of notification. The refund offset does not apply to offers accepted under the provisions of Effective Tax Administration or Doubt as to Collectibility with special circumstances based on public policy/equity considerations.

d) I understand that the amount I am offering may not include part or all of an expected or current tax refund, money already paid, funds attached by any collection action, or anticipated benefits from a capital or net operating loss.

e) The IRS will keep any monies it has collected prior to this offer. Under section § 6331(a) the IRS may levy up to the time that the IRS official signs and acknowledges my offer as pending, which is accepted for processing and the IRS may keep any proceeds arising from such a levy. No levy will be issued on individual shared responsibility payments. However, if the IRS served a continuous levy on wages, salary, or certain federal payments under sections 6331(e) or (h), then the IRS could choose to either retain or release the levy.

f) The IRS will keep any payments that I make related to this offer. I agree that any funds submitted with this offer will be treated as a payment unless I checked the box to treat any amount more than the required initial payment as a deposit. Only amounts that exceed the mandatory payments can be treated as a deposit. I also agree that any funds submitted with periodic payments made after the submission of this offer and prior to the acceptance, rejection, or return of this offer will be treated as payments, unless I identify the amount more than the required payment as a deposit on the check submitted with the corresponding periodic payment. A deposit will be returned if the offer is rejected, returned, or withdrawn. I understand that the IRS will not pay interest on any deposit.

g) If my offer is accepted and my final payment is more than the agreed amount by $50 or less, the IRS will not return the difference, but will apply the entire payment to my tax debt. If my final payment exceeds the agreed amount by more than $50, the IRS will return the excess payment to me.

Section 7 (Continued) — Offer Terms

Pending status of an offer and right to appeal

h) Once an authorized IRS official signs this form, my offer is considered pending as of that signature date and it remains pending until the IRS accepts, rejects, returns, or I withdraw my offer. An offer is also considered pending for 30 days after any rejection of my offer by the IRS, and during the time that any rejection of my offer is being considered by the Appeals Office. An offer will be considered withdrawn when the IRS receives my written notification of withdrawal by personal delivery or certified mail or when I inform the IRS of my withdrawal by other means and the IRS acknowledges in writing my intent to withdraw the offer.

i) I waive the right to an Appeals hearing if I do not request a hearing in writing within 30 days of the date the IRS notifies me of the decision to reject the offer.

I must comply with my future tax obligations and understand I remain liable for the full amount of my tax debt until all terms and conditions of this offer have been met.

j) I will comply with all provisions of the internal revenue laws, including requirements to timely file tax returns and timely pay taxes for the five year period beginning with the date of acceptance of this offer and ending through the fifth year, including any extensions to file and pay. I agree to promptly pay any liabilities assessed after acceptance of this offer for tax years ending prior to acceptance of this offer that were not otherwise identified in Section 1 or Section 2 of this agreement. I also understand that during the five year period I cannot request an installment agreement for unpaid taxes incurred before or after the accepted offer. If this is an offer being submitted for joint tax debt, and one of us does not comply with future obligations, only the non-compliant taxpayer will be in default of this agreement. An accepted offer will not be defaulted solely due to the assessment of an individual shared responsibility payment. I also understand that during the five year period I cannot request an installment agreement for unpaid taxes incurred before or after the accepted offer.

k) I agree that I will remain liable for the full amount of the tax liability, accrued penalties and interest, until I have met all of the terms and conditions of this offer. Penalty and interest will continue to accrue until all payment terms of the offer have been met. If I file for bankruptcy before the terms and conditions of the offer are met, I agree that the IRS may file a claim for the full amount of the tax liability, accrued penalties and interest, and that any claim the IRS files in the bankruptcy proceeding will be a tax claim.

l) Once the IRS accepts my offer in writing, I have no right to challenge the tax debt(s) in court or by filing a refund claim or refund suit for any liability or period listed in Section 1 or Section 2, even if I default the terms of the accepted offer.

I understand what will happen if I fail to meet the terms of my offer (e.g., default).

m) If I fail to meet any of the terms of this offer, the IRS may revoke the certificate of release of federal tax lien and file a new notice of federal tax lien; levy or sue me to collect any amount ranging from one or more missed payments to the original amount of the tax debt (less payments made) plus penalties and interest that have accrued from the time the underlying tax liability arose. The IRS will continue to add interest, as required by section § 6601 of the Internal Revenue Code, on the amount the IRS determines is due after default Shared responsibility payments are excluded from levy.

I agree to waive time limits provided by law.

n) To have my offer considered, I agree to the extension of the time limit provided by law to assess my tax debt (statutory period of assessment). I agree that the date by which the IRS must assess my tax debt will now be the date by which my debt must currently be assessed plus the period of time my offer is pending plus one additional year if the IRS rejects, returns, or terminates my offer or I withdraw it. (Paragraph (h) of this section defines pending and withdrawal.) I understand that I have the right not to waive the statutory period of assessment or to limit the waiver to a certain length or certain periods or issues. I understand, however, that the IRS may not consider my offer if I refuse to waive the statutory period of assessment or if I provide only a limited waiver. I also understand that the statutory period for collecting my tax debt will be suspended during the time my offer is pending with the IRS, for 30 days after any rejection of my offer by the IRS, and during the time that any rejection of my offer is being considered by the Appeals Office.

I understand the IRS may file a Notice of Federal Tax Lien on my property.

o) The IRS may file a Notice of Federal Tax Lien during consideration of the offer. The IRS may file a Notice of Federal Tax Lien to protect the Government's interest on offers that will be paid over time. This tax lien will be released 30 days after the payment terms have been satisfied and the payment has been verified. If the offer is accepted, the tax lien will be released within 30 days of when the payment terms have been satisfied and the payment has been verified. The time it takes to transfer funds to the IRS from commercial institutions varies based on the form of payment. The IRS will not file a Notice of Federal Tax Lien on any individual shared responsibility debt.

Correction Agreement

p) I authorize IRS, to correct any typographical or clerical errors or make minor modifications to my/our Form 656 that I signed in connection to this offer.

I authorize the IRS to contact relevant third parties in order to process my offer.

q) By authorizing the IRS to contact third parties, I understand that I will not be notified of which third parties the IRS contacts as part of the offer application process, including tax periods that have not been assessed, as stated in §7602 (c) of the Internal Revenue Code. In addition, I authorize the IRS to request a consumer report on me from a credit bureau.

I am submitting an offer as an individual for a joint liability.

r) I understand if the liability sought to be compromised is the joint and individual liability of myself and my co-obligor(s) and I am submitting this offer to compromise my individual liability only, then if this offer is accepted, it does not release or discharge my co-obligor(s) from liability. The United States still reserves all rights of collection against the co-obligor(s).

| Shared Responsibility Payment (SRP) | s) If your offer includes any shared responsibility payment (SRP) amount that you owe for not having minimum essential health coverage for you and, if applicable, your dependents per Internal Revenue Code Section 5000A - Individual shared responsibility payment, it is not subject to penalties, except applicable bad check penalty, or to lien and levy enforcement actions. However, interest will continue to accrue until you pay the total SRP balance due. We may apply your federal tax refunds to the SRP amount that you owe until it is paid in full. |

IRS Use Only. I accept the waiver of the statutory period of limitations on assessment for the Internal Revenue Service, as described in Section 7(n).

Signature of Authorized Internal Revenue Service Official	Title	Date (mm/dd/yyyy)

Section 8 — Signatures

Under penalties of perjury, I declare that I have examined this offer, including accompanying schedules and statements, and to the best of my knowledge and belief, it is true, correct and complete.

Signature of Taxpayer/Corporation Name	Phone Number	Today's Date (mm/dd/yyyy)

☐ By checking this box you are authorizing the IRS to contact you at the telephone number listed above and leave detailed messages concerning this offer on your voice mail or answering machine.

Signature of Spouse/Authorized Corporate Officer	Phone Number	Today's Date (mm/dd/yyyy)

☐ By checking this box you are authorizing the IRS to contact you at the telephone number listed above and leave detailed messages concerning this offer on your voice mail or answering machine.

Section 9 — Paid Preparer Use Only

Signature of Preparer	Phone Number	Today's Date (mm/dd/yyyy)

☐ By checking this box you are authorizing the IRS to contact you at the telephone number listed above and leave detailed messages concerning this offer on your voice mail or answering machine.

Name of Paid Preparer	Preparer's CAF no. or PTIN

Firm's Name (or yours if self-employed), Address, and ZIP Code

---

If you would like to have someone represent you during the offer investigation, include a valid, signed Form 2848 or 8821 with this application or a copy of a previously filed form. You should also include the current tax year.

Privacy Act Statement

We ask for the information on this form to carry out the internal revenue laws of the United States. Our authority to request this information is section § 7801 of the Internal Revenue Code.

Our purpose for requesting the information is to determine if it is in the best interests of the IRS to accept an offer. You are not required to make an offer; however, if you choose to do so, you must provide all of the taxpayer information requested. Failure to provide all of the information may prevent us from processing your request.

If you are a paid preparer and you prepared the Form 656 for the taxpayer submitting an offer, we request that you complete and sign Section 9 on Form 656, and provide identifying information. Providing this information is voluntary. This information will be used to administer and enforce the internal revenue laws of the United States and may be used to regulate practice before the Internal Revenue Service for those persons subject to Treasury Department Circular No. 230, Regulations Governing the Practice of Attorneys, Certified Public Accountants, Enrolled Agents, Enrolled Actuaries, and Appraisers before the Internal Revenue Service. Information on this form may be disclosed to the Department of Justice for civil and criminal litigation. We may also disclose this information to cities, states and the District of Columbia for use in administering their tax laws and to combat terrorism. Providing false or fraudulent information on this form may subject you to criminal prosecution and penalties.

APPLICATION CHECKLIST

Review the entire application using the Application Checklist below. Include this checklist with your application.

Forms 433-A (OIC), 433-B (OIC), and 656

- ☐ Did you complete all fields and sign all forms?
- ☐ Did you make an offer amount that is equal to the offer amount calculated on the Form 433-A (OIC) or Form 433-B (OIC)? If not, did you describe the special circumstances that are leading you to offer less than the minimum in the "Explanation of Circumstances" Section 3 of Form 656, and did you provide supporting documentation of the special circumstances?
- ☐ Have you filed all required tax returns and received a bill or notice of balance due?
- ☐ Did you select a payment option on Form 656?
- ☐ Did you sign and attach the Form 433-A (OIC), if applicable?
- ☐ Did you sign and attach the Form 433-B (OIC), if applicable?
- ☐ Did you sign and attach the Form 656?
- ☐ If you are making an offer that includes business and individual tax debts, did you prepare a separate Form 656 package (including separate financial statements, supporting documentation, application fee, and initial payment)?

Supporting documentation and additional forms

- ☐ Did you include photocopies of all required supporting documentation?
- ☐ If you want a third party to represent you during the offer process, did you include a Form 2848 or Form 8821 unless one is already on file? Does it include the current tax year?
- ☐ Did you provide a letter of testamentary or other verification of person(s) authorized to act on behalf of the estate or deceased individual?

Payment

- ☐ Did you include a check or money order made payable to the "United States Treasury" for the initial payment? (Waived if you meet Low Income Certification guidelines—see Form 656.)
- ☐ Did you include a separate check or money order made payable to the "United States Treasury" for the $186 application fee? (Waived if you meet Low Income Certification guidelines—see Form 656.)

Mail your application package to the appropriate IRS facility

Mail the Form 656, 433-A (OIC) and/or 433-B (OIC), and related financial document(s) to the appropriate IRS processing office for your state. You may wish to send it by Certified Mail so you have a record of the date it was mailed.

If you reside in:

AK, AL, AR, AZ, CO, FL, GA, HI, ID, KY, LA, MS, NC, NM, NV, OK, OR, TN, TX, UT, WA, WI

CA, CT, DE, IA, IL, IN, KS, MA, MD, ME, MI, MN, MO, MT, ND, NE, NH, NJ, NY, OH, PA, RI, SC, SD, VT, VA, WY, WV; DC, PR, or a foreign address

Mail your application to:

Memphis IRS Center COIC Unit
P.O. Box 30803, AMC
Memphis, TN 38130-0803
1-866-790-7117

Brookhaven IRS Center COIC Unit
P.O. Box 9007
Holtsville, NY 11742-9007
1-866-611-6191

National Standards: Food, Clothing and Other Items

Disclaimer: IRS Collection Financial Standards are intended for use in calculating repayment of delinquent taxes. These Standards are effective on March 25, 2019 for purposes of federal tax administration only. Expense information for use in bankruptcy calculations can be found on the website for the U.S. Trustee Program.

Download the national standards for food, clothing and other items in PDF format for printing. Please note that the standard amounts change, so if you elect to print them, check back periodically to assure you have the latest version.

National Standards have been established for five necessary expenses: food, housekeeping supplies, apparel and services, personal care products and services, and miscellaneous.

The standards are derived from the Bureau of Labor Statistics (BLS) Consumer Expenditure Survey (CES) and defined as follows:

Food includes food at home and food away from home. Food at home refers to the total expenditures for food from grocery stores or other food stores. It excludes the purchase of nonfood items. Food away from home includes all meals and snacks, including tips, at fast-food, take-out, delivery and full-service restaurants, etc.

Housekeeping supplies includes laundry and cleaning supplies, stationery supplies, postage, delivery services, miscellaneous household products, and lawn and garden supplies.

Apparel and services includes clothing, footwear, material, patterns and notions for making clothes, alterations and repairs, clothing rental, clothing storage, dry cleaning and sent-out laundry, watches, jewelry and repairs to watches and jewelry.

Personal care products and services includes products for the hair, oral hygiene products, shaving needs, cosmetics and bath products, electric personal care appliances, and other personal care products.

The miscellaneous allowance is for expenses taxpayers may incur that are not included in any other allowable living expense items, or for any portion of expenses that exceed the Collection Financial Standards and are not allowed under a deviation. Taxpayers can use the miscellaneous allowance to pay for expenses that exceed the standards, or for other expenses such as credit card payments, bank fees and charges, reading material and school supplies.

Related Topics

- Collection Financial Standards

Taxpayers are allowed the total National Standards amount monthly for their family size, without questioning the amounts they actually spend. If the amount claimed is more than the total allowed by the National Standards for food, housekeeping supplies, apparel and services, and personal care products and services, the taxpayer must provide documentation to substantiate those expenses are necessary living expenses. Deviations from the standard amount are not allowed for miscellaneous expenses. Generally, the total number of persons allowed for National Standards should be the same as those allowed as dependents on the taxpayer's most recent year income tax return.

Expense	One Person	Two Persons	Three Persons	Four Persons
Food	$386	$685	$786	$958
Housekeeping supplies	$40	$72	$76	$76
Apparel & services	$88	$159	$169	$243
Personal care products & services	$43	$70	$76	$91
Miscellaneous	$170	$302	$339	$418
Total	**$727**	**$1,288**	**$1,446**	**1,786**

More than four persons	Additional Persons Amount
For each additional person, add to four-person total allowance:	$420

Rate the Small Business and Self-Employed Website

Page Last Reviewed or Updated: 30-May-2019

National Standards: Out-of-Pocket Health Care

Disclaimer: IRS Collection Financial Standards are intended for use in calculating repayment of delinquent taxes. These Standards are effective on March 25, 2019 for purposes of federal tax administration only. Expense information for use in bankruptcy calculations can be found on the website for the U.S. Trustee Program.

Download the out-of-pocket health care standards in PDF format for printing. Please note that the standard amounts change, so if you elect to print them, check back periodically to assure you have the latest version.

The table for health care expenses, based on Medical Expenditure Panel Survey data, has been established for minimum allowances for out-of-pocket health care expenses.

Out-of-pocket health care expenses include medical services, prescription drugs, and medical supplies (e.g. eyeglasses, contact lenses, etc.). Elective procedures such as plastic surgery or elective dental work are generally not allowed.

Taxpayers and their dependents are allowed the standard amount monthly on a per person basis, without questioning the amounts they actually spend. If the amount claimed is more than the total allowed by the health care standards, the taxpayer must provide documentation to substantiate those expenses are necessary living expenses. Generally, the number of persons allowed should be the same as those allowed as dependents on the taxpayer's most recent year income tax return.

The out-of-pocket health care standard amount is allowed in addition to the amount taxpayers pay for health insurance.

	Out of Pocket Costs
Under 65	$55
65 and Older	$114

Related Topics

- Local Standards Housing and Utilities

Rate the Small Business and Self-Employed Website

Page Last Reviewed or Updated: 29-Jul-2019

Connecticut - Local Standards: Housing and Utilities

Disclaimer: *IRS Collection Financial Standards are intended for use in calculating repayment of delinquent taxes. These Standards are effective on March 25, 2019 for purposes of federal tax administration only. Expense information for use in bankruptcy calculations can be found on the website for the U.S. Trustee Program.*

The housing and utilities standards are derived from U.S. Census Bureau, American Community Survey and Bureau of Labor Statistics data, and are provided by state down to the county level. The standard for a particular county and family size includes both housing and utilities allowed for a taxpayer's primary place of residence. Generally, the total number of persons allowed for determining family size should be the same as those allowed as exemptions on the taxpayer's most recent year income tax return.

Housing and utilities standards include mortgage or rent, property taxes, interest, insurance, maintenance, repairs, gas, electric, water, heating oil, garbage collection, residential telephone service, cell phone service, cable television, and Internet service. The tables include five categories for one, two, three, four, and five or more persons in a household.

The taxpayer is allowed the standard amount, or the amount actually spent on housing and utilities, whichever is less. If the amount claimed is more than the total allowed by the housing and utilities standards, the taxpayer must provide documentation to substantiate those expenses are necessary living expenses.

Related Topic
- Local Standards Housing and Utilities

Maximum Monthly Allowance

County	2019 Published Housing and Utilities for a Family of 1	2019 Published Housing and Utilities for a Family of 2	2019 Published Housing and Utilities for a Family of 3	2019 Published Housing and Utilities for a Family of 4	2019 Published Housing and Utilities for a Family of 5

Fairfield County	2,552	2,998	3,159	3,522	3,579
Hartford County	1,854	2,177	2,294	2,558	2,599
Litchfield County	1,843	2,165	2,281	2,543	2,584
Middlesex County	1,996	2,344	2,470	2,754	2,799
New Haven County	1,925	2,261	2,382	2,656	2,699
New London County	1,809	2,125	2,239	2,496	2,537
Tolland County	1,867	2,193	2,311	2,577	2,618
Windham County	1,660	1,950	2,055	2,291	2,328

Rate the Small Business and Self-Employed Website

Page Last Reviewed or Updated: 15-Mar-2019

Local Standards: Transportation

Disclaimer: IRS Collection Financial Standards are intended for use in calculating repayment of delinquent taxes. These Standards are effective on March 25, 2019 for purposes of federal tax administration only. Expense information for use in bankruptcy calculations can be found on the website for the U.S. Trustee Program.

Download the transportation standards in PDF format for printing. Please note that the standard amounts change, so if you elect to print them, check back periodically to assure you have the latest version.

The transportation standards for taxpayers with a vehicle consist of two parts: nationwide figures for monthly loan or lease payments referred to as ownership costs, and additional amounts for monthly operating costs. The operating costs include maintenance, repairs, insurance, fuel, registrations, licenses, inspections, parking and tolls (These standard amounts do not include personal property taxes).

Ownership Costs

The ownership costs, shown in the table below, provide the monthly allowances for the lease or purchase of up to two automobiles. A single taxpayer is normally allowed one automobile. For each automobile, taxpayers will be allowed the lesser of:

a. the monthly payment on the lease or car loan, or
b. the ownership costs shown in the table below.

If a taxpayer has no lease or car loan payment, the amount allowed for Ownership Costs will be $0.

Operating Costs

In addition to Ownership Costs, a taxpayer is allowed Operating Costs, by regional and metropolitan area, as shown in the table below. For each automobile, taxpayers will be allowed the lesser of:

a. the amount actually spent monthly for operating costs, or
b. the operating costs shown in the table below.

Public Transportation

Related Topic

- Collection Financial Standards

There is a single nationwide allowance for public transportation based on Bureau of Labor Statistics expenditure data for mass transit fares for a train, bus, taxi, ferry, etc. Taxpayers with no vehicle are allowed the standard amount monthly, per household, without questioning the amount actually spent.

If a taxpayer owns a vehicle and uses public transportation, expenses may be allowed for both, provided they are needed for the health and welfare of the taxpayer or family, or for the production of income. However, the expenses allowed would be actual expenses incurred for ownership costs, operating costs and public transportation, or the standard amounts, whichever is less.

If the amount claimed for Ownership Costs, Operating Costs or Public Transportation is more than the total allowed by the transportation standards, the taxpayer must provide documentation to substantiate those expenses are necessary living expenses.

Public Transportation

National	$217

Ownership Costs

	One Car	Two Cars
National	$508	$1,016

Operating Costs

	One Car	Two Cars
Northeast Region	$237	$474
Boston	$230	$460

	One Car	**Two Cars**
New York	$319	$638
Philadelphia	$244	$488
Midwest Region	$191	$382
Chicago	$208	$416
Cleveland	$191	$382
Detroit	$277	$554
Minneapolis-St. Paul	$197	$394
St. Louis	$190	$380
South Region	$210	$420
Atlanta	$240	$480
Baltimore	$258	$516
Dallas-Ft. Worth	$281	$562

	One Car	**Two Cars**
Houston	$287	$574
Miami	$316	$632
Tampa	$236	$472
Washington, D.C.	$242	$484
West Region	$205	$410
Anchorage	$179	$358
Denver	$212	$424
Honolulu	$191	$382
Los Angeles	$273	$546
Phoenix	$233	$466
San Diego	$255	$510
San Francisco	$212	$424
Seattle	$268	$536

For Use with 2019 Allowable Transportation Table

The data for the Operating Costs section of the Transportation Standards are provided by Census Region and Metropolitan Statistical Area (MSA). The following table lists the states that comprise each Census Region. Once the taxpayer's Census Region has been ascertained, to determine if an MSA standard is applicable, use the definitions below to see if the taxpayer lives within an MSA (MSAs are defined by county and city, where applicable). If the taxpayer does not reside in an MSA, use the regional standard.

MSA Definitions by Census Region

Northeast Census Region: Maine, New Hampshire, Vermont, Massachusetts, Rhode Island, Connecticut, Pennsylvania, New York, New Jersey

MSA	Counties
Boston	*in* MA: Essex, Middlesex, Norfolk, Plymouth, Suffolk
	in NH: Rockingham, Strafford
New York	*in* NY: Bronx, Dutchess, Kings, Nassau, New York, Orange, Putnam, Queens, Richmond, Rockland, Suffolk, Westchester
	in NJ: Bergen, Essex, Hudson, Hunterdon, Middlesex, Monmouth, Morris, Ocean, Passaic, Somerset, Sussex, Union
	in PA: Pike
Philadelphia	*in* PA: Bucks, Chester, Delaware, Montgomery, Philadelphia
	in NJ: Burlington, Camden, Gloucester, Salem

	in DE: New Castle
	in MD: Cecil

Midwest Census Region: North Dakota, South Dakota, Nebraska, Kansas, Missouri, Illinois, Indiana, Ohio, Michigan, Wisconsin, Minnesota, Iowa

MSA	Counties (unless otherwise specified)
Chicago	*in* IL: Cook, DeKalb, DuPage, Grundy, Kane, Kendall, Lake, McHenry, Will
	in IN: Jasper, Lake, Newton, Porter
	in WI: Kenosha
Cleveland	*in* OH: Ashtabula, Cuyahoga, Geauga, Lake, Lorain, Medina, Portage, Summit
Detroit	*in* MI: Lapeer, Livingston, Macomb, Oakland, St. Clair, Wayne
Minneapolis-St. Paul	*in* MN: Anoka, Carver, Chisago, Dakota, Hennepin, Isanti, Le Sueur, Mille Lacs, Ramsey, Scott, Sherburne, Sibley, Washington, Wright
	in WI: Pierce, St. Croix
St. Louis	*in* MO: Franklin, Jefferson, Lincoln, St. Charles, St. Louis county, Warren, St. Louis city

in IL: Bond, Calhoun, Clinton, Jersey, Macoupin, Madison, Monroe, St. Clair

South Census Region: Texas, Oklahoma, Arkansas, Louisiana, Mississippi, Tennessee, Kentucky, West Virginia, Virginia, Maryland, District of Columbia, Delaware, North Carolina, South Carolina, Georgia, Florida, Alabama

MSA	Counties (unless otherwise specified)
Atlanta	*in GA*: Barrow, Bartow, Butts, Carroll, Cherokee, Clayton, Cobb, Coweta, Dawson, DeKalb, Douglas, Fayette, Forsyth, Fulton, Gwinnett, Haralson, Heard, Henry, Jasper, Lamar, Meriwether, Morgan, Newton, Paulding, Pickens, Pike, Rockdale, Spalding, Walton
Baltimore	*in MD*: Anne Arundel, Baltimore county, Carroll, Harford, Howard, Queen Anne's, Baltimore city
Dallas-Ft. Worth	*in TX*: Collin, Dallas, Denton, Ellis, Hood, Hunt, Johnson, Kaufman, Parker, Rockwall, Somervell, Tarrant, Wise
Houston	*in TX*: Austin, Brazoria, Chambers, Fort Bend, Galveston, Harris, Liberty, Montgomery, Waller
Miami	*in FL*: Broward, Miami-Dade, Palm Beach
Tampa	*in FL*: Hernando, Hillsborough, Pasco, Pinellas
Washington, D.C.	*in DC*: District of Columbia

	in MD: Calvert, Charles, Frederick, Montgomery, Prince George
	in VA: Arlington, Clarke, Culpeper, Fairfax county, Fauquier, Loudoun, Prince William, Rappahannock, Spotsylvania, Stafford, Warren, Alexandria city, Fairfax city, Falls Church city, Fredericksburg city, Manassas city, Manassas Park city
	in WV: Jefferson

West Census Region: New Mexico, Arizona, Colorado, Wyoming, Montana, Nevada, Utah, Washington, Oregon, Idaho, California, Alaska, Hawaii

MSA	Counties (unless otherwise specified)
Anchorage	*in* AK: Anchorage, Matanuska-Susitna
Denver	*in* CO: Adams, Arapahoe, Broomfield, Clear Creek, Denver, Douglas, Elbert, Gilpin, Jefferson, Park
Honolulu	*in* HI: Honolulu
Los Angeles	*in* CA: Los Angeles, Orange, Riverside, San Bernardino
Phoenix	*in* AZ: Maricopa, Pinal
San Diego	*in* CA: San Diego

San Francisco	*in* CA: Alameda, Contra Costa, Marin, San Francisco, San Mateo
Seattle	*in* WA: King, Pierce, Snohomish

Rate the Small Business and Self-Employed Website

Page Last Reviewed or Updated: 29-Jul-2019

Department of the Treasury

Date of this Letter: NOV 6 2016

Internal Revenue Service
Centralized OIC
PO Box 9011 Stop 682
Holtsville, NY 11742

Person to Contact:
Mr. Exmployee
Employee #: 0xxxxxxx
Phone#: (866) 611-6191
08:00am-08:00pm Mon-Fri

Taxpayer ID#: ***-**-xxxx
Offer Number: 1001xxxxxx

Taxpayer Name
Taxpayer Address
City, CT xxxxx

Dear Mrs. Taxpayer,

    We received your Offer in Compromise. You will be contacted by 03/06/2017.

    While investigating your offer, we will determine whether a notice of federal tax lien should be filed in order to protect the government's interests. If we determine to file a notice of federal tax lien we will provide you with notification within five days of the filing. You will have the opportunity to request a hearing with Appeals at which you may propose alternative methods for protecting the government's interest.

    If you have any questions, please contact the person whose name and telephone number are shown in the upper right hand corner of this letter.

                      Since

                        Process Examiner Manager

Enclosure:
Publication 594
Publication 1
Copy of this letter
cc: POA   WI Letter Combination (1-2015)

Exhibit 22

Department of the Treasury
Internal Revenue Service
Appeals Office
150 Court Street, Room 312
New Haven, CT 06510

Date: MAR 21 2017

Person to contact:
Name: Employee Name
Employee ID number: 100xxxxxx
Telephone: 203-xxx-xxxx
Fax: 855-xxx-xxxx
Hours: 8:00 - 4:30

Tax period(s) ended:
12/2007 12/2008 12/2009 12/2010
12/2011

Re:
Offer in Compromise

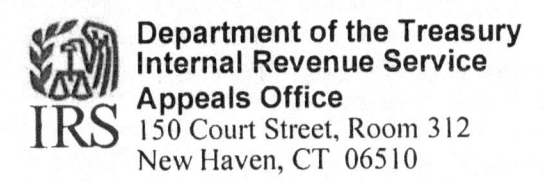

Taxpayer name
Taxpayer Address
City, CT, Zip

Dear Mr. _____:

We accepted your offer in compromise signed and dated by you on 12/03/2014 and as modified by an addendum dated 02/01/2017. The date of acceptance is the date of this letter and our acceptance is subject to the terms and conditions on the enclosed Form 656, *Offer in Compromise*.

Please note that the conditions of the offer require you to file and pay all required taxes for five tax years, beginning from the date of this letter.

If you are required to make payments under this agreement, make your check or money order payable to the United States Treasury and send it to:

IRS - OIC
P.O. Box 24015
Fresno, CA 93779

You must promptly notify the IRS of any change in your address or marital status. That way we'll have the correct address to advise you of your offer status.

If you submitted a joint offer with your spouse or former spouse and you personally are meeting or have met all the conditions of your offer agreement, but your spouse or former spouse fails to adhere to the conditions of the offer agreement, your offer agreement will not be defaulted.

If you fail to meet any of the terms and conditions of the offer, the IRS will issue a notice to default the agreement. If the offer defaults, the original tax including all penalties and interest will be due. After issuance of the notice the IRS may:

- Immediately file suit to collect the entire unpaid balance of the offer.
- Immediately file suit to collect an amount equal to the original amount of the tax liability as liquidating damages, minus any payments already received under the terms of this offer.
- Disregard the amount of the offer and apply all amounts already paid under the offer against the original amount of the tax liability.
- File suit or levy to collect the original amount of the tax liability.

Please remember that as a condition of the offer, we'll retain any refunds you may be entitled to receive for 2017, or earlier tax years. This includes refunds you receive in 2018 for any overpayments you made

Letter 5490 (Rev. 12-2015)
Catalog Number 67202S

Exhibit 23

toward tax year 2017, or earlier tax years. These refunds will be applied to your liability, not to your accepted offer amount. If a Notice of Federal Tax Lien was filed on your account, we'll release it when the offer amount is paid in full. If the final payment is by credit or debit card, we cannot release the Notice of Federal Tax Lien for up to 120 days from the date of the credit or debit payment.

Appeals will send your case for processing to Brookhaven, NY. If you have questions, you can contact the IRS at 1-631-447-4018.

Sincerely,

IRS Employee Name
Appeals Team Manager

Enclosure(s):
Form 656 and Form 14640
cc: Eric L Green

Letter 5490 (Rev. 12-2015)
Catalog Number 67202S

Department of the Treasury

Internal Revenue Service
Centralized OIC
PO Box 9011 Stop 682
Holtsville, NY 11742

Date of this Letter: JUN - 1 2017

Person to Contact:
Mr. Employee
Employee #:1000XXXXXX
Phone#: (866) 611-6191 EXT. 3366 08:00am-03:30pm Mon-Fri

Taxpayer ID#:***-**-XXXX
Offer Number:1001XXXXXX

Taxpayer Name
Taxpayer Address
City, CT Zip

Dear Mr. Taxpayer,

    We have investigated your offer dated 11/28/2016 in the amount of $250.00.

    We are rejecting the offer for the following reason(s):

    The amount offered is less than your reasonable collection potential. Copies of worksheets showing our calculations are enclosed for your review.

    Based on the financial information you submitted, we have determined you can pay the amount due in full.

    We have considered the special circumstances you raised but they did not warrant a decision to accept your offer.

    If you disagree with our findings, please provide any additional information in writing to support your position within 30 days of the date of this letter. If you also want your case considered by the Office of Appeals, you must include a written statement in your response asking that your case be sent to the Office of Appeals after our reconsideration. If you do not send this written statement within 30 days of the date of this letter you will not receive consideration by the Office of Appeals.

    Include any additional information that you want Appeals to consider. You may still appeal without additional information, but including it will help us to process your request promptly. You should send a letter requesting Appeals consideration. Please complete the enclosed Form 13711 or include the following information in your written protest:

1. Your name, address, social security number (if applicable, Employer identification number) and daytime telephone number;

2. A statement that you want to appeal the IRS findings to the Appeals Office;

3. A copy of this letter;

continued on next page

Exhibit 24

4. The tax periods or years involved;

5. A list of the specific items you don't agree with and a statement of why you don't agree with each item;

6. The facts supporting your position on any issue that you don't agree with;

7. Any law or other authority, if any, on which you are relying;

8. You must sign the letter, stating that it is true, under penalties of perjury as follows:

    "Under penalties of perjury, I declare that I have examined the facts stated in this protest, including any accompanying documents, and to the best of my knowledge and belief, they are true, correct, and complete."

If your representative prepares and signs the protest for you, he or she may substitute a declaration stating either:

1. Under penalties of perjury, I declare that I have submitted the protest and accompanying documents and to the best of my knowledge, the information is true, correct, and complete.

   or

2. Under penalties of perjury, I declare that I have submitted the protest and accompanying documents, but have no personal knowledge concerning the facts stated in the protest and the accompanying documents.

You may represent yourself at your appeals conference or you may be represented by an attorney, certified public accountant, or an individual enrolled to practice before the IRS. Your representative must be qualified to practice before the IRS. If your representative appears without you, he or she must file a power of attorney or tax information authorization with the IRS before receiving or inspecting confidential information. You may use Form 2848, Power of Attorney and Declaration of Representative, or any other properly written power of attorney or authorization for this purpose. Copies of these forms are available from any IRS office, or by calling 1-800-TAX-FORM (1-800-829-3676). You may also bring another person(s) with you to support your position.

If you don't send your written response within 30 days from the date of this letter, our file on this offer will be closed. The date of this letter will be the legal rejection date of your offer.

We may file a notice of federal tax lien in order to protect

continued on next page

the government's interests. In order to prevent this action, please pay your liability in full. If you wish to discuss the filing of the notice of federal tax lien and any pre-filing Appeal rights provided via the Collection Appeal Program (CAP), please contact the person named above. After we file a notice of federal tax lien you will have the opportunity to request a hearing with Appeals.

Any payments received with your offer or after your offer is closed, will be applied to your liability unless specified elsewhere in this letter.

If you have any questions, please contact the person whose name and telephone number are shown in the upper right hand corner of this letter.

Sincerely,

Enclosure: Worksheets
Form 13711

SB Letter 238(AOIC) (9-2015)

TAXPAYER'S NAME: TAXPAYER NAME

Date: 02/17/2016

EIN/TIN: XXX-XX-XXXX

ASSET/EQUITY TABLE (AET)
(Rev. 3-2014)

ASSETS	Fair Market Value	Quick Sale Reduction Percentage	Quick Sale Value	Encumbrances or Exemptions	Net Realizable Equity
1. Cash/Bank Accounts	$649.02			$1,000.00	
2. Offer Deposit					
3. Loan Value Life Insurance					
4. Pensions / IRA/401(k)					
5. Real Estate	$379,400.00	20	$303,520.00	$382,209.06	
6. Furniture/Personal Effects					
7. Vehicles	$12,148.00	20	$9,718.40	$7,932.93	$1,785.47
8. Accounts Receivable					
9. Tools and/or Equipment					
Other - Other - Value of TPs business - bank accts	$34,219.00		$34,219.00		$34,219.00
2006 Saab	$4,572.00	20	$3,657.60		$3,657.60
Corp assets	$4,800.00	20	$3,840.00		$3,840.00
Trust - TPs 1/2 interest	$21,053.33		$21,053.33		$21,053.33
Future Income Value (see Income and Expense Table (IET) attached)					$17,102.52
TOTAL MINIMUM VALUE					$81,657.92

Item 1 Cash/Bank accounts has been reduced by $1,000. Net equity should not be less than -0-.
Item 6 IRC 6334(a)(2) allows an exemption of $8,940 for fuel, provisions, furniture and personal effects.
Item 7 Vehicle equity has been reduced by $3,450. Net equity should not be less than -0-.
Item 9 IRC 6334(a)(3) allows an exemption of $4,470 for tools of the trade.

REMARKS:

Exhibit 25

TAXPAYER: TAXPAYER NAME

TIN/EIN: XXX-XX-XXXX
Date: 02/16/2016

INCOME/EXPENSE TABLE (IET) (Rev. 1-2014)

The Internal Revenue Service uses established National and Local standards for necessary living expenses when considering Offers in Compromise. Only necessary living expenses will be allowed. Other expenses, such as charitable contributions, education, credit cards, and voluntary retirement allotments are generally not considered as necessary living expenses.

Total Income		Necessary Living Expenses		
Source	Gross		Claimed	Allowed
20. Wages (T/P)	$1,041.67	35. Food, Clothing, and Misc	$1,092.00	$1,092.00
21. Wages (Spouse)		36. Housing and Utilities	$2,281.00	$2,281.00
22. Interest - Dividend	$26.58	37. Vehicle Ownership Costs	$417.00	$417.63
23. Net Business Income	$6,361.58	38. Vehicle Operating Costs	$478.00	$342.00
24. Net Rental Income		39. Public Transportation		
25. Distributions		40. Health Insurance	$480.00	$480.47
26. Pension/Soc. Sec. (TP)		41. Out of Pocket Health Care Costs	$410.00	$185.01
27. Pension/Soc. Sec. (Spouse)		42. Court ordered payments		
28. Social Security (Taxpayer)		43. Child/dependent care		
29. Social Security (Spouse)		44. Life Insurance	$229.00	$165.51
30. Child Support		45. Current Year Taxes (Income/FICA)	$2,230.00	$1,041.00
31. Alimony		46. Secure Debts (Attach list)		
Other Income (Specify below)		47. Del. State or Local Taxes		
32.		48 Other Expenses (Attach list)		
33.		49. Total Living Expenses	$7,617.00	$6,004.62
34. Total Income	$7,429.83	50. Net Difference	($ 187.17)	$1,425.21

50. Net difference times (a,b or c) = Amount that could be paid from future income:

| Net difference = $1,425.21 | Months 12 | Amount that could be paid = $17,102.52 |

a) For cash offers, if the offer is payable in 5 or fewer installments within 5 months, project the payment by multiplying the amount that could be paid times 12 months or times the number of months remaining in the collection statute, whichever is shorter.

b) For cash offers, payable in 5 or fewer installments within 24 months or a periodic payment offer payable within 24 months project the payments by multiplying the amount that could be paid times 24 months or times the number of months remaining in the collection statute, whichever is shorter.

The total offer amount must be equal to, or greater than, the sum of the equity in assets and the amount that could be paid from future income unless special circumstance considerations have been approved.

NOTES:
Line 35 National Standard expenses: Maximum allowable by IRS National Expense Standard for food, housekeeping supplies, apparel and services, and personal care products, based upon the number of persons in the household.

Line 36 Housing & Utilities expenses: Housing and utility expenses are limited to standards established for the county of residence and the number of household members.

Line 37 & 38 Transportation expenses: Transportation expenses are limited to the standards established for zero, one or two vehicles, and to a maximum allowable amount for lease or purchase of one or two vehicles.

Months: The number of months shown may be greater than 24 months in order to determine the taxpayer's ability to fully pay the liability through an installment agreement.

Form **14640**
(January 2016)

Department of the Treasury–Internal Revenue Service

Addendum to Form 656

Part 1

Taxpayer Name
TAXPAYER NAME

Offer Number
1001XXXXXX

Primary Taxpayer SSN/EIN *(last 4 digits)*
xxxx

Secondary Taxpayer SSN/EIN *(last 4 digits)*

I/We submitted an offer dated 12/03/2014 in the amount of $ 12,864 to compromise unpaid income tax *(kind of tax)*, plus statutory additions for the tax periods 2007, 2008, 2009, 2010, 2011. The purpose of this addendum is to amend the above offer amount I/we are offering to pay and/or to specify the payment terms if the offer is accepted.

Part 2. Revised Offer in Compromise Amount

Accordingly, I/we offer to pay $ 44,600, which includes the following amounts already paid or included with this addendum:

A. $ 2,573, paid with original offer dated 12/03/2014

B. $ _____, paid with an amended/revised Form 656 dated _____

C. $ 6,347, additional payment, if any, to be included with this addendum

D. $ _____, periodic payments, if any, made since original offer was submitted

Part 3. Revised Offer in Compromise Payment Amount

E. $ 35,680 payable within 5 months after acceptance

F. $ _____ payable within _____ months after acceptance

G. $ _____ payable within _____ months after acceptance

H. $ _____ payable within _____ months after acceptance

I. $ _____ payable within _____ months after acceptance

Part 4. Revised Offer in Compromise Payment Terms—Periodic Payment Offer payable in 6–24 months

$ _____ will be sent beginning on the _____ of _____, _____
                                        (day)   (month after the addendum is submitted)   (year)

and then $ _____ will be sent on the _____ of each month for a total of _____ months with a
                                       (day)

final payment of $ _____ due on the _____ of the _____ month of the agreement.
                                      (day)

Part 5. Reason for the Offer

[X] Doubt as to Collectibility — IRS has determined that I have insufficient assets and income to pay the full amount.

[ ] Exceptional Circumstance (Effective Tax Administration) — IRS has determined that I owe this amount and have sufficient assets to pay the full amount, but due to my exceptional circumstances, requiring full payment would cause an economic hardship or would be unfair and inequitable.

Date 2/1/17

Date _____   Signature of Taxpayer/Authorized Corporate Officer

Catalog Number 66857X   www.irs.gov   Form **14640** (Rev. 1-2016)

Exhibit 26

MAY 2 4 2017

Department of the Treasury

Internal Revenue Service
PO Box 9006, Stop 663
Holtsville, NY 11742

Date of this Letter:

Person to Contact:
NAME
Employee #:xxxxxxx
Phone#:(631)447-4279 EXT.
07:00am-03:30pm Mon-Fri

Taxpayer ID#:***-**-xxxx
Offer Number:1001xxxxxx

Taxpayer Name
Taxpayer Address
_____, CT Zip

Dear Mr._____,

    Thank you for your payment. You have met the payment provisions for your Offer in Compromise contract. Please remember that we will apply any overpayments from the year we accepted your Offer in Compromise to the tax periods specified in your offer contract.

REMINDER: Compliance is an important part of your Offer in Compromise contract. You must file and pay your taxes timely for five years following the date we accepted the offer or during an extended installment offer payment period, whichever is later. If you don't comply, we will terminate your offer and reinstate the original amount of your liability, less payments made.

    We are processing your lien release and it should be effective within 30 days.

    If you write, please include your telephone number, the hours we can reach you, and a copy of this letter. Keep a copy of this letter for your records. We've enclosed an envelope for your convenience.

    If you have any questions, please contact the person whose name and telephone number are shown in the upper right hand corner of this letter.

                         Sincerely,

                           Name
                           Tax Examining Technician

Enclosure:Envelope
cc:POA   SB Letter 2908(SC/CG)(1-2000)

Exhibit 27

Department of the Treasury

Internal Revenue Service
PO Box 9006, Stop 663
Holtsville, NY 11742

JUL 25 2019

Date of this Letter:

Person to Contact:
Name
Employee #:0000000000
Phone#:(631)977-3492 EXT.
03:00pm-11:30pm Mon-Fri

Taxpayer ID#:***-**-XXXX
Offer Number:1001XXXXXX

NAME
STREET
CITY,STATE,ZIP

Dear Mr. Client,

NOTICE OF INTENT TO DEFAULT OFFER

When we accepted your Offer in Compromise, you agreed to file all tax returns and pay all taxes on time for the five years following the date we accepted your offer or until you pay the offered amount in full, whichever is later.

Our records show that there is an outstanding balance due for the period(s) listed below. You need to pay $2,218.79 within 30 days from the date of this letter to prevent termination of your Offer In Compromise. If you cannot full pay within 30 days, please call the number shown at the top of this letter to determine if you qualify for extension to pay. If eligible, you may request an extension to pay up to 120 days.

Form 1040 for tax year 2018

It is important that you comply with the terms of the agreement. If you don't comply with the above request, we will terminate your offer and will reinstate the original amount of your liability, less any offer payments you made.

If you write, please include your telephone number, the hours we can reach you, and a copy of this letter. Keep a copy of this letter for your records. We've enclosed an envelope for your convenience.

If your offer defaults, the shared responsibility payment (SRP) amount that you owe is not subject to penalties or to lien and levy enforcement actions. The SRP amount that you owe is the assessed payment for not having minimum essential health coverage for you and, if applicable, your dependents per Internal Revenue Code Section 5000A - Individual shared responsibility payment. Interest will continue to accrue and we may apply your federal tax refunds, in accordance with the terms of your offer, to the SRP amount that you owe until it is paid in full.

continued on next page

Exhibit 28

If you have any questions, please contact the person whose name and telephone number are shown in the upper right hand corner of this letter.

Sincerely,

IRS EMPLOYEE NAME
Tax Examining Technician

Enclosure:Envelope
cc:POA

SB Letter 2909c(SC/CG)(2-2018)

Department of the Treasury

Internal Revenue Service
Offer In Compromise Group 1100
2888 Woodcock Blvd. Stop 313-D
Atlanta, Ga 30341

Date of this Letter:

Person to Contact:
Name
Employee #:1000xxxxxx
Phone#: (EXT.
07:00am-04:30pm Mon-Thu

Taxpayer   ID#:**-***xxxx
Offer Number:1001xxxxxx

TAXPAYER INC
STREET
CITY, STATE

Dear Mr.TAXPAYER,

We have investigated your offer dated 05/02/2016 in the amount of $xx,000.00.

We are rejecting the offer for the following reason(s):

The amount offered is less than your reasonable collection potential. Copies of worksheets showing our calculations are enclosed for your review.

Based on the financial information you submitted, we have determined you can pay the amount due in full.

If you disagree with our findings, please provide any additional information in writing to support your position within 30 days of the date of this letter. If you also want your case considered by the Office of Appeals, you must include a written statement in your response asking that your case be sent to the Office of Appeals after our reconsideration. If you do not send this written statement within 30 days of the date of this letter you will not receive consideration by the Office of Appeals.

Include any additional information that you want Appeals to consider. You may still appeal without additional information, but including it will help us to process your request promptly. You should send a letter requesting Appeals consideration. Please complete the enclosed Form 13711 or include the following information in your written protest:

1. Your name,address,social security number (if applicable, Employer identification number) and daytime telephone number;

2. A statement that you want to appeal the IRS findings to the Appeals Office;

3. A copy of this letter;

4. The tax periods or years involved;

continued on next page

Exhibit 29

5. A list of the specific items you don't agree with and a statement of why you don't agree with each item;

6. The facts supporting your position on any issue that you don't agree with;

7. Any law or other authority, if any, on which you are relying;

8. You must sign the letter, stating that it is true, under penalties of perjury as follows:

   "Under penalties of perjury, I declare that I have examined the facts stated in this protest, including any accompanying documents, and to the best of my knowledge and belief, they are true, correct, and complete."

If your representative prepares and signs the protest for you, he or she may substitute a declaration stating either:

1. Under penalties of perjury, I declare that I have submitted the protest and accompanying documents and to the best of my knowledge, the information is true, correct, and complete.

   or

2. Under penalties of perjury, I declare that I have submitted the protest and accompanying documents, but have no personal knowledge concerning the facts stated in the protest and the accompanying documents.

You may represent yourself at your appeals conference or you may be represented by an attorney, certified public accountant, or an individual enrolled to practice before the IRS. Your representative must be qualified to practice before the IRS. If your representative appears without you, he or she must file a power of attorney or tax information authorization with the IRS before receiving or inspecting confidential information. You may use Form 2848, Power of Attorney and Declaration of Representative, or any other properly written power of attorney or authorization for this purpose. Copies of these forms are available from any IRS office, or by calling 1-800-TAX-FORM (1-800-829-3676). You may also bring another person(s) with you to support your position.

If you don't send your written response within 30 days from the date of this letter, our file on this offer will be closed. The date of this letter will be the legal rejection date of your offer.

We may file a notice of federal tax lien in order to protect the government's interests. In order to prevent this action, please pay your liability in full. If you wish to discuss the filing of the notice of federal tax lien and any pre-filing Appeal

continued on next page

rights provided via the Collection Appeal Program (CAP), please contact the person named above. After we file a notice of federal tax lien you will have the opportunity to request a hearing with Appeals.

Any payments received with your offer or after your offer is closed, will be applied to your liability unless specified elsewhere in this letter.

If you have any questions, please contact the person whose name and telephone number are shown in the upper right hand corner of this letter.

name
Acting Group Manager

Enclosure: Worksheets
　　　　　　Form 13711
cc:POA　　　　　　　　　　　　SB Letter 238(AOIC) (9-2015)

Form **4180**
(August 2012)

Department of the Treasury - Internal Revenue Service

Report of Interview with Individual Relative to Trust Fund Recovery Penalty or Personal Liability for Excise Taxes

Instructions: The interviewer *must* prepare this form either in person or via telephone.
Do not leave any information blank. Enter "N/A" if an item is not applicable.

Section I - Person Interviewed

1. Name	2. Social Security Number *(SSN)*

3. Address *(street, city, state, ZIP code)*	4. Home telephone number ( )
	5. Work telephone number ( )

6. Name of Business and Employer Identification Number *(EIN)*	7. Did you use a third-party payer, such as a payroll service? ☐ Yes *(If yes complete Section VI A)* ☐ No

8. What was your job title and how were you associated with the business? *(Describe your duties and responsibilities and dates of employment.)* If person being interviewed is a payroll service provider or a professional employer organization, complete Section VI B

Section II - Responsibilities

1. State whether you performed any of the duties / functions listed below for the business and the time periods during which you performed these duties.

Did you...	Yes	No	Dates From	Dates To
a. Determine financial policy for the business?	☐	☐		
b. Direct or authorize payments of bills/creditors?	☐	☐		
c. Prepare, review, sign, or authorize transmit payroll tax returns?	☐	☐		
d. Have knowledge withheld taxes were not paid?	☐	☐		
e. Authorize payroll?	☐	☐		
f. Authorize or make Federal Tax Deposits?	☐	☐		
g. Authorize the assignment of any EFTPS or electronic banking PINS/passwords?	☐	☐		

h. Could other individuals do any of the above? *(Complete Section IV and V)* ☐ ☐

Name	Contact Number

i. Have signature authority or PIN assignment on business bank accounts?

Bank Name(s)	Account Number(s)

Section III - Signatures

I declare that I have examined the information given in this interview and to the best of my knowledge and belief, it is true, correct, and complete.

Signature of person interviewed	Date

Signature of Interviewer	Date

Date copy of completed interview form given to person interviewed ▶

Taxpayer Statement on Page 4: ☐ Yes ☐ No	Interview Continued on subsequent pages? ☐ Yes ☐ No

Interview Handouts *("X" if given or explain why not in case history.)*

☐ **Notice 609**, Privacy Act Notice   ☐ **Notice 784**, Could You be Personally Liable for Certain Unpaid Federal Taxes?

Catalog Number 22710P   www.irs.gov   Exhibit 30   Form **4180** (Rev. 8-2012)

Section IV - Business Information

1. List corporate positions below, identifying the persons who occupied them and their dates of service.

Position (e.g. president, director)	Name	Address	Dates

2. Did/does the business use the Electronic Federal Tax Payment System (EFTPS) to make Federal Tax Deposits (FTD's) or payments?
- [ ] No
- [ ] Yes   If yes, to whom are the PINS or passwords assigned

3. Other than the EFTPS, does the business do any other banking electronically?
- [ ] No
- [ ] Yes   Where _____
              To whom are the PINs/passwords assigned

4. Does the business file Form 941 electronically?
- [ ] No   Who is authorized to sign Form 941
- [ ] Yes   Who files the returns electronically

Section V - Knowledge / Willfulness

1. During the time the delinquent taxes were increasing, or at any time thereafter, were any financial obligations of the business paid? *(such as rent, mortgage, utilities, vehicle or equipment loans, or payments to vendors)*
- [ ] No
- [ ] Yes   Which obligations were paid?

   Who authorized them to be paid?

2. Were all or a portion of the payrolls met?
- [ ] No
- [ ] Yes

Who authorized

3. Did any person or organization provide funds to pay net corporate payroll?
- [ ] No
- [ ] Yes *(explain in detail and provide name)*

4. When and how did you first become aware of the unpaid taxes?

5. What actions did you attempt to see that the taxes were paid?

6. Were discussions ever held by stockholders, officers, or other interested parties regarding nonpayment of the taxes?
- [ ] No
- [ ] Yes

Identify who attended, dates, any decisions reached, and whether any documentation is available.

7. Who handled IRS contacts such as phone calls, correspondence, or visits by IRS personnel?

When did these contacts take place, and what were the results of these contacts?

Catalog Number 22710P   www.irs.gov   Form **4180** (Rev. 8-2012)

Page 3

Section VI - Payroll Service Provider (PSP) or Professional Employer Organization (PEO)

A - Third-Party Payer Arrangements
(complete this section only if you are interviewing a taxpayer who used a third-party payer)

1. Who signed the service contract or entered into the agreement for services with the third-party payer?	2. Who in the business handled the contacts with the third-party payer?
3. Who was your contact at the third-party payer?	4. How were funds to be made available for the third-party payer to pay the taxes? Name of Bank(s) and Account number(s) from which funds were to be transferred.
5. What actions did you take to verify the third-party payer was filing returns, or making required payments?	6. Were funds available for the third-party payer to use for payment of the taxes? ☐ Yes ☐ No If yes, explain in detail how and when the money was transferred to the third-party.
7. Were you aware that the third-party payer was not making the required payments? ☐ Yes ☐ No	8. Did you receive IRS notices indicating that the employment tax returns were not filed, or that the employment taxes were not paid? ☐ Yes ☐ No

B - Third-Party Payer Companies
(complete this section only if you are interviewing a Third-Party Payroll Service Payer)

1. Who in your organization handled the contacts with the client?	2. Who was your contact at the client business?
3. Who at the client business signed the service contract or entered into the agreement for services?	4. Who had control over the payments of the client's employment taxes?

5. How were funds to be made available from the client business to pay the taxes?

Bank Name(s)	Account Number(s)

6. Were there funds actually available for you to make the tax payments?
☐ Yes ☐ No
If yes, explain in detail how and when the money was transferred to the third-party.

If no, what actions did you take to attempt to collect the funds from the client?

Section VII - Personal Liability for Excise Tax Cases
(Complete only if Business is required to file Excise Tax Returns)

1. Are you aware of any required excise tax returns which have not been filed? ☐ No ☐ Yes *(list periods)*	2. With respect to excise taxes, were the patrons or customers informed that the tax was included in the sales price? ☐ No ☐ Yes
3. If the liability is one of the "collected" taxes *(transportation of persons or property and communications)*, was the tax collected? ☐ No ☐ Yes	4. Were you aware, during the period tax accrued, that the law required collection of the tax? ☐ No ☐ Yes

Catalog Number 22710P www.irs.gov Form **4180** (Rev. 8-2012)

Additional Information

Section VIII - Signatures

I declare that I have examined the information given in this interview and to the best of my knowledge and belief, it is true, correct, and complete.

Signature of person interviewed	Date
Signature of Interviewer	Date
Date copy of completed interview form given to person interviewed ▶	

Interview Handouts *("X" if given or explain why not in case history.)*

☐ **Notice 609**, Privacy Act Notice   ☐ **Notice 784**, Could You be Personally Liable for Certain Unpaid Federal Taxes?

Internal Revenue Service   **Department of the Treasury**

Date: Number of this Letter:

                                                 Person to Contact:

                                                 Employee Number:

                                                 IRS Contact Address:

                                                 IRS Telephone Number:

                                                 Employer Identification Number:

                                                 Business Name and Address:

Dear

Our efforts to collect the federal employment or excise taxes due from the business named above have not resulted in full payment of the liability. We therefore propose to assess a penalty against you as a person required to collect, account for, and pay over withhold taxes for the above business.

Under the provisions of Internal Revenue Code section 6672, individuals who were required to collect, account for, and pay over these taxes for the business may be personally liable for a penalty if the business doesn't pay the taxes. These taxes, described in the enclosed Form 2751, consist of employment taxes you withheld (or should have withheld) from the employees' wages (and didn't pay) or excise taxes you collected (or should have collected) from patrons (and didn't pay), and are commonly referred to as "trust fund taxes."

The penalty we propose to assess against you is a personal liability called the Trust Fund Recovery Penalty. It is equal to the unpaid trust fund taxes which the business still owes the government. If you agree with this penalty for each tax period shown, please sign Part 1 of the enclosed Form 2751 and return it to us in the enclosed envelope.

If you don't agree, have additional information to support your case, and wish to try to resolve the matter informally, contact the person named at the top of this letter within ten days from the date of this letter.

You also have the right to appeal or protest this action. To preserve your appeal rights you need to mail us your written appeal within 60 days from the date of this letter (75 days if this letter is addressed to you outside the United States). The instructions below explain how to make the request.

Exhibit 31

Letter 1153 (DO) (Rev. 3-2002)
Catalog Number: 40545C

APPEALS

You may appeal your case to the local Appeals Office. Send your written appeal to the attention of the Person to Contact at the address shown at the top of this letter. The dollar amount of the proposed liability for each specific tax period you are protesting affects the form your appeal should take.

For each period you are protesting, if the proposed penalty amount is:	You should:
$25,000 or less	Send a letter listing the issues you disagree with and explain why you disagree. (Small Case Request).
More than $25,000	Submit a formal Written Protest.

One protest will suffice for all the periods listed on the enclosed Form 2751, however if any one of those periods is more than $25,000, a formal protest must be filed. Include any additional information that you want the Settlement Officer/Appeals Officer to consider. You may still appeal without additional information, but including it at this stage will help us to process your request promptly.

A SMALL CASE REQUEST should include:

1. A copy of this letter, or your name, address, social security number, and any information that will help us locate your file;

2. A statement that you want an Appeal's conference;

3. A list of the issues you disagree with and an explanation of why you disagree. Usually, penalty cases like this one involve issues of responsibility and willfulness. Willfulness means that an action was intentional, deliberate or voluntary and not an accident or mistake. Therefore, your statement should include a clear explanation of your duties and responsibilities; and specifically, your duty and authority to collect, account for, and pay the trust fund taxes. Should you disagree with how we calculated the penalty, your statement should identify the dates and amounts of payments that you believe we didn't consider and or/ any computation errors that you believe we made.

Please submit two copies of your Small Case Request.

A formal **WRITTEN PROTEST should** include the items below. Pay particular attention to item 6 and the note that follows it.

Letter 1153 (DO) (Rev. 3-2002)
Catalog Number: 40545C

1. Your name, address, and social security number;

2. A statement that you want a conference;

3. A copy of this letter, or the date and number of this letter;

4. The tax periods involved (see Form 2751);

5. A list of the findings you disagree with;

6. A statement of fact, signed under penalties of perjury, that explains why you disagree and why you believe you shouldn't be charged with the penalty. Include specific dates, names, amounts, and locations which support your position. Usually, penalty cases like this one involve issues of responsibility and willfulness. Willfulness means that an action was intentional, deliberate or voluntary and not an accident or mistake. Therefore, your statement should include a clear explanation of your duties and responsibilities; and specifically, your duty and authority to collect, account for, and pay the trust fund taxes. Should you disagree with how we calculated the penalty, your statement should identify the dates and amounts of payments that you believe we didn't consider and/or any computation errors you believe we made;

   NOTE:

   To declare that the statement in item 6 is true under penalties of perjury, you must add the following to your statement and sign it:

   "Under penalties of perjury, I declare that I have examined the facts presented in this statement and any accompanying information, and, to the best of my knowledge and belief, they are true, correct, and complete."

7. If you rely on a law or other authority to support your arguments, explain what it is and how it applies.

REPRESENTATION

You may represent yourself at your conference or have someone who is qualified to practice before the Internal Revenue Service represent you. This may be your attorney, a certified public accountant, or another individual enrolled to practice before the IRS. If your representative attends a conference without you, he or she must file a power of attorney or tax information authorization before receiving or inspecting confidential tax information. Form 2848, Power of Attorney and Declaration of Representative, or Form 8821, Tax Information Authorization, may be used for this purpose. Both forms are available from any IRS office. A properly written power of attorney or authorization is acceptable.

Letter 1153 (DO) (Rev. 3-2002)
Catalog Number: 40545C

If your representative prepares and signs the protest for you, he or she must substitute a declaration stating:

1. That he or she submitted the protest and accompanying documents, and

2. Whether he or she knows personally that the facts stated in the protest and accompanying documents are true and correct.

CLAIMS FOR REFUND AND CONSIDERATION BY THE COURTS

CONSIDERATION BY THE COURTS

If you and the IRS still disagree after your conference, we will send you a bill. However, by following the procedures outlined below, you may take your case to the United States Court of Federal Claims or to your United States District Court. These courts have no connection with the IRS.

Before you can file a claim with these courts, you must pay a portion of the tax liability and file a claim for refund with the IRS, as described below.

SPECIAL BOND TO DELAY IRS COLLECTION ACTIONS FOR ANY PERIOD AS SOON AS A CLAIM FOR REFUND IS FILED

To request a delay in collection of the penalty by the IRS for any period as soon as you file a claim for refund for that period, you must do the following within 30 days of the date of the official notice of assessment and demand (the first bill) for that period:

1. Pay the tax for one employee for each period (quarter) of liability that you wish to contest, if we've based the amount of the penalty on unpaid employment taxes; or pay the tax for one transaction for each period that you wish to contest, if we've based the amount of the penalty on unpaid excise tax.

2. File a claim for a refund of the amount(s) you paid using Form(s) 843, Claim for Refund and Request for Abatement.

3. Post a bond with the IRS for one and one half times the amount of the penalty that is left after you have made the payment in Item 1.

If the IRS denies your claim when you have posted this bond, you then have 30 days to file suit in your United States District Court or the United States Court of Federal Claims before the IRS may apply the bond to your trust fund recovery penalty and the interest accruing on this debt.

Letter 1153 (DO) (Rev. 3-2002)
Catalog Number: 40545C

CLAIM FOR REFUND WITH NO SPECIAL BOND

If you do not file a special bond with a prompt claim for refund, as described above, you may still file a claim for refund following above action items 1 and 2, except these action items do not have to be taken in the first 30 days after the date of the official notice of assessment and demand for the period.

If IRS has not acted on your claim within 6 months from the date you filed it, you can file a suit for refund. You can also file a suit for refund within 2 years after IRS has disallowed your claim.

You should be aware that if IRS finds that the collection of this penalty is in jeopardy, we may take immediate action to collect it without regard to the 60-day period for submitting a protest mentioned above.

For further information about filing a suit you may contact the Clerk of your District Court or the Clerk of the United States Court of Federal Claims, 717 Madison Place, NW, Washington, D.C. 20005.

If we do not hear from you within 60 days from the date of this letter (or 75 days if this letter is addressed to you outside the United States), we will assess the penalty and begin collection action.

Sincerely yours,

Revenue Officer

Enclosures:
Form 2751
Publication 1
Envelope

Letter 1153 (DO) (Rev. 3-2002)
Catalog Number: 40545C

Form **2751**
(Rev. 7-2002)

Department of the Treasury-Internal Revenue Service

Proposed Assessment of Trust Fund Recovery Penalty

(Sec. 6672, Internal Revenue Code, or corresponding provisions of prior internal revenue laws)

Report of Business Taxpayer's Unpaid Tax Liability

Name and address of business

BUSINESS NAME
STREET ADDRESS
CITY, STATE, ZIP

Tax Return Form Number	Tax Period Ended	Date Return Filed	Date Tax Assessed	Identifying Number	Amount Outstanding	Penalty
941	12/31/2016	05/18/2017	07/10/2017	xx-xxx-1111	$31,928.62	$25,939
941	03/31/2017	05/18/2017	07/10/2017	xx-xxx-1111	$56,143.81	$34,929

Totals: $88,072.43 $60,869.

Agreement to Assessment and Collection of Trust Fund Recovery Penalty

Name, address, and social security number of person responsible

Responsible person's name
xxx-xx-1111
Street Adress
City, State Zip

I consent to the assessment and collection of the penalty shown for each period, which is equal either to the amount of federal employment taxes withheld from employees' wages or to the amount of federal excise taxes collected from patrons or members, and which was not paid over to the Government by the busine named above. I waive the 60 day restriction on notice and demand set forth in Internal Revenue Code Section 6672(b).

Signature of person responsible   Date

Part 1— Please sign and return this copy to Internal Revenue Service   Catalog No. 21955U   www.irs.gov   Form **2751** (Rev. 7-2002

Exhibit 32

Department of the Treasury
Internal Revenue Service
Appeals Office

Date:
February 24, 2016
Taxpayer ID number:

Re:
Collection Due Process - Levy
Tax period(s) ended:
12/2011
Person to contact:
 Name:
 Employee number:
 Telephone:
 Fax:

TAXPAYER
ADDRESS
CITY, STATE ZIP

Appeals Received Your Request for a Collection Due Process Hearing

Dear Taxpayer:

We received your request for a Collection Due Process (CDP) and/or Equivalent Hearing in our New Haven Appeals office on 02/24/2016.

Your levy hearing request regarding the proposed levy action for the tax periods shown above was timely. The legal period for collection is suspended and generally no levy action may be taken from the date you sent your request until any Appeals' decision becomes final for the tax period(s) shown above.

I have scheduled a telephone conference for you. Please call me on 03/23/2016 at 10:00 am.

This is your opportunity to discuss with me the reasons you disagree with the collection action or to discuss alternatives to the collection action. If this time is not convenient for you, or you would prefer another type of conference (telephone, correspondence or face-to-face), please call or write me within 14 days from the date of this letter.

Our office is separate from, and independent of, the IRS office taking the action that you disagree with. We review and resolve disputes in a fair and impartial manner by weighing the facts according to the law and judicial decisions.

During the hearing, I must consider:

- Whether the IRS met all the requirements of any applicable law or administrative procedure

- Any relevant issue(s) you wish to discuss. These can include

    1. Collection alternatives to levy, such as full payment of the liability, an installment agreement, or an offer in compromise. Although these collection options may not necessarily be considered an "alternative" to a notice of lien filing, they may be discussed at a lien hearing.

    2. Challenges to the appropriateness of collection action. If this is a lien hearing, you may ask us to determine if the notice of lien filing was appropriate and if you qualify for a notice of lien withdrawal or other lien options.

    3. Spousal defenses, when applicable.

Exhibit 33

Letter 4837 (Rev. 6-2013)
Catalog Number 58666E

4. Whether you owe the amount due, but only if you did not receive a statutory notice of deficiency or have not otherwise had an opportunity to dispute your liability with Appeals.

In considering your case, I will balance the IRS' need for efficient tax collection and your legitimate concern that the collection action be no more intrusive than necessary.

You are entitled to have your conference with an Appeals employee who has had no prior involvement with the tax period(s) at issue (other than a prior CDP Hearing), either in Appeals or in the Compliance (Collection or Examination) division. I don't recall any previous involvement with these tax periods; however, if you believe I've had previous involvement, please notify me immediately to discuss. If I've been involved but you still want me to conduct your hearing, you may waive your right to have another Appeals employee consider your case.

For me to consider alternative collection methods such as an installment agreement or offer in compromise, you must provide any items listed below.

The items to be provided are:

- Signed tax return(s) for the following tax periods. Our records indicate they have not been filed:

    Type of Tax: Form 1040

    Tax Periods: 2012

If you did not file a return because your yearly income was below the amount for which a return is required to be filed, please let me know.

Please send me the items listed above within 14 days from the date of this letter. For tax returns, please send them to me within 21 days from the date of this letter. I can't consider collection alternatives without the information requested. I am enclosing the necessary forms and a return envelope for your convenience.

At the conclusion of the hearing process, we will issue a determination letter as required by law for the tax periods for which your CDP hearing request was received timely. If you do not agree with our determination, you may appeal the case to the United States Tax Court.

The Office of Appeals may ask the Collection function to review, verify and provide their opinion on any new information you submit. You will receive any comments, and you will have an opportunity to respond.

If you do not participate in a conference or respond to this letter, the determination or decision letter that we issue will be based on your CDP request, any information you previously provided to this office, and any information we have on file regarding the applicable tax period(s).

We strongly urge you to read the enclosed Publication 4227, *Overview of the Appeals Process,* which includes details about the Appeals process and your right to representation. Please note that while you are in Appeals and until you pay your tax liability in full, interest will continue to be added on any balance due, including prior accruals of penalty and interest.

At the conclusion of the Appeals process, you may be asked to participate in an Appeals customer satisfaction survey. Participation is voluntary and the survey will not ask for personal or financial information of any kind. The results of the survey will be used to further improve the Appeals process and service to our customers.

Letter 4837 (Rev. 6-2013)
Catalog Number 58666E

Please contact me with any questions or concerns you have regarding this letter or the CDP procedures. My telephone number is listed in the heading to this letter.

Appeals Officer

Enclosures:
Publication 4227 Welcome to Appeals

cc: Eric L Green

Internal Revenue Service
Appeals Office
P.O. Box
Fresno, CA

Date: July 26, 2016

MR & MRS CLIENT
CLIENT ROAD
CLIENT CITY, STATE ZIP

Department of the Treasury

Person to Contact:
APPEALS OFFICER NAME
Employee ID Number:
Tel:
Fax:
Contact Hours: 8:30AM - 4:00PM
Refer Reply to:

In Re:
Collection Due Process - Levy
Tax Period(s) Ended:
12/2014

Dear Mr. & Mrs. CLIENTS NAMES HERE:

Please find enclosed a Form 12257, Waiver of Right to Judicial Review of a Collection Due Process Determination and Waiver of Suspension of Levy Action. If you agree to sign this waiver, please sign it and fax it back to me **by August 9, 2016.**

The terms and effects of your account while in *currently not collectible status* are as follows:

- There will be no levy or other enforced collections while your account is in currently not collectible status.
- If your current financial circumstances improve, you will be contacted and collection action considerations will resume.
- Your tax refunds will be applied to the outstanding balance(s).
- You will receive an annual reminder notice of the balance due.

Upon receipt of the signed Form 12257, I will close out the case and send you a copy of the waiver approved by the Appeals team manager and immediately return the file to Compliance for necessary action.

Please note if I don't hear from you by August 9, 2016, your hearing may consist of a review by Appeals of the administrative file, including information you already provided. We may issue you a determination letter based upon that review.

If you have question or concerns, please call me at the number above.

Enclosures: Form 12257
Envelope

cc: Eric L. Green

Exhibit 34

Form 12257
(September 2012)

Department of the Treasury - Internal Revenue Service

Summary Notice of Determination, Waiver of Right to Judicial Review of a Collection Due Process Determination, Waiver of Suspension of Levy Action, and Waiver of Periods of Limitation in Section 6330(e)(1)

Taxpayer name(s)
CLIENT NAMES

Address (street)
CLIENT ADDRESS

City
CLIENT CITY

State
CONNECTICUT

Zip code

Type of tax/tax form
INCOME / 1040

Tax period(s)
12/2014

Social Security/Employer Identification Number(s)
XXX-XX-XXXX

This waiver concerns the following Collection Due Process (CDP) Notice(s):

☐ Notice of Federal Tax Lien Filing and Your Right to a Hearing *(IRC Section 6320)*

☒ Notice of Intent to Levy and Your Right to a Hearing *(IRC Section 6330)*

I understand that IRC Sections 6320 and 6330 require the Office of Appeals to issue a Notice of Determination after a CDP Hearing. Those sections allow me 30 days to seek judicial review of Appeals determination with Tax Court. A longer period may apply to file a lawsuit with the Tax Court to contest determinations by Appeals regarding innocent spouse (section 6015) or interest abatement (section 6404).

I understand that, if I have requested an IRC Section 6330 hearing, the IRS may not levy to collect the taxes at issue for the period of the hearing, during the 30-day period for seeking judicial review of Appeals' determination and while any timely-requested appeal is pending *(unless an exception to the levy prohibition applies)*. If I have only requested an IRC Section 6320 hearing, the IRS may not levy unless an exception to the levy prohibition applies or I already have been given my IRC Section 6330 hearing rights.

I agree that the Appeals determination shown on the following page, as a Summary Notice of Determination, is appropriate and correct. Because of my agreement, I recognize there is no need for judicial review of the determination, or for the continuation of the levy prohibition or suspension of the statute of limitation on collection and other suspended periods referred to in section 6330(e)(1).

- I waive my right under Sections 6320 and 6330 to request judicial review of an Appeals' Notice of Determination.
- I waive the 30-day suspension of levy action described in section 6330(e)(1) if I have requested an IRC Section 6330 hearing.
- I waive the 30-day suspension of the statute of limitations on collection and other suspended periods referred to in section 6330(e)(1).

If, in accordance with the Appeals' determination, I entered into an offer in compromise, installment agreement, or other collection alternative, I understand that the IRS will not levy my property so long as I comply with the terms of the Appeals' determination, unless levy action is part of the Appeals' determination. If I fail to abide by the terms of the Appeals' determination, the IRS may begin enforced collection actions, including the filing of a lien and/or a levy.

I do not waive my right under Appeals' retained jurisdiction to receive another hearing with Appeals if I disagree with the IRS over how it followed the Appeals' determination.

I do not waive my right under Appeals retained jurisdiction to receive another hearing with Appeals if my circumstances change in a way that affects this determination. I understand that I must first exhaust my administrative remedies before I request a hearing.

Catalog Number 27780L   www.irs.gov   Form **12257** (Rev. 9-2012)

Page 2

I do not give up any other administrative appeal rights I'm entitled to, such as appeal rights under the Collection Appeals Program (CAP).

My agreement to the Summary Notice of Determination shown below, to waive judicial review and to waive the suspension of levy action under section 6330(e)(1) is effective upon the written approval by a person in the Office of Appeals with authority to bind the IRS to (1) the installment agreement, offer in compromise or other collection alternative I have requested, (2) the Summary Notice of Determination shown below, and (3) any other agreement described in the Summary Notice of Determination that has been signed by me and requires separate written approval.

Appeals has verified whether applicable laws and administrative procedures have been met, has considered the issues raised, and has balanced the proposed collection action with the legitimate concerns that such action be no more intrusive than necessary as required by IRC Section 6330(c)(3).

The determination of Appeals is:
We have advised Compliance to close your account as currently not collectible since you currently do not have the ability to pay the tax in full nor make monthly installment payments; and you do not have the ability to file an Offer in Compromise.

The Collections department is required to make a lien determination and may file a Notice of Federal Tax Lien.

Since penalties and interest continue to accrue until your account is paid in full you may make voluntary payments at any time. You will receive an annual reminder notice of the balance due and all refunds will be applied to the outstanding balance(s). No levy or other enforced collections may occur while your account is in currently not collectible status. You will submit a corrected W-4 wage statement to your employer changing your filing and withholding status to indicate: "Single with zero dependents" so that you do not have future tax liabilities.

If in the future your income exceeds your monthly expenses, if you fail to timely file tax returns or if you have additional tax liabilities the Internal Revenue Service may take the account out of currently not collectible status. Compliance must first contact you to solicit your cooperation to determine whether or not you have an ability to pay prior to the service of any levy or other enforced collections action. They may, at their discretion, ask you at that time to complete a current Form 433A, Collection Information Statement for Wage Earners and Self-Employed Individuals. If and when a determination is made that you have an ability to pay the tax, you should work with Compliance to resolve the tax liability. If at any time after there is a determination that you have an ability to pay the tax and you do not continue to cooperate or propose an acceptable collection alternative, Compliance may proceed with enforced collections.

The Settlement Officer who conducted the hearing had no prior involvement with this taxpayer with respect to these liabilities in either Compliance or Appeals.

The proposed intent to levy action is not sustained.

No other issues raised.

Taxpayer's signature	Date
Spouse's signature *(if applicable)*	Date
Signature of Taxpayer's Authorized Representative *(if applicable)*	Date
Team Manager, Office of Appeals	Date

Catalog Number 27780L www.irs.gov Form **12257** (Rev. 9-2012)

Page 5

Form **656-L**
(May 2017)

Department of the Treasury - Internal Revenue Service

Offer in Compromise *(Doubt as to Liability)*

OMB Number
1545-1686

IRS Received Date

▶ **To: Commissioner of Internal Revenue Service**

In the following agreement, the pronoun "we" may be assumed in place of "I" when there are joint liabilities and both parties are signing this agreement.
I submit this offer to compromise the tax liabilities plus any interest, penalties, additions to tax, and additional amounts required by law for the tax type and period(s) marked below:

Section 1 — Individual Information (Form 1040 filers)

Your First Name, Middle Initial, Last Name

Social Security Number (SSN)

If a Joint Offer: Spouse's First Name, Middle Initial, Last Name

Social Security Number (SSN)

Your Physical Home Address *(Street, City, State, ZIP Code)*

Your Mailing Address *(if different from your Physical Home Address or Post Office Box Number)*

Is this a new address?
☐ Yes ☐ No

If yes, would you like us to update our records to this address?
☐ Yes ☐ No

Employer Identification Number *(For self-employed individuals only)*

Individual Tax Periods

☐ **1040** U.S. Individual Income Tax Return [List all year(s); for example 2009, 2010, etc.]

☐ **941** Employer's Quarterly Federal Tax Return [List all quarterly period(s); for example 03/31/2010, 06/30/2010, 09/30/2010, etc.]

☐ **940** Employer's Annual Federal Unemployment (FUTA) Tax Return [List all year(s); for example 2010, 2011, etc.]

☐ **Trust Fund Recovery Penalty** as a responsible person of *(enter business name)* _____,
for failure to pay withholding and Federal Insurance Contributions Act taxes (Social Security taxes), for period(s) ending [List all quarterly period(s); for example 03/31/2009, 06/30/2009, etc.]

☐ **Other Federal Tax(es)** [specify type(s) and period(s)]

Section 2 — Business Information (Form 1120, 1065, etc., filers)

Business Name

Business Physical Address *(Street, City, State, ZIP Code)*

Business Mailing Address *(Street, City, State, ZIP Code)*

Employer Identification Number (EIN)

Name and Title of Primary Contact

Telephone Number
( ) -

Business Tax Periods

☐ **1120** U.S. Corporate Income Tax Return [List all year(s); for example 1120 2010, 1120 2013, etc.]

☐ **941** Employer's Quarterly Federal Tax Return [List all quarterly period(s); for example 03/31/2010, 06/30/2010, 09/30/2010, etc.]

☐ **940** Employer's Annual Federal Unemployment (FUTA) Tax Return [List all year(s); for example 2010, 2011, etc.]

☐ **Other Federal Tax(es)** [specify type(s) and period(s)]

Note: If you need more space, use a separate sheet of paper and title it "Attachment to Form 656-L Dated _____." Sign and date the attachment following the listing of the tax periods.

Catalog Number 47516R

Exhibit 35

www.irs.gov

Form **656-L** (Rev. 5-2017)

Page 6

Section 3 — Amount of the Offer

I offer to pay $ _____

Must be $1 or more and payable within 90 days of the notification of acceptance, unless an alternative payment term is approved at the time the offer is accepted. **Do not send any payment with this form.** If you do not offer at least $1, your offer will be returned without consideration.

Section 4 — Terms

By submitting this offer, I have read, understand and agree to the following terms and conditions:

Terms, Conditions, and Legal Agreement

a) The IRS will apply payments made under the terms of this offer in the best interest of the government.

IRS will keep my payments and fees

b) I voluntarily submit all payments made on this offer.

c) The IRS will keep all payments and credits made, received, or applied to the total original tax debt before I send in the offer or while it is under consideration, including any refunds from tax returns and/or credits from tax years prior to the year in which the offer was accepted.

d) The IRS may levy under section 6331(a) up to the time that the IRS official signs and acknowledges my offer as pending, which is accepted for processing, and the IRS may keep any proceeds arising from such a levy.

e) If the Doubt as to Liability offer determines that I do not owe the taxes, or the IRS ultimately over-collected the compromised tax liability, the IRS will return the over-collected amount to me, unless such refund is legally prohibited by statute.

f) If the IRS served a continuous levy on wages, salary, or certain federal payments under sections 6331(e) or (h), then the IRS could choose to either retain or release the levy. No levy may be made during the time an offer in compromise is pending.

I agree to the time extensions allowed by law

g) To have my offer considered, I agree to the extension of time limit provided by law to assess my tax debt (statutory period of assessment). I agree that the date by which the IRS must assess my tax debt will now be the date by which my debt must currently be assessed plus the period of time my offer is pending plus one additional year if the IRS rejects, returns, or terminates my offer, or I withdraw it. [Paragraph (m) of this section defines pending and withdrawal]. I understand I have the right not to waive the statutory period of assessment or to limit the waiver to a certain length or certain periods or issues. I understand, however, the IRS may not consider my offer if I decline to waive the statutory period of assessment or if I provide only a limited waiver. I also understand the statutory period for collecting my tax debt will be suspended during the time my offer is pending with the IRS, for 30 days after any rejection of my offer by the IRS, and during the time any rejection of my offer is being considered by the Appeals Office.

I understand I remain responsible for the full amount of the tax liability

h) The IRS cannot collect more than the full amount of the tax debt under this offer.

i) I understand I remain responsible for the full amount of the tax debt, unless and until the IRS partially or fully abates the tax, or accepts the offer in writing and I have met all the terms and conditions of the offer. The IRS will not remove the original amount of the tax debt from its records until I have met all the terms of the offer.

j) I understand the tax I offer to compromise is and will remain a tax debt until I meet all the terms and conditions of this offer. If I file bankruptcy before the terms and conditions of this offer are completed, any claim the IRS files in bankruptcy proceedings will be a tax claim.

k) Once the IRS accepts the offer in writing, I have no right to contest, in court or otherwise, the amount of the tax debt.

Pending status of an offer and right to appeal

l) The offer is pending starting with the date an authorized IRS official signs this form. The offer remains pending until an authorized IRS official accepts, rejects, returns, or acknowledges withdrawal of the offer in writing. If I appeal an IRS rejection decision on the offer, the IRS will continue to treat the offer as pending until the Appeals Office accepts or rejects the offer in writing. If an offer is rejected, no levy may be made during the 30 days of rejection. If I do not file a protest within 30 days of the date the IRS notifies me of the right to protest the decision, I waive the right to a hearing before the Appeals Office about the offer.

I understand if IRS fails to make a decision in 24-months my offer will be accepted

m) I understand under Internal Revenue Code (IRC) § 7122(f), my offer will be accepted, by law, unless IRS notifies me otherwise, in writing, within 24 months of the date my offer was initially received.

I understand what will happen if I fail to meet the terms of my offer (e.g. default)

n) If I fail to meet any of the terms of this offer, the IRS may levy or sue me to collect any amount ranging from the unpaid balance of the offer to the original amount of the tax debt (less payments made) plus penalties and interest that have accrued from the time the underlying tax liability arose. The IRS will continue to add interest, as required by Section § 6601 of the Internal Revenue Code, on the amount of the IRS determines is due after default.

I understand the IRS may file a Notice of Federal Tax Lien on my/our property

o) The IRS may file a Notice of Federal Tax Lien to protect the Government's interest during the offer investigation. The tax lien will be released 30 days after the payment terms have been satisfied and the payment has been verified. If the offer is accepted, the tax lien will be released within 30 days of when the payment terms have been satisfied and the payment has been verified. The time it takes to verify the payment varies based on the form of payment.

Catalog Number 47516R   www.irs.gov   Form **656-L** (Rev. 5-2017)

Page 7

Section 4 — Terms (continued)

I authorize the IRS to contact relevant third parties in order to process my/our offer

p) I understand that IRS employees may contact third parties in order to respond to this request, and I authorize the IRS to make such contacts. Further, in connection with this request, by authorizing the IRS to contact third parties, I understand that I will not receive notice of third parties contacted as is otherwise required by IRC § 7602(c).

Section 5 — Explanation of Circumstances

THIS SECTION MUST BE COMPLETED.

Explain why you believe the tax is incorrect. Reminder: if your explanation indicates you cannot afford to pay, do not file a Form 656-L. Refer to page 4 "What if I agree with the tax debt but cannot afford to pay in full?", for additional information. **Note: You may attach additional sheets if necessary. Please include your name and SSN and/or EIN on all additional sheets or supporting documentation.**

_____
_____
_____
_____
_____
_____
_____
_____
_____
_____

Section 6 — Signature(s)

Taxpayer Attestation: If I submit this offer on a substitute form, I affirm this form is a verbatim duplicate of the official Form 656-L, and I agree to be bound by all the terms and conditions set forth in the official Form 656-L. Under penalties of perjury, I declare that I have examined this offer, including accompanying schedules and statements, and to the best of my knowledge and belief, it is true, correct and complete.

▶ Signature of Taxpayer/Corporation Name | Daytime Telephone Number ( ) - | Today's date (mm/dd/yyyy)

☐ The IRS may contact you by telephone about this offer. By checking this box, you authorize the IRS to leave detailed messages concerning your offer on your voice mail or answering machine.

▶ Signature of Spouse/Authorized Corporate Officer | Today's date (mm/dd/yyyy)

☐ The IRS may contact you by telephone about this offer. By checking this box, you authorize the IRS to leave detailed messages concerning your offer on your voice mail or answering machine.

Section 7 — Application Prepared by Someone Other than the Taxpayer

If this application was prepared by someone other than you (the taxpayer), please fill in that person's name and address below.

Name

Address (Street, City, State, ZIP Code) | Daytime Telephone Number ( ) -

Section 8 — Paid Preparer Use Only

Signature of Preparer

☐ The IRS may contact you by telephone about this offer. By checking this box, you authorize the IRS to leave detailed messages concerning your offer on your voice mail or answering machine.

Name of Preparer | Today's date (mm/dd/yyyy) | Preparer's CAF no. or PTIN

Firm's Name, Address, and ZIP Code | Daytime Telephone Number ( ) -

If you would like to have someone represent you during the offer investigation, include a valid, signed Form 2848 or 8821 with this application, or a copy of a previously filed form.

Catalog Number 47516R | www.irs.gov | Form **656-L** (Rev. 5-2017)

IRS Use Only		
I accept the waiver of the statutory period of limitations on assessment for the Internal Revenue Service, as described in Section 4(h).		
Signature of Authorized IRS Official	Title	Today's date (mm/dd/yyyy)

Privacy Act Statement

We ask for the information on this form to carry out the internal revenue laws of the United States. Our authority to request this information is contained in Section 7801 of the Internal Revenue Code.

Our purpose for requesting the information is to determine if it is in the best interests of the IRS to accept an offer. You are not required to make an offer; however, if you choose to do so, you must provide all of the information requested. Failure to provide all of the information may prevent us from processing your request.

If you are a paid preparer and you prepared the Form 656-L for the taxpayer submitting an offer, we request that you complete and sign Section 8 on the Form 656-L, and provide identifying information. Providing this information is voluntary. This information will be used to administer and enforce the internal revenue laws of the United States and may be used to regulate practice before the Internal Revenue Service for those persons subject to Treasury Department Circular No. 230, Regulations Governing the Practice of Attorneys, Certified Public Accountants, Enrolled Agents, Enrolled Actuaries, and Appraisers before the Internal Revenue Service. Information on this form may be disclosed to the Department of Justice for civil and criminal litigation.

We may also disclose this information to cities, states and the District of Columbia for use in administering their tax laws and to combat terrorism. Providing false or fraudulent information on this form may subject you to criminal prosecution and penalties.

APPLICATION CHECKLIST

☐ Did you include supporting documentation and an explanation as to why you doubt you owe the tax?

☐ Did you complete all fields on the Form 656-L?

☐ Did you make an offer amount that is $1 or more?

Note: The amount of your offer should be based on what you believe the correct amount of the tax debt should be. However, you must offer at least $1. If you do not want to offer $1 or more, you should pursue the alternative solutions provided under "What alternatives do I have to sending in an Offer in Compromise (Doubt as to Liability)?" found on page 3.

☐ If someone other than you completed the Form 656-L, did that person sign it?

☐ Did you sign and include the Form 656-L?

☐ If you want a third party to represent you during the offer process, did you include a Form 2848 or Form 8821 unless one is already on file?

Note: There is no application fee or deposit required for a Doubt as to Liability offer. Do not send any payments with this offer.

Mail your package to:

Brookhaven Internal Revenue Service
COIC Unit
P.O. Box 9008
Stop 681-D
Holtsville, NY 11742-9008

Catalog Number 47516R   www.irs.gov   Form **656-L** (Rev. 5-2017)

UNITED STATES DISTRICT COURT
DISTRICT OF CONNECTICUT

USA,

V.   **SUMMONS IN A CIVIL CASE**

CASE NUMBER:

TO:
Defendant's Address:

▬▬▬▬▬▬▬▬▬ Road
▬▬▬▬ CT ▬▬▬

A lawsuit has been filed against you.

Within **21** days after service of this summons on you (not counting the day you received it) – or 60 days if you are the United States or a United States agency, or an officer or employee of the United States described in Fed. R. Civ. P. 12 (a)(2) or (3) – you must serve on the plaintiff an answer to the attached complaint or a motion under Rule 12 of the Federal Rules of Civil Procedure. The answer or motion must be served on the plaintiff or plaintiff's attorney, whose name and address are:

Unites States Dept of Justice, Tax Div –pob 55
P.O. Box 55, Ben Franklin Station
Washington, DC 20044

If you fail to respond, judgment by default will be entered against you for the relief demanded in the complaint. You also must file your answer or motion with the court.

CLERK OF COURT

/s/ – P. Malone
Signature of Clerk or Deputy Clerk

ISSUED ON 2015-03-12 15:49:39.0, Clerk
USDC CTD

Exhibit 36

PROOF OF SERVICE
(This section should not be filed with the court unless required by Fed. R. Civ. P. 4 (l))

This summons for *(name of individual and title, if any)* _____
was received by me on *(date)* _____.

☐ I personally served the summons on the individual at *(place)* _____
_____ on *(date)* _____; or

☐ I left the summons at the individual's residence or usual place of abode with *(name)* _____
_____, a person of suitable age and discretion who resides there,
on *(date)* _____, and mailed a copy to the individual's last known address; or

☐ I served the summons on *(name of individual)* _____, who is
designated by law to accept service of process on behalf of *(name of organization)* _____
_____ on *(date)* _____; or

☐ I returned the summons unexecuted because _____
_____; or

☐ Other *(specify)* _____
_____
_____

My fees are $_____ for travel and $_____ for services, for a total of $_____ 0.00

I declare under penalty of perjury that this information is true.

Date: _____

_____
Servers signature

_____
Printed name and title

_____
Servers address

Additional information regarding attempted service, etc:

IN THE UNITED STATES DISTRICT COURT FOR THE
DISTRICT OF CONNECTICUT

UNITED STATES OF AMERICA,)
       Plaintiff,) Case No. ███
       v.)
███)
       Defendants.)

NOTICE OF LIS PENDENS

Notice is hereby given that the above entitled case was filed in the United States District Court for the District of Connecticut, on the 12th day of March, 2015, in which the United States of America seeks to enforce federal tax liens against real property more fully described hereunder, and is now pending in the Court.

Notice is further given that the subject property affected by the said action is, as follows:

ALL THAT CERTAIN piece, parcel or tract of land, with the buildings and improvements thereon, located in the City of ███ and State of Connecticut, known and designated as Lot 5A on a certain map entitled ███, which map is on file in the office of the Town Clerk of said City of ███ together with the benefits flowing from those certain agreements, covenants and reservations set forth in that certain Executor's Deed from the ███ Said premises conveyed subject to the following:

CPSIA information can be obtained
at www.ICGtesting.com
Printed in the USA
FSHW021651051020
74413FS